God's Whisper to my Heart

Bible Teachings to

Strengthen Your Faith

and Give You Hope

**By
Julia Brown**

TURN TO ME AND BE SAVED,
ALL THE ENDS OF THE EARTH!
FOR I AM GOD,
AND THERE IS NO OTHER
ISAIAH 45:22

ISBN 978-1-64492-012-1 (paperback)
ISBN 978-1-64492-013-8 (digital)

Copyright © 2019 by Julia Brown

All rights reserved. No part of this publication may be reproduced, distributed, or transmitted in any form or by any means, including photocopying, recording, or other electronic or mechanical methods without the prior written permission of the publisher. For permission requests, solicit the publisher via the address below.

Christian Faith Publishing, Inc.
832 Park Avenue
Meadville, PA 16335
www.christianfaithpublishing.com

Printed in the United States of America

Acknowledgments

I want to especially thank Pastors Jackie and Donna Chavers' for encouraging me to write these bible teachings which ended up being a blessing for me and for all those that read them. I really wanted to share these messages with as many people as I could because I found them helpful in my life and my walk with the Lord. Even when I re-read them I feel hopeful and encouraged. I also want to thank my very good friend Patty Prezzavento who really encouraged me to publish this book, and I will forever be grateful to her. But I cannot forget to thank my loving husband, Rhett Brown, who not only patiently sat down and read each bible study, but contributed by helping me to modify and edit it when necessary. He encouraged me through it all.

There would not have even been a book without the Holy Spirit. I feel so blessed to be used by my Heavenly Father in helping to edify and encourage others. All the honor and glory for this book goes to God. My prayer is that everyone who reads this book will not only find it helpful and encouraging, but I pray that they will be blessed! "Give Thanks to the Lord for He is good; Love endures forever." Ps. 107:1

Foreword

When Julia Brown asked my wife and I if we would write a foreward for her new book, we felt honored to do so. She is such a loving and compassionate person that has such a passion to share the Good News of Jesus Christ. When she and her husband, Rhett Brown (who is a lifelong friend of ours) were members of our church, she was always an ambitious and gifted person with so many things on her heart she wanted to do and to share about our Lord Jesus Christ. So we put her right to work. She began ministering in music worship with flags and then we ask her to put together our bulletins for our Sunday morning service. It was unbelievable how God used her talent in this ministry. She would sit down and just let God begin flowing through her with a message of the Cross, there were times she struggled, but God always came through! She put heart and soul in to this ministry and people's lives were touched. She has put together this book from many thoughts of what God had put on her heart to write down on paper. We pray that everyone who reads this book will be as blessed as we the people of Gospel Lighthouse Church were touched by her love for Christ.

Pastor Jackie and Donna Chavers
Gospel Lighthouse Church
Ridgeland, South Carolina

Introduction

This book of Bible teachings was given to me by the Holy Spirit, not only to encourage and edify others, but to help me grow in my own personal relationship and walk with Jesus. I pray that the Lord will speak to you through these teachings as He has spoken to me.

First, I would like to tell you that *Jesus loves you* and that *"He will never leave you or forsake you"* (Deuteronomy 31:6).

Jesus said that at the end it would be like the days of Noah. In the days of Noah, the earth was filled with violence and corruption. I believe that today we are truly living in these troubling times. However, we do have *"hope" that* comes from Jesus Christ! We are overcomers by the Blood of the Lamb!

> ***"For God so loved the world, that he gave his only Son, that whoever believes in him should not perish but have eternal life." -John 3:16***
>
> ***Jesus said, "I came that they may have life, and have it abundantly." -John 10:10***

Do you really understand what God has done for us by sacrificing His only Son? *Apart from the blood of Jesus, you and I could not have had a relationship with Our Heavenly Father.* Jesus's sacrificial death made it possible for sinful man to approach a Holy God. Because of His blood, believers are redeemed, forgiven, justified, and sanctified, and they have access to their Creator. The blood of Jesus is precious because of *who* Jesus is. Christ was not just a man, but the Son of God, born of a virgin. Because Jesus was conceived by the Holy Spirit, He was wholly man and wholly God and without any spots or blemishes. He was the perfect Lamb of God. His perfection was Holiness. The blood of Jesus is precious because of *why* He came. From Genesis to Revelation, the Bible has one main theme—the Father's redeeming love for mankind. Christ came as the Son of God with the purpose of dying for the sins of humanity. *The blood of Jesus Christ is absolutely essential to our relationship with God.* Those who refuse it will spend eternity in the lake of fire, forever separated from God.

When you accept Jesus as your personal Savior you become a child of God. This means you don't have to wait until you get to Heaven to experience Heaven on earth. In the Lord's Prayer it says, *"Our Father who art in heaven, hallowed be thy name,* **thy kingdom come, thy will be done, on earth as it is in heaven.** *Give us today our daily bread. And forgive us our debts, as we also have forgiven our debtors. And lead us not into temptation, but deliver us from evil."* This prayer tells us that you can have Heaven on Earth, and be in the presence of the Almighty God by the following:

- Accepting Jesus Christ as your personal Savior
- Having a personal and intimate relationship with God by reading and studying the Bible
- Having no unforgiveness in your heart
- Being content and thankful in all things
- Praising and worshiping Him and giving Him all the glory
- Spending quiet time in His Presence…*just listening*
- Keeping your eyes always on Jesus

We all have a choice to *"accept or reject"* Jesus as our Savior. The choice is *yours*. Whatever you have done in your past—God loves you! He accepts you right where you are. Get down on your knees and ask God to forgive you and ask Jesus into your hear as your personal Savior. Then submit yourselves to Him and allow Him to change you and give you eternal life!

I hope that you will get to know Jesus and accept Him as your personal Savior. He is your *only hope! Jesus wants to give you the free gift of eternal life and all you have to do is say "YES."*

We have been given these *two most important* commandments: *"...Love the Lord your God with all your heart and with all your soul and with all your mind. This is the first and greatest commandment. And the second is like it: Love your neighbor as yourself"* (Matthew 22:37-39).

Don't wait too long... because Jesus is coming back soon!

My Personal Prayer for You:

"The LORD your God is in your midst, A mighty one who will save; He will rejoice over you with gladness; He will quiet you by his love; He will exult over you with loud singing."
-Zephaniah 3:17

I pray that from His glorious, unlimited resources He will empower you with inner strength through His Spirit. Then Christ will make His home in your hearts as you trust in Him. Your roots will grow down into God's love and keep you strong. And may you have the power to understand, as all of God's people should, how wide, how long, how high and how deep His love is. May you experience the love of Christ, though it is too great to understand fully. Then you will be made complete with all the fullness of life and power that comes from God. Now all glory to God, who is able, through His mighty power at work within us, to accomplish infinitely more than we might ask or think. (Ephesians 3:16-20)

I ask God to give you complete knowledge of His will and to give you spiritual wisdom and understanding. Then the way you live will always honor and please the Lord, and your lives will produce every kind of good fruit. All the while, you will grow as you learn to know God better and better. We also pray that you will be strengthened with all His glorious power so you will have all the endurance and patience you need. May you be filled with joy, always thanking the Father. He has enabled you to share in the inheritance that belongs to His people, who live in the light. (Colossians 1:9-12)

Lord, Help Me Be Grateful And to Rejoice in You In All My Circumstances!

This is a story of a man who had every right to be bitter—but he wasn't:
    The next footsteps in the corridor, he knew, might be those of the guards taking him away to his execution. His only bed was the hard, cold stone floor of the dark, cramped prison cell. Not an hour passed when he was free from the constant irritation of the chains and the pain of the iron manacles cutting into his wrists and legs. Separated from friends, unjustly accused, brutally treated—if ever a person had a right to complain, it was this man, languishing almost forgotten in a harsh Roman prison. But instead of complaints, his lips rang with words of praise and thanksgiving! This man was the Apostle Paul—a man who had learned the meaning of true thanks-giving, even in the midst of great adversity. Earlier, when he had been imprisoned in Rome, Paul wrote, *"Sing and make music in your heart to the Lord, always giving thanks to God the Father for everything, in the name of our Lord Jesus Christ"* (Ephesians 5:19-20).
    Thanksgiving—*the giving of thanks*—to God for all His blessings should be one of the most distinctive marks of the believer in Jesus Christ. We must not allow a spirit of ingratitude to harden our heart. Nothing turns us into bitter, selfish, dissatisfied people more quickly than an ungrateful heart. And nothing will do more to restore contentment and the joy of our salvation than *a true spirit of thankfulness.* From one end of the Bible to the other, we are commanded to be thankful. In fact, thankfulness is the natural outflowing of a heart that is attuned to God. The psalmist declared, *"Sing to*

the Lord with thanksgiving" (Psalms 147:7). Paul wrote, *"Be thankful"* (Colossians 3:15). A spirit of thanksgiving is always the mark of a joyous Christian. Paul declared, *"I have learned the secret of being content in any and every situation, whether well fed or hungry, whether living in plenty or in want"* (Philippians 4:12). A spirit of thankfulness makes all the difference. Are you constantly preoccupied with what you do not have? Or have you learned to thank God for what you do have? We know that He can use times of suffering to draw us closer to Him.

> *"Consider it pure joy, my brothers, whenever you face trials of many kinds, because you know that the testing of your faith develops perseverance." -James 1:2-3*

I don't know what trials you may be facing right now, but God does, and He loves you and is with you by His Holy Spirit. Cultivate a spirit of thankfulness even in the midst of trials and heartaches. "God has given us the greatest Gift of all—His Son, Jesus Christ!" We should not let a day go by without thanking God for His mercy and His grace to us in Jesus Christ. We can thank God for His Continued Presence and Power in our lives.

When we come to Christ, it is not the end but the beginning of a whole new life! He is with us, and He wants to help us follow Him and His Word. In ourselves we do not have the strength that we need to live the way God wants us to live. But when we turn to Him, we discover that *"it is God who works in [us] to will and to act according to his good purpose"* (Philippians 2:13).

We *can* rejoice, every second of every day of every week of every month of every year because *The Lord is at hand—He is near*. We're not rejoicing because we are happy about our situation, but because the Lord is *with* us. In that horrible, terrifying, and seemingly hopeless moment, the Lord is right there by our side. I'm sure you have been in a moment like that or maybe you are there right now. A storm may still be a ways off, but it is coming. The clouds are looming in the distance and the forecast is bleak at best… but your joy and hope comes in God's word.

"Rejoice in the Lord always. I will say it again: Rejoice!… for the Lord is near." -Philippians 4:4-5

There is no greater joy than to give praise to God!

> *Rejoice in the Lord always!*
>
> *Be continually happy; this happiness you can find only in the Lord. Genuine happiness is spiritual; as it can only come from God*

Every Time You Grumble You Will Stumble!

> *"Rejoice always, pray continually, give thanks in all circumstances; for this is God's will for you in Christ Jesus."*
> *-1 Thessalonians 5:16-18*

Only three days after being miraculously delivered through the parted Red Sea, the Israelites started to grumble. God gave them a decree and law to listen to His voice, do right in His eyes, and pay attention to and keep his commands and decrees. Even though they grumbled God graciously and miraculously supplied all their needs. God decreed that no one who disobeyed and tested Him would ever see the Promised Land. Because of all their grumbling and their unbelief, the rebellious Israelites wandered in the desert for forty years and died there. God only allowed Caleb and Joshua and those younger than twenty to enter the Promised Land (Numbers 14:26-35).

Through this review of the scriptures, we can see how grumbling can start small but end up having a very big and very bad affect. We can surely identify with some of these examples ourselves. It can seem so *natural* to grumble. We can even delude ourselves into thinking that we *need* to grumble or are even *entitled* to grumble. But the fact of the matter is that God does *not* want us to grumble. He does want us to share our problems with Him, but it's all in our attitude. Even though God is very patient and loving, scripture makes it clear that there is a limit to the grumbling that He will endure before there are some serious consequences. *All* grumbling is sin and unacceptable in

God's eyes. Murmuring is a sign of distrust of God. It leads to greater sin and can test the patience of the Lord.

God doesn't want us to fall—so He gives us a warning from Israel's history:

> *"For I do not want you to be ignorant of the fact, brothers and sisters, that our ancestors were all under the cloud and that they all passed through the sea. They were all baptized into Moses in the cloud and in the sea. They all ate the same spiritual food and drank the same spiritual drink; for they drank from the spiritual rock that accompanied them, and that rock was Christ. Nevertheless, God was not pleased with most of them; their bodies were scattered in the wilderness. Now these things occurred as examples to keep us from setting our hearts on evil things as they did… we should not test Christ, as some of them did—and were killed by snakes. And do not grumble, as some of them did—and were killed by the destroying angel. These things happened to them as examples and were written down as warnings for us, on whom the culmination of the ages has come. So, if you think you are standing firm, be careful that you don't fall!"-1 Corinthians 10:1-6, 9-12*

God has not only warned us but He *commands us* not to grumble.

> *"Don't grumble against one another, brothers and sisters, or you will be judged. The Judge is standing at the door!" -James 5:9*

Like the Israelites in the wilderness, the Christian today is between promise and fulfillment. We have been delivered from slavery, but we have not reached our final destination and resting place. The "promised land" symbolizes the place of ultimate blessing in the presence of God. You cannot enter the "promised land" (God's rest) without leaving "Egypt" (Sin). The Bible says that only Jesus Christ can set you free. The Israelites "turned back" when the road ahead looked difficult. They failed to obey God's instructions and to trust in his promises. Is there something in your life that you know God wants you to do, but you have not been obedient to Him because of fear, or lack of faith? Humble yourself before the Lord, seek His help, and--make every effort to enter that rest.

> *"Let us, therefore, make every effort to enter that rest, so that no one will fall by following their example of disobedience." -Hebrews 4:11*
>
> *"Therefore, since the promise of entering his rest still stands, let us be careful that none of you be found to have fallen short of it. For we also have had the gospel preached to us, just as they did; but the message they heard was of no value to them, because those who heard did not combine it with faith. Now we who have believed enter that rest." -Hebrews 4:1-3*

Stop grumbling today and start TRUSTING GOD!

A THANKFUL HEART is a flood-gate opener to blessings, joy and peace. With thankful hearts,

WE CAN TOUCH THE VERY HEART OF GOD!

Have You Sinned So Much That You Wonder HOW Could God Still Love Me?

> *"For I am persuaded, that neither death, nor life, nor angels, nor principalities, nor powers, nor things present, nor things to come, nor height, nor depth, nor any other creature, shall be able to separate us from the love of God, which is in Christ Jesus our Lord."*
> *-Romans 8:39*

No truth will transform your life more than God's gracious love for you in Christ. To the extent that you understand it, feel it, and live daily with a deep sense of its reality--you will live in victory over temptation and sin and be able joyfully to persevere through trials. If God saved us while we were still sinners, knowing full well that we would sin after He saved us, then we can trust that He will not cast us off as His children, even when we disobey. He will discipline us as a loving Father, but our sin will not cause Him to diminish His love for us. God's great love for us in Christ Jesus our Lord enables us to be more than conquerors through every trial that comes.

> *"I give them eternal life, and they will never perish, and no one will snatch them out of my hand. My Father, who has given them to me, is greater than all." -John. 10:28-29*

The Word of God equips us with the knowledge that we need not only to *persevere* through trials for Christ's sake, but to *overwhelmingly conquer* in all these difficulties. We may face many trials and even death before Christ's return. By having an intimate relationship with the Lord…you will be more than conquerors—*you will be able to endure* any difficulties that you may go through for His sake. God's love for us is why He sent his only Son to die on the cross for us.

> ***"He loved us so much that He delivered up His own Son for us on the cross. God did all of this for us while we were yet sinners." -Romans 5:8***

When you choose Jesus Christ as your personal Savior… you become a child of God. And there isn't anything you can do or say that will separate you from God's love.

> ***"The Lord himself goes before you and will be with you; he will never leave you nor forsake you…" -Deuteronomy 31:8***

God's great love for you will not diminish or be terminated by your failures. His love for us is not conditioned on our worthiness or our performance. *PRAISE GOD!*

Your obedience to Christ reflects your love for Him. And we will only experience the love of the Lord… as we obey Him. God has written a comprehensive instruction manual… *THE BIBLE—so* that we will know exactly how to live our lives for HIM. Once we are saved, we must not only read, but meditate on His Word… HE WILL DO THE REST! He will change our hearts and He will transform them into the image of His Son. The more you seek Him….the more He will reveal His heart to you and His blessings and favor will rest upon you.

Satan will lie and use anything to try to get us to doubt God's love. No matter how difficult any trials may be, God's love for us is rock solid. Whatever the trial, by faith, not by feelings, we must come back to God's love for us in Christ Jesus our Lord. We need to *unceasingly repent* of our sins and ask God for forgiveness when we have done something that is not pleasing to Him. We are to die to our sin; and LIVE FOR CHRIST.

Ask the Lord to put the desire in your heart to fervently read and study His Word so that you will grow spiritually. God's purpose for us is that we grow and become more like the Lord Jesus Christ in our daily lives to reflect more of Him and less of us. You will only experience God's great love…if Jesus Christ is *your* Lord. God's great love for us will be consummated in heaven, but we can begin to taste His grace and love now… *through the cross.*

You don't have to wait until you go to Heaven… you can start living life abundantly *today*… in Jesus Christ!

> *"The LORD hath appeared of old unto me, saying, Yea, I have loved thee with an everlasting love: therefore with lovingkindness have I drawn thee." -Jeremiah 31:3*

Imagine Never Thirsting Again...
HOW IS THAT POSSIBLE?

> *"If anyone is thirsty, let him come to Me and drink. Whoever believes in Me, as the Scripture has said, streams of living water will flow from within him."*
>
> *-John 7:37-38*

The Bible speaks of both physical water necessary for life here on earth, and living water necessary for eternal life. One is for temporary relief, the other for eternal satisfaction. Jesus said in the Gospel of John, *"Everyone who drinks this water (physical water) will be thirsty again, but whoever drinks the water I give him will never thirst. Indeed, the water I give him will become in him a spring of water welling up to eternal life."* In the Bible, God promises those who come to Christ will never thirst again.

Salvation comes only to those who recognize their desperate need for …the spiritual life they *do not* have. Living water can be obtained only by those who recognize that they are spiritually thirsty. And Salvation comes only to those who confess and repent of their sin and desire forgiveness. You must accept Jesus Christ as your Savior…for salvation can be found in no one else.

> *"Jesus saith unto him, I am the way, the truth, and the life: no man cometh unto the Father, but by me." -John 14:6*

> *"Salvation is found in no one else, for there is no other name under heaven given to mankind by which we must be saved." -Acts 4:12*

The heavenly water of life is readily available to… *"…whoever is thirsty, let him come; and whoever wishes, let him take the free gift of the water of life"* (Revelation 22:17). These words of Jesus's invitation echo in our ears. Jesus stands at the doors of our hearts and speaks to the heart of each person on earth, offering the water of eternal life--the life that flows from God. Those with a desire for God may find *the God who is offering himself.* Jesus invites those who know their need, those who are poor in spirit (Matthew 5:3), to take the initiative and come to him and drink. Drinking refers to believing which means aligning oneself with him, trusting him, receiving his teaching, and obeying his commands.

Such faith will enable one to receive the Spirit and enter an abiding relationship with Jesus Christ. When we believe, we open our hands to receive what His grace offers—we come and drink. The one who has placed their faith in Jesus Christ has tapped into *The Fountain of Living Water* which is never exhausted, but one that abundantly satisfies. It is everlasting and always there to continuously refresh the life of the believer. This living water gives us power, joy and gives the only hope you can have in this world. Without this living water there isn't a Christian who can live a truly holy life. Only when the Spirit of God lives in us and lives through us—*will all things be possible.*

> *"I can do all things through Christ who strengthens me." -Philippians 4:13*

His well is never dry… *if you will only come to Him…* He will demonstrate His great saving power in your life. He loves you more than you could ever know, and He longs to save your eternal soul. All He requires is that you come to Him in faith.

So many are satisfied in their sins and content with their lives and have no thought for God. Salvation *will not come* for them!

Before a person can be saved, he/she must sense their need of salvation. Only when they see their need of thirst for salvation and realize that satisfaction can only come from Jesus—only then can they come to Christ and be saved by the grace of God.

> *"For whosoever shall call upon the name of the Lord shall be saved."-Romans 10:13*

Have you been searching everywhere for things that simply do not and cannot satisfy the soul? Are you longing for true peace in your heart?

Why not come to Jesus today?

> *Jesus is the water that brings life to the soul. By drinking the living water one can live and never thirst again.*
>
> ***JESUS IS ... THE ONLY SOURCE OF LIVING WATER.***

How Can I Receive God's Grace... When Grace is an Undeserved Free Gift, Undeserved Favor and Undeserved Love

> *"But grow in grace, and in the knowledge of our Lord and Savior Jesus Christ. To him be glory both now and forever. Amen."*
> *- 2 Peter 3:18*

We are offered grace *only* through Jesus Christ. *All that we are—all that we have ever been—all that we will ever be—*is totally one hundred percent a result of God's awesome grace. God's grace does not depend on our efforts or works… it totally depends upon God.

> *"I will have mercy on whom I have mercy, and I will have compassion on whom I have compassion. It does not, therefore, depend on man's desire or effort, but on God's mercy."-Romans 9:15-16*

If we are willing to allow the Holy Spirit to work in us then God does the work of changing our heart to love Him and love others, so that we can be obedient to His Word. We must always understand that our failures and weaknesses are no match for God's grace and love that He has for us.

"And you He made alive, who were dead in trespasses and sins, in which you once walked according to the course of this world, according to the prince of the power of the air, the spirit who now works in the sons of disobedience, among whom also we all once conducted ourselves in the lusts of our flesh, fulfilling the desires of the flesh and of the mind, and were by nature children of wrath, just as the others. But God, who is rich in mercy because of His great love with which He loved us, even when we were dead in trespasses, made us alive together with Christ and raised us up together, and made us sit together in the heavenly places in Christ Jesus, that in the ages to come He might show the exceeding riches of His grace in His kindness toward us in Christ Jesus. For by grace you have been saved through faith, and that not of yourselves; it is the gift of God, not of works, lest anyone should boast." -Ephesians 2:1-9

The works that we do for God are the works that He has prepared in advance that we should walk in them; they are not a result of our efforts. They are God's works that we move in being guided by His Holy Spirit. The first step toward accepting God's grace is to understand that you don't deserve it. God does not love you because you are good. God loves you because He is good. Everything about our relationship with God depends upon us trusting Him in faith, by resting in His grace. We are to come to Him as a little child saying, "Daddy pick me up", and He does, Then He carries us. *"Even to your old age and gray hairs I am he, I am he who will sustain you. I have made you and I will carry you; I will sustain you and I will rescue you"* (Isaiah 46:4). Out of His grace comes freedom, authority, power, love, worship, and life in abundance (John 10:10).

The *GRACE OF GOD* is what God has already done for us. He has already laid all our sin on Jesus. Jesus has already purged us from all of our sins. God has laid the righteousness of Christ upon us. He sees us, as believers, as perfectly righteous before him, as though sin had never existed. *How do we respond to this good news of God's grace?* We place our faith, our trust, and our dependence wholly upon Jesus and his finished work, and we receive for ourselves the abundance of grace and of the gift of righteousness. God's Grace is *the power of God to do for us what we cannot do for ourselves.*

Jesus says, *"...without me ye can do nothing"* (John 15:5). Grace is God's unmerited favor that is extended to all mankind. God's grace supplies— *ALL THAT WE WILL EVER NEED.* You can live above your circumstances, problems, trouble, and weakness when you understand His grace. God will exalt you in your weakness and humility. What God requires is that we abide in Him (John 15:4-5). His Grace will save you from sin's penalty and give you an inheritance that will never fade away.

Jesus already paid the price for this FREE GIFT...

SO RECEIVE IT... simply by FAITH!!

> *"...My grace is sufficient for you, for my power is made perfect in weakness. Therefore I will boast all the more gladly about my weaknesses, so that Christ's power may rest on me." -2 Corinthians 12:9*

Only God's Love
Can and Will Sustain You!

God said, have not I commanded you: *"Be strong and courageous. Do not be terrified; do not be discouraged, for the Lord your God will be with you wherever you go."*
-Joshua 1:9

Only with God's Love... will you be able to BEAR all things, BELIEVE all things, HOPE all things and ENDURE all things.

How comforting it is to know that wherever we go God is there with us. Sometimes we find ourselves in situations and we wonder if God is paying attention. We may feel so alone and even depressed. We can't feel God's presence, and we need His guidance and help. Often others don't really understand what we are going through, but *God does and He cares.* God told Joshua to be strong and to have courage. Then He told him a wonderful truth: *"The Lord your God will be with you wherever you go."* You heard it—WHEREVER! We don't have to feel all alone. God is with us. He is working out the problems, and we don't even realize it.

But now... the Lord who created you says: *"Do not be afraid, for I have ransomed you. I have called you by name; you are mine. When you go through deep waters and great trouble, I will be with you. When you go through rivers of difficulty, you will not drown! When you walk through the fire of oppression, you will not be burned up; the flames will not consume you. For I am the Lord, your God, the Holy One of Israel, your Savior... From eternity to eternity I am God. No one can oppose what I do. No one can reverse my actions"* (Isaiah 43:1-3, 13).

God is with us, leading us, guiding us, loving us, and providing for us all with His unlimited resources. What do we need? Do we need strength, peace, love, joy, or hope? He has it all. He is longing to pour out His favor and blessing upon us. We need to be open to Him and to trust Him. We need, by faith, to receive what He has for us. It is essential that we realize how much He loves us and that He has a good purpose and plan for us.

When you think about God's plan for you, it should make you want to fall to your knees and pray to the Father, the Creator of everything in heaven and on earth. There is nothing that God doesn't know and can't do for us. He walks with us every moment of every day. The devil can't stand it when we, in confidence, speak God's Word... but if you declare His Word it will build your faith and give you the strength to stand.

> *"O Lord, you have examined my heart and know everything about me. You know when I sit down or stand-up. You know my every thought when far away. You chart the path ahead of me and tell me where to stop and rest. Every moment you know where I am. You know what I am going to say even before I say it, Lord. You both precede and follow me. You place your hand of blessing on my head. Such knowledge is too wonderful for me, too great for me to know!"* -Psalms 139:1-6

Ask the Lord to show you the path where you should walk, and to point out the right road for you to follow. Ask Him to lead you in His truth.

> *"Show me your ways, Lord, teach me your paths. Guide me in your truth and teach me,*

for you are God my Savior, and my hope is in you all day long." -Psalms 25:4-5

You can trust God. No matter what is going on in your life, He is there! God goes wherever you go.

"So do not throw away this confident trust in the Lord. Remember the great reward it brings you! Patient endurance is what you need now, so that you will continue to do God's will. Then you will receive all that He has promised." -Hebrews 10:35-36

There is only one way to fill any void in your life...

HIS NAME IS JESUS!

Without God... everything is impossible,
But WITH GOD...
EVERYTHING IS POSSIBLE!
If you don't have God in your life...
you will live a life without hope!

We Are Called to Be a Light in This Dark World!

> *"I do not ask You to take them out of the world, but to keep them from the evil one. They are not of the world, even as I am not of the world. Sanctify them in the truth; Your word is truth. As You sent Me into the world, I also have sent them into the world."*
> *- John 17:15-17*

So we are to be *in the world* as Jesus was in the world, yet also *not* to be *of the world*, even as Jesus was not of the world. The way to keep this fine balance is to be sanctified (set apart) by God's Word of truth. We are to walk as *children of light* in this dark world, exposing the deeds of darkness.

> *"You are all the children of light, and the children of the day: we are not of the night, nor of darkness." -1 Thessalonian 5:5*

The Bible tells us that *darkness* symbolizes Satan's evil domain and the sinful deeds of those who do not obey God. It also represents the spiritual ignorance of those whose sin has blinded their eyes from the light of God's truth. (Ephesians 4:18, 2 Corinthians 4:4) The *Light* pictures the knowledge of the truth that comes when God shines into our lives. *"For God, who said, 'Light shall shine out of darkness,' is the One who has shone in our hearts to give the Light of the knowledge of the glory of God in the face of Christ"* (2 Corinthians 4:6). *Light* also pictures the holiness of God, (1 John 1:5) who dwells in unapproachable light. (1 Timothy 6:16) So as believers, we are called to walk in the light, just as He Himself is in the light, (1 John 1:7) living with every area of our lives exposed to God.

We formerly were darkness. We were spiritually blind. We not only didn't see God's glory and truth, we didn't have the ability or desire to see such things. We didn't sense our need for the Savior, because we thought we were good enough to go to heaven and we didn't understand the absolute holiness and justice of God. So we lived entirely for ourselves and our own pleasure, avoiding the thought of death and eternity. But… when God saved us, He opened the eyes of our understanding so that we saw *"the Light of the knowledge of the glory of God in the face of Christ."* We saw our true condition as guilty sinners, but we also saw the all sufficiency of Jesus and His death on the cross to cover all our sins. We had a new understanding of God's Word and a new desire to know God and His truth more and more. We now hate the sin that we formerly lived in and we long to be like our Savior, holy in all our ways. We now walk in the light, rather than in darkness, because God has made us light in the Lord.

> *"For you were once darkness, but now you are light in the Lord. Live as children of light."*
> *-Ephesians 5:8*

If we're no different in our thinking, attitudes, words, and behavior than those that do not know Christ, we have no message to give them. Jesus said, *"Let your light shine before men in such a way that they may see your good works, and glorify your Father who is in heaven"* (Matthew 5:16). We are called to tell people the message of the gospel. But that message must be backed up with genuine concern for the whole person. If someone is hungry, feed him and tell him about Jesus. The fruit of the light consists in goodness, which means doing good deeds that show love for people.

We are to live and share the Word of God with those in darkness—It is indeed a poor testimony to put into God's service the "leftovers" of our time, energy, and resources, after being preoccupied with making sure that all of our own selfish desires have been met. Jesus declared, *"By this is My Father glorified, that You bear much fruit, and so prove to be My disciples"* (John 15:8).

If we walk as *children of light*, we will be people of truth. We are to speak the truth in love. (Ephesians 4:15, 25) We are to be people of our word, maintaining integrity in all things. We shouldn't have anything to hide, because we walk in the light. *We are people of all truth*!

God is LOVE and—
only with His <u>LOVE</u> can good fruit come forth!

> *"And do not be conformed to this world, but be transformed by the renewing of your mind, so that you may prove what the will of God is, that which is good and acceptable and perfect."*
> *-Romans 12:2*

You Must Be Able to Face Your Giants!

> *"Be sober, be vigilant; because your adversary the devil, as a roaring lion, walketh about, seeking whom he may devour."*
> *-1 Peter 5:8*

Goliath was an impressive man. He seemed unstoppable. He presented himself as someone who would not go down. We see that Goliath didn't think much of David. In fact, from an earthly stand point, David looked outclassed and outmanned. But from a Heavenly stand point, Goliath was no match for David's God! David faced Goliath *in the name of the Lord!*

> *"Then said David to the Philistine, Thou comest to me with a sword, and with a spear, and with a shield: BUT I COME IN THE NAME OF THE LORD OF HOSTS, the God of the armies of Israel, whom thou hast defied."*
> *-1 Samuel 17:45*

David knew that the battle was in the hands of the Lord. As David ran at Goliath, he knew that Goliath had to fall. David could challenge Goliath because he knew that since God took care of him in the past, God could and would take care of him in the present. David had nothing to fear in his present because of what God did for him in his past. David trusted God completely with his life!

> *"Through thee we will push down our enemies: through thy name will we tread them under that rise up against us." -Psalm 44:5*

Giants are real! *GIANTS* are problems, pressures, pains, and persecutions that we have to face. A *giant* is anything that distracts us from our focus on God; anything that detours us from our service for God; and anything that drains us of our driving passion for God. Some of the *giants* that people face include: resentment, fear, loneliness, guilt and shame, worry, jealousy, discouragement, depression, hopelessness, bitterness, pride, selfishness, and doubt. The devil is on the prowl and he will taunt you with bills you can't pay, people you can't please, habits you can't break, failures you can't forget, and a future you can't face.

The same thing that happened to David can happen to you. Great struggles are taking place in the lives of God's people. But just like David, you can face your giant. The same God that helped David will help you! The giants that are before us must be slain and removed. If you will just *trust* and *depend* upon the Lord, you *can* face, fight, and finish off your giant. Don't just throw a stone at your Goliath and hit him in the forehead; go over to your giant and take the sword and cut its head off and completely finish it. Don't give the giant that you are facing in your life an opportunity to live again in your life. CONQUER YOUR GIANT! You can conquer your giant by *placing your faith in the hands of God who can do all things*. Don't look at your giant from an earthly point of view; look at it from Heaven's point of view. *God is bigger than any giant that you will ever face.* Your 'giant' can be defeated and removed with the help of the Lord!

> *"You, dear children, are from God and have overcome them, because the one who is in you is greater than the one who is in the world." -1 John 4:4*

If you are a member of the body of Christ and made Jesus the Lord of your life, Satan has marked you for destruction. He is going to flood your life with troubles of all kinds. But the good news is that we have a God who loves us and we have victory in Him!

David chose to stand confident *in the name of the Lord*. David did not strategize or contemplate what weapons he needed to use against Goliath. David moved with God. As a result of following God—Goliath was defeated.

You may have many giants that you are facing, but I encourage you to stand strong *in the name of the Lord*. Do not stand against your giant in your own power, but stand against your giant *in the name of the Lord*. It is time to stand up *in the name of the Lord* and defeat the *GIANTS* that have been trying to control your life.

Focus on giants—you stumble;

Focus on GOD—your giants tumble

> *"We wrestle not against flesh and blood, but against principalities, against powers, against the rulers of the darkness of this world, against spiritual wickedness in high places." -Ephesians 6:12*

Get Right with God...
For the Day of the Lord is at Hand!

> *"The great day of the LORD is near, it is near, and hastens quickly, Listen! The cry on the day of the Lord will be bitter..."*
>   *-Zephaniah 1:14*

The hour is very late. *"...the end of all things is at hand..."* (1 Peter 4:7). The Bible tells us that judgment and the wrath of God will be unleashed upon our world. Sooner than most think or care to even see, we shall see our world be destroyed through fire, war, famine, plagues, natural and supernatural disasters *(Matthew 24)*. As men cry, *"peace, peace... then sudden destruction will come!"* (1 Thessalonians 5:3). This Word of God will come to pass and many will not heed the warnings.

> *"But because of your stubbornness and unrepentant heart you are Storing up wrath for yourself in the day of wrath and revelation of the righteous judgment of God." -Romans 2:5*

Just as in Noah's day, God warned the people—*"Flee from the wrath to come!"* The world was once destroyed by a great flood of water. God's word tells us that the earth will be soon be destroyed by fire. We need to heed this warning because it will happen as God's Word will *always* come to pass.

> ***"So shall my word be that goeth forth out of my mouth: it shall not return unto me void, but it shall accomplish that which I please, and it shall prosper whereto I sent it."* -Isaiah 55:11**

The person who fears God will take His word seriously. He will not lightly dismiss the word of God, turn a deaf ear to it, or attempt to alter it—but he will tremble and meekly receive it as the word of The Living God. The individual who takes seriously the word of God does not approach the word with a *"take-it-or-leave-it"* attitude. He does not pick and choose what to affirm and what to deny. Taking God's word seriously is a matter of *paying attention to Scripture, taking it personally, listening to it and being conscious that God is speaking to us through it.*

The Lord Jesus who came to bring mercy once before as a meek lamb, a sin offering to God, will come back very soon as *"The Lion of Judah"* bringing judgment on all those who refused His mercy and His love. *"The Day of the Lord"* will be a fearful and dark day as God pours out his wrath against all the ungodly, the unbelievers, and all those who do not know Him.

But there is HOPE! *"Every word of God is pure: He is a shield unto them that put their trust in him"* (Proverbs 30:5). JESUS IS OUR HOPE! Jesus took *our* punishment! The Gospel is simply this—Jesus, the Lamb of God took upon Himself your debt of sin. He paid for it in full. You can be forgiven and have fellowship with the Holy God that you once offended with your sin.

However, to receive God's forgiveness, eternal salvation and blessings, you are required to believe the gospel of the Lord Jesus Christ and confess your sins to God. Be specific in confessing what you have done to offend His holiness. Show Him that you are sincerely sorry for your sins by making a commitment to turn from those sins. Repentance is not about promises to be good, but working with God as He molds us into His image. It is trusting God to have mercy on you. It is trusting God to fix your evil heart. It is trusting God to be who he says he is—Creator, Savior, Redeemer, Teacher, Lord and Sanctifier.

Many have hardened their hearts to God and the gospel. If you have never made a total commitment to follow Jesus, or if you need to recommit your life to Him—*do it now*! Do not harden your heart to God's love and mercy! There is no other choice left to you but His wrath and indignation! This is a very serious decision you must make. Your eternal destiny depends upon it! Jesus loves you… enough to warn you and provide for you a way out.

"It is better to take refuge in the LORD than to trust in man." -Psalm 118:8

Don't wait until it is too late…

get right with God today!

> *"For whatsoever things were written aforetimewere written for our learning, that we through patience and comfort of the scriptures might have HOPE."*
> *-Romans 15:4*

What Kind of Food Are You Eating...???

> *"Keep this Book of the Law always on your lips; meditate on it day and night, so that you may be careful to do everything written in it. Then you will be prosperous and successful."*
> *-Joshua 1:8*

With the New Year beginning, many are preparing and thinking about new ways to get healthier—new diets, exercise programs, and even new creative ideas for healthier eating. Most people are considering new health goals to improve their physical health. This is a good thing because we *should* take care of our bodies. God the Father created our bodies, God the Son redeemed them, and God the Holy Spirit indwells them. This makes our body—the very temple of the Holy Spirit of God.

> *"Do you not know that your body is a temple of the Holy Spirit, who is in you, whom you have received from God? You are not your own; you were bought at a price. Therefore honor God with your body." -1 Corinthians 6:19-20*

Although this is all good—it is even more important to be looking at your spiritual health! As you are looking at the junk you need to remove from your diet, consider looking at what spiritual junk food that needs to go as well. Junk food is usually delicious in flavor, but low in nutritional value, and high in fat and calories. If you fill up with junk food on a daily basis, you won't be hungry for nutritious food. In the same way junk food derails your health goals, succumbing to the temptations of spiritual junk food throws us off track and curbs our appetite for God. We should be filling ourselves with God's Word instead of the temptations of the world.

After the death of Moses, God appointed Joshua to lead the Israelites. To prepare Joshua for the task, God gave him instructions and encouragement. God explained the importance of meditating on His Word to avoid temptation and sin, and the importance of keeping His commands on Joshua's lips. God knew that the distractions and discouragements of the world could easily derail Joshua from His chosen path. He commanded Joshua to have a daily menu of His truth and to meditate on the Law every day and talk about it often so that His ways would always be fresh in Joshua's mind. In other words, God wanted Joshua to be *filled with His Word*, so that he would have no hunger for the temptations of the world.

An infinite amount of spiritual junk food tickles our fingertips every day through television, movies, computers, smart phones, books, radio and more. Even though these things can offer good "food" as well, if we don't use spiritual discernment to selectively choose what we are consuming, we may find ourselves filled with the wrong things, and a curbed appetite for what is spiritually nutritious. If we aren't careful, the spiritual junk food the world offers might inadvertently become our primary source of nourishment, diminishing our appetite for God's Word, and lessening our desire for healthy portions of His instruction. Too much junk food of any kind will weaken our bodies and our spirits. But spending time with God and keeping His Word on our lips will bring strength and health, inside and out.

> *"Like newborn babies, you must crave pure spiritual milk so that you will grow into a full experience of salvation. Cry out for this nourishment, now that you have had a taste of the Lord's kindness." -1 Peter 2:2-3*

Ponder these questions and judge for yourself. What are you being fed?

1. In *what ways* do I feed my heart and mind on a daily basis? (TV, radio, books, God's Word, devotions, etc.)
2. Does my *hunger for God* outweigh my hunger for other "foods"?
3. What *changes* can I make in my daily life to increase my appetite for God?

Ask God to open your eyes to the spiritual junk food you are feeding your heart and mind. Ask Him to help you see where you need to make some changes in your life in order to be spiritually healthier.

Give up the "spiritual junk food" and Feast on God's Word!

> *"It is written: 'Man should not live on bread alone, but on EVERY WORD that comes from the MOUTH OF GOD.'"*
> *-Matthew 4:4*

If You Are Walking in the Light...
You Must Love Your Brother!

"Whoever says he is in the light and hates his brother is still in darkness. Whoever loves his brother abides in the light, and in Him there is no cause for stumbling. But whoever hates his brother is in the darkness and walks in the darkness, and does not know where he is going, because the darkness has blinded his eyes."
-1 John 2:9–11

As Christians, we are commanded to love one another. It is not a question of whether or not we want to love other believers. This is a command from God. If we choose not to love another believer, we are disobeying Him. The Lord Jesus said, *"A new commandment I give to you, that you love one another; as I have loved you, that you must love one another"* (John 13:34).

- Leviticus 19:17 : S 1Jn 2:9
- Leviticus 19:17 : S Mt 18:15
- Leviticus 19:18 : S Ge 4:23; Ro 12:19; Heb 10:30
- Leviticus 19:18 : Ps 103:9
- Leviticus 19:18 : S Ex 12:48
- Leviticus 19:18 : S Ex 20:16
- Leviticus 19:18 : ver 34; S Mt 5:43*; 19:16*; 22:39*; Mk 12:31*; Lk 10:27*; Jn 13:34; Ro 13:9*; Gal 5:14*; Jas 2:8*

This command that we love one another is given special importance by the Lord Jesus Himself. Jesus said that obedience to this command would be the identifying mark of His disciples. He said, *"By this all will know that you are My disciples, if you have love for one another"* (John 13:35).

The Apostle John said that loving one another is the proof that we have been truly born again.

> ***"We know that we have passed from death unto life, because we love the brethren." -1 John 3:14***

Each of us needs to examine ourselves to see if we are treating our fellow-Christians in the right way. And when we fall short, we need to immediately repent, and then go to the person or persons we have mistreated and seek forgiveness.

> ***"Let all bitterness, wrath, anger, clamor, and evil speaking be put away from you, with all malice. And be kind to one another, tenderhearted, forgiving one another, just as God in Christ forgave you. Therefore be imitators of God as dear children. And walk in love, as Christ also has loved us and given Himself for us, an offering and a sacrifice to God for a sweet-smelling aroma." -Ephesians 4:31; 5:2***

When Christians are vitally yoked to Christ and in relationship with God and walking in the Spirit, loving Him with all your hearts, souls and minds—*only then* will you be fulfilling God's command to love others as you love yourselves. It is love for God and for others that results in righteousness, in fruit, and in glory to Christ.

God enables us to love one another with His love by giving us the indwelling of the Holy Spirit. The same Spirit that dwells in the Father and in the Lord Jesus now dwells in us. The AGAPE love, which is in God's heart, flows to us and through us to others by the power of the Holy Spirit. The Bible says, *"…the love of God has been poured out in our hearts by the Holy Spirit who was given to us"* (Romans 5:5).

Also, you were commanded to love others because such love testifies to your relationship with the Father. You demonstrate that you belong to Christ by that love.

Jesus said our love for one another would be one way to show the world His love *(John 13:34-35)*. The church is indeed a miracle – people from varied backgrounds and different races, all loving each other as a family brought together by the blood of Jesus. Being family means we must love even those who seem to be unlovable. It is essential for us to grow together in love for each other and service to our Father. We have all been created by God and made in His image. GOD LOVES EACH ONE OF US AND HE SACRIFICED HIS ONLY SON *TO DIE FOR US!*

Should we not love everyone… AS JESUS DID?

Cross references:
- A) John 13:34 : Jn 15:12; 1Jn 2:7-11; 3:11
- b) John 13:34 : Lev 19:18; 1Th 4:9; 1Pe 1:22
- c) John 13:34 : Jn 15:12; Eph 5:2; 1Jn 4:10, 11

> *"Dear friends, let us continue to love one another, for love comes from God. Anyone who loves is a child of God and knows God." -1 John 4:7*

"Is There Anything Too Hard for God?" Absolutely Nothing!

> *"Ah, Sovereign LORD, you have made the heavens and the earth by your great power and outstretched arm. Nothing is too hard for you."*
> *-Jeremiah 32:17*

God is ready, willing, and able to help us; He is ready, willing, and able to be our Lord and our God. No matter what is going on in your life, you can trust that God is in control, and is working *everything* out for your good (Romans 8:28). When you wake up in the morning and wonder how you will face the day, God is working it out. When you wonder how you can get through and overcome this difficult time, God is working it out. And when you lay down at night, wondering how you will face the challenges of tomorrow, whatever they may be, God is already working it out. God knows intimately the concerns of your heart.

> *"You have searched me, LORD, and you know me. You know when I sit and when I rise; you perceive my thoughts from afar. You discern my going out and my lying down; you are familiar with all my ways" -Psalm 139:1-3.*

GOD CAN PROVIDE ALL THE PEACE, STRENGTH, AND COURAGE YOU NEED. Confidently hope in Him. HOPE AND PERSEVERE! God is the God of promise. *He keeps His Word,* even when you feel that your circumstances seem impossible. When you feel like running for shelter; a place to hide; a place where anyone facing tragedy can go; a place that provides our spirits never-ending shelter from danger, and offers powerful strength to weather any storm life may bring our way... THAT SECRET PLACE IS FOUND ONLY IN JESUS. In Psalm 32:7 David says this of God: *"You are my hiding place; you preserve me from trouble; you surround me with songs of deliverance."*

Though life is sometimes difficult and painful, when we take shelter in Him, God is there. God promises to be with the one who trusts in Him. He alone can truly rescue you and keep you from falling. Just as Jesus rescued Peter when He invited him to walk on water in the midst of a storm... He will stretch out His hand and rescued you. All you need do is take a deep breath of faith, reach out, and take hold of the mighty hand of God. Do not fear the deep, murky waters of uncertainty surrounding you. Though the way seems difficult, and at times impossible, you can be confident in this, *"Nothing will be impossible with God"* (Luke 1:3). Every time your situation seems too difficult or impossible, take this scripture and speak to it as a reminder that God can handle whatever is troubling you. Cast your cares upon the Lord. *Call on Jesus!* For your only HOPE is found in Him.

> If you take from a man his wealth— *you hinder him.*
> If you take from him his purpose—*you slow him down.*
> But if you take from man *his HOPE—you will stop him.*

You may go on without wealth, and even without purpose, for a while. But you will not go on without hope. When looking at your own circumstances, you may feel completely discouraged. The reality of what you are facing can seem so overwhelming; you might feel like giving up. But don't give up. The circumstances may be too difficult for us to handle, but in Christ there is *always* hope.

> ***"For I know the plans I have for you, says the Lord. They are plans for good and not for evil, to give you a future and a hope" -Jeremiah 29:11***

Some other scriptures you may want to meditate on and write them on the tablets of your heart:

"God is our refuge and strength, a very present help in trouble" -Psalm 46:1

"My flesh and my heart fail, but God is the strength of my heart and my portion forever." -Psalm 73:26

"Be strong and take heart, all you who hope in the LORD." -Psalm 31:24

"Therefore let us draw near with confidence to the throne of grace, so that we may receive mercy and find grace to help in time of need." -Hebrews. 4:16

Let Jesus calm the storms in your life…
Trust in Him! Cross references:

> *Don't keep focusing on the bigness of your circumstances because it will keep you from seeing*
>
> **THE BIGNESS OF GOD!**

Do You Realize Who You Are?
You Are Sons and Daughters of the King!
You Are Royalty!

> *"I have told you these things, so that in me you may have peace. In this world you will have trouble. But take heart! I have overcome the world."*
>
> *-John 16:33*

Jesus willingly died for each one of us, (*who are guilty of sin*) so that we could have eternal life. *Become the children of God--Heirs to the Royal Kingdom*!

We can have a life of peace and joy *right now* here on earth. But we must turn toward the true light *Jesus Christ*. As the Spirit of Christ lives in us, by His power we will overcome the world. We are no longer slaves to sin. It is time we rid ourselves of slave mentality and start to think like our Heavenly Father thinks, to see as He sees, to see ourselves redeemed and righteous and no longer slaves to sin!

As Christians, we are children of God, and yet most of us forget to live that way. We live defeated lives, keeping our heads down and believing the lies of the devil. We don't have to live in the past anymore since we can't change what has happened. Sometimes the things that we did will bring pain and discomfort and we feel haunted by them. We often hold ourselves back from moving forward in our walk with God simply because we have never dealt with our past. We often find it easier to bury these things than to deal with them.

Remember that the only power your past has over you—is the power *you* give it. Living in the past is bondage …it is not of God. Because of what Jesus did at the cross, we no longer have to be haunted and tormented by the past anymore. We are FREE from condemnation. Not just some condemnation, but ALL condemnation of the past, present and future.

> ***"There is therefore now no condemnation to them which are in Christ Jesus, who walk not after the flesh, but after the Spirit." -Romans 8:1***

Faith always looks at the future and says, *"It can be done, and according to the promises of God, it is done!"* Lay down all your past failures at the feet of Jesus and let your faith step out and act like you have victory. YOU DO HAVE VICTORY! It's already been won at the cross at Calvary. We can proclaim with confidence: *"I can do all things through Christ who strengthens me* (Philippians. 4:13).

Not only are we Children of the most High God, we now take our place as royal priests and the holy nation, as the children of Israel were called to be!

> ***"But you are a chosen generation, a royal priesthood, a holy nation, His own special people, that you may proclaim the praises of Him who called you out of the darkness into His marvelous light." -1 Peter 2:9***

It is time to stop thinking with the world's mentality. It is time to stop seeing things the way the world does. Learn what God thinks and train your mind to think like Him. We serve a Father who is the King of all things. As adopted children of God, we belong to royalty and will one day live as such in His Kingdom. The enemy wants us to forget this truth so he plants all kinds of deceit in our minds. He knows that as long as he can keep us from thinking like royalty, he can interfere with our acting like royalty. God expects us to follow His lead in handling out mercy, grace, love, compassion, forgiveness, hope, and truth.

Therefore, we must be Christ minded. Our overcoming began with the Blood of the Lamb. It is only by the cross that the enemy's power was and is broken. When the perfect, sinless Son of God gave up His pure life on the cross to die for all sin, the penalty for all sin was and is forever paid. From that point forward, the enemy has no further hold, no further right to impose evil on you... except as we allow it. Don't let doubt and unbelief keep you under bondage, and don't miss out on any more blessings.

> *"But as many as received Him, to them He gave the right to become children of God, to those who believe in His name."-John 1:12*

God has called us to be Royalty so why not walk in your Heritage that He has provided.
See yourself how God sees you...
AS A BELOVED CHILD OF GOD!

Are the Words Coming Out of Your Mouth Blessing You or Cursing You???

> *"For he that will love life and see good days, let him refrain His tongue from evil, and his lips that they speak no guile."*
> *-1 Peter 3:10*

What are your words saying about yourself and your circumstances? Your words will determine whether you see blessings or curses in your life. If you want to see blessings in your life, you will need to keep your tongue from speaking curses.

Deuteronomy 30:19 says, "I call heaven and earth to record this day against you, that I have set before you death and life, blessing and cursing: therefore choose life that both thou and thy seed may live." You choose death or life and blessing or cursing by your tongue. Death and life are in the power of the tongue: and they that love it shall eat the fruit thereof (Proverbs 18:21). Out of the same mouth comes blessing and cursing—so don't use the power of the tongue to speak death and curses. God instructs you to speak life and blessings, because He knows you will eat the fruit of your lips. That's why God told the people *"Let the weak say, I am strong"* (Joel 3:10). So what are you speaking? Let the words of your mouth speak only that which is useful for edification and God-honoring purposes. *"Let no unwholesome word proceed from your mouth, but only such a word as is good for edification according to the need of the moment, so that it will give grace to those who hear"* (Ephesians 4:29). Let the words of your mouth make your way prosperous—speak to and bless your finances, your body, and your family.

Because our words are very powerful, we need to objectively evaluate our walk with Christ by taking a look at what we laugh at, what we say, and whether our words are abusive to others or offensive to God in any way. Our words should edify, minister grace, and demonstrate how thankful we are to be changed from the inside out and freed from language that defiles, debases, an dehumanizes.

Are you speaking words to *build up yourself and others?* Are your words filled with *hate or love, bitterness or blessing, complaining or compliments, lust or love, victory or defeat?* Speaking curses will affect your quality of life. They can bring failure, shame, sickness and even physical death. Do not let the words of your mouth snare you. Don't live your life one more day trapped in the wilderness. Do not let your tongue keep you in bondage anymore… free yourself with your words of praise and worship unto the Lord.

Jesus reminds us that the words we speak are actually the overflow of our hearts (Matthew 12:34-35). What our tongue produces has eternal implications: *"Men will have to give account on the Day of Judgment for every careless word they have spoken"* (Matthew 12:36). When one becomes a Christian there is an expectancy that a change of speech follows because living for Christ makes a difference in one's choice of words. The sinner's mouth is "full of cursing and bitterness" (Romans 3:14); but when we turn our lives over to Christ, we gladly confess that "Jesus is Lord" (Romans. 10:9-10). As condemned sinners, our mouths are silenced before the throne of God (Romans 3:19), but as believers, our mouths are opened to praise and glorify God (Romans. 15:6).

Those whose hearts have been changed by the power of God will be recognized by the words that they speak. When our *hearts* are full of blessing our *words* also will be full of blessing. So if we fill our hearts with the love of Christ, only truth and purity can come out of our mouths.

Let the power of our words be used of God to manifest all the blessings that He has prepared for us who have accepted Jesus as our Savior. Let your word's demonstrate the power of God's grace and the indwelling of the Holy Spirit in your live. May God enable us all to use our words as an instrument of His *Love* and His *Saving Grace*.

Psalm 31:24 : Ps 27:14

If you will choose your words carefully and speak only blessings, you will change your life forevermore. You will be living the true Blessed Hope that Our Father in Heaven has freely given to us right here on earth… *RIGHT NOW.*

> *"Let the words of my mouth, and the meditation of my heart, be acceptable in thy sight, O Lord, my strength, and my redeemer." -Psalm 19:14*

START *speaking blessings into your life* **TODAY**… *and watch your life change!*

The Fruit That You Are Producing IS VERY Important!

> *"Make a tree good and its fruit will be good, or make a tree bad and its fruit will be bad, for a tree is recognized by its fruit."*
> *-Matthew 12:33*

The Bible tells us that we are known by our fruits. God measures our character by these fruits. It is important that we recognize what kind of fruit that we are producing.

> *"Who is wise and understanding among you? Let them show it by their good life, by deeds done in the humility that comes from wisdom. But if you harbor bitter envy and selfish ambition in your hearts, do not boast about it or deny the truth. Such "wisdom" does not come down from heaven but is earthly, unspiritual, demonic. For where you have envy and selfish ambition, there you find disorder and every evil practice. But the wisdom that comes from heaven is first of all pure; then peace-loving, considerate, submissive, full of mercy and good fruit, impartial and sincere..." -James 3:13-18*

Jesus warns us what will happen if we don't produce good fruit:

"The ax is already at the root of the trees, and every tree that does not produce good fruit will be cut down and thrown into the fire."
-Matthew 3:10

Jesus exhorts us to *remain in Him* so we can bear good fruit:

"If anyone does not remain in me, he is like a branch that is thrown away and withers; such branches are picked up, thrown into the fire and burned. If you remain in me and my words remain in you, ask whatever you wish, and it will be given you. This is to my Father's glory that you bear much fruit, showing yourselves to be my disciples." -John 15:6-8

Our fruitfulness *does* matter to God. The Father rejoices when His children produce fruit. He takes special care to prune and cleanse those who produce fruit so that they will be more fruitful. The Father does not want us to just have branches…He wants us to have ABUNDANT fruitful branches —that give fruit to their full potential. To do this we *need* to abide in the Vine, that is to abide in the Lord Jesus Christ (John 15:4-5). We must passionately desire an intimate relationship with Him. For us to truly abide in Christ, His living words must abide in us. Abiding in Christ is to abide in His *light*, in His *presence* and in His *living Word*. We must go to Him and quietly sit waiting on Him; and then listen for Him to speak to us and watch for what He shows us.

The Bible tells us what a life characterized by the fruit of the Spirit looks like.

"But the fruit of the Spirit is love, joy, peace, longsuffering, kindness, goodness, faithfulness, gentleness, self-control…" -Galatians 5:22-23

These are the fruits that you must desire and produce. These are the fruits you must present yourself with to be identified with Christ. Bearing good fruit essentially is becoming like Jesus. Spiritual fruit will show itself in our lives as a change in our character and outlook. As we spend time with Jesus and get to know Him better, His thoughts will become our thoughts. His purpose will become our purpose. We will become like Jesus.

Faithful Christians look to God and they want to grow in Him. They want to get closer and closer to Him and His Son. They want to manifest Christ as much as possible in their lives. These Christians have passion for fruit and vision for Christ. And the good news is that God wants *you* to be one of them. He wants you to be a fruitful branch, blossoming and giving fruit in its full potential. This is what the Christian life is all about. God has already prepared the good works in which we should walk; He has already gifted each one of us uniquely, like a tree planted and destined to make fruit. All that we have to do is to walk in what God has already prepared. Doing this is destined to please the Father and bring forth good fruit.

Is that what others see in your life? If not, then either you don't know God or you are living outside of fellowship with Him. If that is the case, then a commitment or a recommitment to Him would be in order. God is not asking for a perfect life, but He *is* asking that these fruits be primary characteristics of a life that is lived for Him. Jesus is trying to tell us that we *must* bear good fruit. *When we bear fruit that is good*, we identify ourselves as <u>HIS</u>!

> *"You did not choose me, but I chose you and appointed you to go and bear fruit— fruit that will last..."* -John 15:16

Where Do We Go For Help... Google... or God?

"Cast all your anxiety on Him because He cares for you."
-1 Peter 5:7

In this age of technology, the internet has become the default source of wisdom for making decisions. Have we replaced God with a computer, when we really need to learn how to access the Author of all knowledge? Technology seems to have taken priority over a better source of wisdom. So whom do you search first, Google or God?

How often do we run into a decision making process *without* consciously asking God about it, right at the beginning? But even before asking God for wisdom in your circumstances, ask Him to help you see yourself the way that He sees you. It is so easy to get caught up in what we do, or don't do, or used to do. Ask God to give *you* insight into *who He has made you to be, the gifts He has given you, and the path He has placed you on.* God sees each of us as worthy of His Son's sacrifice – that's a lot more value than we sometimes put on ourselves. Ask for a *heart of gratitude* for your current situation and then for *wisdom* as you consider a change. Seek godly counsel from a trusted friend or church leader and ask them to pray through this journey with you.

Why limit the Lord when He offers to help us in *all* of our cares and concerns? Jesus said, *"Everyone who asks receives; the one who seeks finds; and to the one who knocks, the door will be opened"* (Matthew 7:8).

> *"When He, the Spirit of truth, has come, He will guide you into all truth; for He will not speak on His own authority, but whatever He hears He will speak; and He will tell you of things to come." -John 16:13*

God created us for relationship. He wants His sheep to hear His voice and does not restrict Himself in how He talks to us. Jeremiah instructs us that when we call upon God, He will not only respond but show us great and mighty things, fenced in and hidden, which you do not know.

> *"Call to me and I will answer you and tell you great and unsearchable things you do not know." -Jeremiah 33:3*

There is no problem or decision too insignificant for God. Start *believing* that God cares about your concerns—big and small! The closer you get to God's heart, the more you will be encouraged to seek His wisdom for your needs. God is our burden bearer. He wants to take care of us; He wants to bear our burdens, if only we will cast them on Him. It is evident that God wants to father us; He desires to sustain us because He loves us. God made us with the capacity to trust Him for our daily provisions. When you have *any* decisions to make, you must go to the Lord and ask for His guidance, and then the next crucial step is to *listen for His directions*. If you don't—you are in danger of missing His will and His plans for your life. God is looking for people who want to spend time in His presence. Spending time in His presence—*waiting, watching and listening* is the most important key to accessing His wise counsel—if you do this *it will be life changing!* Incredible joy and peace accompany the Lord's plans for us.

> *"As the heavens are higher than the earth, so are my ways higher than your ways and my thoughts than your thoughts." -Isaiah 55:9*

Without the Holy Spirit guiding our thinking, our minds will produce thoughts that are in opposition to God. Believers can be filled with the Holy Spirit and still have fleshly thoughts, but as we mature spiritually our minds are progressively renewed by the Word of God. As that Word takes root in our hearts, it changes our way of thinking and making decisions so that carnal thoughts are fewer and fewer. We are not to conform to the world, but to be transformed into the image of Christ by the renewing of our minds.

"Do not conform to the pattern of this world, but be transformed by the renewing of your mind. Then you will be able to test and approve what God's will is—His good, pleasing and perfect will." -Romans 12:2

Jesus modeled the way God *wants* us to live our lives. He spent long hours in the night seeking His Father's will through prayer and listening.

Do as Jesus did—don't go to google…
Go to God Our Father!

"Whether you turn to the right or to the left, your ears will hear a voice behind you, saying, "This is the way; walk in it." -Isaiah 30:21

Not Feeling Close to God? Maybe It Is Time to Have a Checkup On Your Heart... Could It Possibly Be Hardened?

> *"For the heart of these people has become dull, and with their ears they scarcely hear, and they have closed their eyes, otherwise they might see with their eyes, and hear with their ears, and understand with their heart, and return, and I would heal them."*
>
> *-Acts 28:27*

Because the heart is so important to what we think, say, and do, we each need to regularly do open heart surgery with the scalpel of the Word under the guiding hand of the great physician, our Lord Jesus Christ. We accomplish this through the teaching, guiding, convicting ministry of the Holy Spirit. Like a sharp two-edged sword, the Word divides the inner man asunder to reveal the true condition and needs of our hearts (Hebrew 4:12). If we aren't careful about our daily spiritual walk, we can easily suffer from a hardened heart. Anyone's heart can harden, even the faithful. — *Too often we forget* how God has blessed us and what He has done for us.

What does a hardened heart look like? A hardened heart keeps pace with the world more than it does with Jesus. It doesn't seek out or listen to Godly counsel or wisdom from the Bible. It stops communicating with God and seals off the work of the Holy Spirit. It loses faith in God's abilities to bless us and work miracles. It is selfish and sows bitterness, anger, resentment jealously, malice, discontent and other evils. It causes more harm than good. It calls evil good and good evil and justifies evil actions. It silences the conscience and suppresses truth. It does not desire forgiveness, healing, faith and hope in God. It substitutes pleasure for righteousness. A hardened heart, without treatment, could fall away from God entirely and be left spiritually corrupted and bankrupt, deprived of spiritual nutrients and every good and amazing thing God had planned.

Sin causes hearts to grow hard. If we relentlessly continue to engage in sin, there will come a time when God will give us over to our "debased mind" and let us have it our way. The apostle Paul writes about God's wrath of abandonment in his letter to the Romans where we see that godless and wicked "men who suppress the truth" are eventually given over to the sinful desires of their hardened hearts (Romans 1:18–24).

God will help us to see our heart's condition when we ask Him. Pray and ask God to show you where your heart is vulnerable and weak.

> *"Search me, O God, and know my heart: test me and know my thoughts. See if there is any offensive way in me, and lead me along the path of everlasting life." -Psalm 139:23-24*

God can heal any heart once we recognize our disobedience and repent of our sins. But true repentance is more than simply a resolute feeling of steadfast determination. Repentance manifests itself in a changed life.

> *"If we confess our sins, [Jesus] is faithful and just and will forgive us our sins." -1 John 1:9*

After repenting of our sins, hard hearts begin to be cured. When we study God's Word, fill your heart daily with God's Word. *"How can a young person stay on the path of purity? By living according to your word, I seek you with all my heart; do not let me stray from your com-*

mands. I have hidden your word in my heart that I might not sin against you" (Psalm 119:1-11). The Bible is our manual for living, as it is written: *"God-breathed and is useful for teaching, rebuking, correcting, and training in righteousness"* (2 Timothy 3:16).

If we are to live life to the fullest as God intended, we need to study and obey God's written Word, which not only keeps a heart soft and pure but allows us to be "blessed" in whatever we do.

> *"Keep this Book of the Law always on your lips; meditate on it day and night, so that you may be careful to do everything written in it. Then you will be prosperous and successful."*
> *-Joshua 1:8*

God can change any heart, no matter how hard, *if we let Him*. The Bible tells us that God *can* and *will* change our hearts if we let Him. He wants to mold our hearts into His image (Genesis 1:27).

> *"Blessed is the one who does not walk in step with the wicked or stand in the way that sinners take or sit in the company of mockers, but whose delight is in the law of the Lord… whatever they do prospers" -Psalm 1:1-3*

Filling our hearts with good things—
will leave no room for evil things!

"Create in me a pure heart, O God, and renew a steadfast spirit within me." -Psalm 51:10

Is Your Bible Sitting on a Shelf Getting Dusty?

> *"This book of the law shall not depart out of your mouth; but you shall Meditate therein day and night, that you may observe to do according to all that is written therein; for then you shall make your way prosperous, and then out shall have good success."*
> *-Joshua 1:8*

So how dusty is your Bible? Have you incorporated reading the Bible daily as part of your spiritual discipline? Or maybe the question is, when was the last time you sat down with your Bible to read it? To study it? To share it? All too often the days get busy and we struggle to get even the basic chores done. Sometimes we add in appointments, special projects, yard work, or even volunteer work at/for the church. Suddenly we are exhausted, ready to call it a day, and sit down for a little TV. The Bible remains closed and sitting on the shelf—*getting dusty*.

Reading the Bible daily is a discipline and it takes a commitment to follow it. As Christians we are responsible for knowing the Bible. We are responsible for listening to God sharing His wisdom through scripture. The Bible tells us that God exists and is real. The Bible tells us that salvation is by faith. Faith can only come by hearing and believing in the Word of God.

> *"So then faith cometh by hearing, and hearing by the word of God."-Romans 10:17*

The Bible is the only book that gives you understanding of God and His will. God proclaims the power of His Word:

> *"So will My Word be which goes forth from My mouth; it will not Return to Me empty, without accomplishing what I desire, and without Succeeding in the matter for which I sent it."*
> *-Isaiah 55:11*

If you desire to have an intimate relationship with Jesus, you *must* read and study the Bible. As a Christian, we should be growing to be more like Jesus daily.

> *"Make every effort to add to your faith goodness; and to goodness, knowledge; and to knowledge, self-control; and to self-control, perseverance; and to perseverance, godliness; and to godliness, brotherly kindness; and to brotherly kindness, love. For if you possess these qualities in increasing measure, they will keep you from being ineffective and unproductive in your knowledge of our Lord Jesus Christ." -2 Peter 1:5-8*

We cannot grow without staying connected to Jesus: *"Abide in Me, and I in you. As the branch cannot bear fruit of itself, unless it abides in the vine, neither can you, unless you abide in me. I am the vine, you are the branches. He who abides in me, and I in him, bears much fruit, for without me you can do nothing"* (John 15:4-5).

Jesus is the source of spiritual growth:

> *"And now just as you trusted Christ to save you, trust Him, too, for each day's problems; live in vital union with Him. Let your roots grow down into Him and draw up nourishment from Him. See that you go on growing in the Lord, and become strong and vigorous in the*

truth you were taught. Let your lives overflow with joy and thanksgiving for all He has done."
-Colossians 2:6-7

THE SCRIPTURES WERE WRITTEN TO HELP US LEARN AND GROW IN FAITH: *"For whatever things were written before were written for our learning, that we through the patience and comfort of the Scriptures might have hope"* (Romans 15:4).

GOD'S WORD IS A LIGHT TO GUIDE US AND TO KEEP US FROM DARKNESS: *"And we have something more sure, the prophetic word, to which you will do well to pay attention as to a lamp shining in a dark place, until the day dawns and the morning star rises in your hearts"* (2 Peter 1:19).

THE WORD OF GOD IS MEANT TO GET US RIGHT WITH GOD... IF WE ALLOW IT TO: *"Holding forth the word of life; that I may rejoice in the day of Christ, that I have not run in vain, neither laboured in vain"* (Philippians 2:16).

The Bible gives us instructions on how to live righteously and become more like Jesus. Your insight into spiritual things, and into life itself, will only be as deep as your Bible knowledge. For the Bible to get into our hearts and lives, we need to get into the Bible.

> *"And this is my prayer: that your love may abound more and more in knowledge and depth of insight." -Philippians 1:9*

We have got to *change* from being a BIBLE OWNER to a BIBLE READER!

> *"You study the Scriptures diligently because you think that in them you have eternal life. These are the very Scriptures that testify of me." -John 5:39*

What Type of Seeds Are You Sowing?

"Be not deceived; God is not mocked: for whatsoever a man soweth, that shall he also reap."
-Galatians 6:7

Whether we realize it or not in our daily actions and interactions we sow seeds that will at some point bring forth fruit. God is not like man, He is just, righteous and very fair. Unlike man, God cannot be fooled or deceived. It is therefore very important that each of us daily keep in mind that our deeds and words will reap consequences of either good or bad, depending on the seeds that we sow.

The Bible warns us not to sow seeds of wickedness, injustice, hatred, jealousy, envy, discord… and expect to reap love, blessings and favour. *"Even as I have seen, they that plow iniquity, and sow wickedness, reap the same"* (Job 4:8). In the book of Proverbs 6:16-19 it states *"These six things doth the LORD hate: yea, seven are an abomination unto him: A proud look, a lying tongue, and hands that shed innocent blood, a heart that deviseth wicked imaginations, feet that be swift in running to mischief, A false witness that speaketh lies, and he that soweth discord among brethren."* Discord is strife, confusion, contention and it is not of God. God is a God of love but He is also a God of judgment and sowing wickedness of any sort will bring a harvest of wickedness.

It is therefore very important for us to be led by the Holy Spirit at all times and in all things be careful what we say and do. Trials are not always a result of sowing bad seeds but in some cases people reap all the bad deeds and actions they have done to others multiplied and it not only affects them but their children and grandchildren.

Now is the time to examine the seeds we are sowing and take responsibility for them. Are they seeds that will cause the Kingdom of God to flourish within us, or are they seeds of the flesh that will produce corruption in body, soul, and spirit? We have the choice on whether we sow to the Spirit or flesh. *Rather than sowing fear and unbelief, let us sow a pure faith – for faith alone accesses the benefits of our covenant in the Kingdom.*

God is calling us to sow seeds of righteousness.

> ***"Sow to yourselves in righteousness, reap in mercy; break up your follow ground: for it is time to seek the LORD, till he come and rain righteousness upon you." -Hosea 10:12***

Thank God for his mercies and His grace. He causes the blessings to fall on the just and the unjust, but we should never ever take God for granted or trample on His mercies. God is calling us to live holy lives and walk in the path of righteousness. We must abide in Jesus Christ so that we will not only sow good seeds but bring forth good fruit.

> ***"Even so every good tree bringeth forth good fruit; but a corrupt tree bringeth forth evil fruit." Matt. 7:17***

> ***"And the fruit of righteousness is sown in peace of them that make peace." -James 3:18***

The fruit that the Holy Spirit produces is love, joy, peace, patience, kindness, goodness, faithfulness, gentleness, and self-control. So if you are saved, sanctified, and filled with the Holy Ghost, then your life should be exhibiting the fruit the Holy Spirit produces. When we sow the seeds of the Kingdom, the Lord will water them with His Spirit and cause our relationship with Him to flourish in abundant productivity. He will be exalted, and His glory will fill the earth. Amen!

The Word declares that a harvest is promised for every seed sown – whether good or bad. Every day you can sow good seeds in all areas of your life. Sow your work into the company of people you serve as unto the Lord. Each day demonstrate God's love in kindness and mercy. Think of all you do as seeds sown into God's kingdom.
Look at the fruit that you are sowing in your life… GOD DOES!

> *"I the LORD search the heart and test the mind to give every man according to his ways according to the fruit of his deeds." -Jeremiah 17:10*

Cross references:
- A) Romans 15:13 : Ro 14:17
- B) Romans 15:13 : ver 19; 1Co 2:4; 4:20; 1Th 1:5

If you are looking for an abundant harvest,
Sow the Seeds of God's Word *in the ears and hearts… of all who will listen.*

Is Your Daily life Filled with the Joy of the Lord or Are You Walking Around Feeling Troubled and Hopeless?

> *"My peace I leave with you; my peace I give to you. Not as the world gives do I give to you. Let not your hearts be troubled, neither let them be afraid."*
>
> *-John 14:27*

Proverbs 16:9 says, *A man's mind plans his way, but the Lord directs his steps and makes them sure."* Proverbs 20:24 says, *"Man's steps are ordered by the Lord. How then can a man understand his way?"* When God directs our paths, He sometimes leads us in ways that don't make sense to us so we're not always going to understand everything. If we try to reason out everything, we will experience struggle, confusion and misery, but there is a *better way*. Proverbs 3:5-6 says, *"Lean on, trust in, and be confident in the Lord with all your heart and mind and do not rely on your own insight or understanding. In all your ways know, recognize, and acknowledge Him, and He will direct and make straight and plain your paths."*

Many make the mistake of trying to figure everything out for themselves and have spent their lives trying to take care of themselves, but when we accept Christ as our Savior, we must learn to trust our lives to His care. When we do, we can say… *"I trusted in, relied on, and was confident in You, O Lord; I said, you are my God. My times are in your hands"* (Psalm 31:14-15).

If you are discontent, worried, anxious, bewildered, perplexed, confused, or agitated, you may not be trusting God like you should or maybe you are trusting in *something or someone* else to satisfy you. Even when your trial seems huge…the joy of knowing Jesus is far greater. When you start feeling hopelessness and feel that you have not anywhere to turn, reach out for a promise of God, and lay hold of it by the power of Jesus, and your fear will vanish.

God has a plan for our lives; his promises are firm, they do not come and go, they don't get tossed about according to our faithfulness but are irrevocable according to his grace and holiness—*His promises are true*. Our God is THE GOD OF HOPE — which means those who trust Christ always have reason to be full of hope.

> *"May the God of hope fill you with all joy and peace in believing, so that by the power of the Holy Spirit you may abound in hope."*
> *-Romans 15:13*

If you want to live a life filled with joy and comfort, you must trust in Jesus with all of your heart. If you are truly trusting Jesus, you will not be living a life of doom and gloom but instead will be rejoicing in the Glory of God.

> *"We are pressed on every side by troubles, but we are not crushed and broken. We are perplexed, but we don't give up and quit. That is why we never give up. Though our bodies are dying, our spirits are being renewed every day. For our present troubles are quite small and won't last very long. Yet they produce for us an immeasurably great glory that will last forever!" -2 Corinthians 4:8, 16-17*

God makes promises and He never breaks them. Because God never lies, His promises are everlasting. HIS PROMISES ARE FOR YOU! You can make excuses, lack faith to believe or even refuse to believe that you are included in the promises of the written word. That is up to you. You alone are accountable for what you do with this knowledge. The Bible has all the answers to *ALL of your problems and needs*. You need to ask God to work in your finances, your employment, your health, your wayward child, etc. But at the same time, fight the fight of faith to keep trusting Christ as your all-satisfying Savior.

As a Christian you should have joy in your heart in all circumstances. Joy is a part of your inheritance. Your heart should be filled with it. Joy is a spring of living water from God's own heart—and this fountain can never fail. This joy of the Lord is said to be our strength. It makes us strong. Sadness makes us weak. When joy departs—strength leaves us, and we faint by the way. When the joy of the Lord is in your heart—the wilder the storm, the fiercer the tempest… the more gladly your heart should sing!

This life is like a vapor which appears for a time and vanishes away. Paul tells us that our trials here are momentary and light compared to the eternal weight of glory we will have in Christ (2 Corinthians 4:16-18).

GOD PROMISES US eternal bliss in Heaven with Him; a perfect everlasting life where there are none of the trials, failures and disappointments of our earthly existence…

> *Do not let your hearts be troubled…*
> **Hold on to the Promises of God!**

What Are You Really Seeking...
In YOUR Life?

Many Christians are living in a continual state of anxiety and frustration. They are turning in all directions looking for help yet nothing seems to improve their situations. As their anxiety increases, they cry out from the depths of their heart. They continue to live with the pain of despair and frustration and feel that their situation is hopeless. If you are living your life like this...it could be the result of what you are truly seeking. So are you seeking God or are you looking for satisfaction in other places, in other things or maybe in other people? If you are seeking things of this world you will never be satisfied—you will always stay restless within your soul and never really reach your goal. Your goal must be to seek Jesus Christ and to desire a fuller knowledge of Him and His Will.

When you seek Jesus... you will be *more* than satisfied. Jesus *promises* to give us something that the world cannot give us. He *promises* that when you come to Him, He *will* give you PEACE, HOPE and LOVE *that will last and that will satisfy your soul* more than you could ever imagine. Jesus *promises* that if you come to Him—He will put in your heart something incredible that this world cannot give—neither your own mind nor your brain nor your acts of goodness, nor the worldly wealth you have, neither something that anyone or anything can ever give to you—*only* through God are these things possible. It is only through Jesus that your soul will find rest and *when you find Him* seeking for satisfaction in other places will end.

If what we really desire is to be worthy of Christ and to be His disciples, we are to hate everything that prevents us from keeping Jesus in first place in our lives. We are to hate everything that prevents us from seeking Him all the time—anything that prevents us from praying, prevents us from worshipping Him, prevents us from reading the Bible and everything that prevents us from concentrating on Him. We need to see Him as crucified in our eyes all the time not just once in a while, *but all the time*. Thus, we are called to seek His Face and His Presence without ceasing. We are to hate everything that prevents us from doing God's will in our lives.

WHAT GOD REQUIRES OF US IS THAT WE ABIDE IN HIM.

> *"Remain in me, and I will remain in you. No branch can bear fruit by itself; it must remain in the vine. Neither can you bear fruit unless you remain in me. I am the vine; you are the branches. If a man remains in me and I in him, he will bear much fruit; apart from me you can do nothing."-John 15:4-5*

Without God we can do nothing, thus the fruits of being a Christian are the result of God's work of grace in our lives, not by our efforts. We must understand that our failures and weaknesses are no match for God's grace and love that He has for us. Our works will always end in failure and suffering, demonstrating our weaknesses, and as we come to the end of our *self*. We can call out to our Father of Compassion and He will give us His strength and the ability to overcome, causing us to love Him and trust Him more and more—in doing this God is Glorified.

> *But he said to me, "My grace is sufficient for you, for my power is made perfect in weakness." Therefore I will boast all the more gladly about my weaknesses, so that Christ's power may rest on me. That is why, for Christ's sake, I delight in weaknesses, in insults, in hardships, in persecutions, in difficulties. For when I am weak, then I am strong."-2 Corinthians 12:9-10*

Sometimes as Christians we are not receiving God's best because we are willing to settle for less. We have to get sick and tired of being sick and tired before we will aggressively pursue all that God has for us. God has far more for all of us than we are experiencing. Seeking God does not end after we become born-again... If we want to live a life of joy and peace right here, right now—the key is to SEEK HIM WITH ALL OF OUR HEART. Jesus is the *only* One who can truly satisfy the very depths of your soul and strengthen you through the many trials this world has to offer. Jesus is all you need. Jesus will forever satisfy you! Jesus will bring you fullness of joy that nothing else in this world can bring. We are called to seek God's wisdom and understanding, and His Kingdom, and that is Jesus Christ Himself, who is the fullness of GOD'S LOVE.

> *"O taste and see that the LORD is good: blessed is the man that trusteth in Him." -Psalm 34:8*

> *Seek* **ONLY THE KINGDOM OF GOD** *and* **ALL** *will be given unto you!*

Are You Standing at a Crossroads Not Knowing Which Path You Should Take? One Day... You Will Have to Choose!

In one direction you see a wide gate alluring you into promises of wealth, power, and happiness. This gate can be entered with no difficulty. It can be entered with all your baggage... No repentance is necessary and no surrender to Christ is necessary. This is the gate of self-indulgence. You can bring your pride, your self-righteousness and your sins—all of these things are welcomed here. Along the way there are hordes of people, places, and things that presume to offer all the paraphernalia that would make your life very comfortable, uncomplicated, and appealing. It must be good because there are masses of people wandering here. This road looks enticing. The wide gate is tempting. It promises that you can be your own god, directing your own affairs, and living by your own conscience. Jesus said that many will choose the wide gate, the easy life—the life full of self. Yet He also said... that road *always* leads to personal destruction and ultimately eternal destruction.

Many will travel through the wide gate, down the wide road only to find that *life without Jesus is meaningless.* The wide road is littered with those who have tried to find peace, goodness, and truth within themselves and have realized that self could not fulfill.

THERE IS ONLY *ONE* OTHER GATE TO CHOOSE FROM... THE NARROW GATE!

> *"Enter through the narrow gate. For wide is the gate and broad is the road that leads to destruc-*

tion, and many enter through it. But small is the gate and narrow the road that leads to life, and only a few find it" -Matthew 7:13, 14

Jesus said, *"I am the gate; whoever enters through me will be saved. They will come in and go out, and find pasture." John 10:9.* The narrow gate will lead you to the Kingdom of God, to salvation, to eternal joy and bliss in heaven. *"There is no salvation in any other name, for there's no other name under heaven given among men whereby we must be saved"* (Acts 4:12).

You must enter the gate of salvation through faith in Jesus Christ.

"Jesus said to him, 'I am the way, the truth, and the life. No one comes to the Father except through Me." - John 14:6

You must enter this gate naked. You and your sins *must* separate, or you cannot become one with God. Not one sin… may you keep… they must all be recognized for what they are. You must forsake them, abhor them and ask the Lord to help you overcome them. *You must enter this gate alone with difficulty and in full surrender to Christ.* Jesus said, *"Deny yourself… take up your cross and follow Me."*—that's repentance. Joyfully submit yourself to your Master—Jesus. Don't see it as burdensome, but see it as *a cherished opportunity to give honor to the One who has given grace to us.*

"Come to Me, all you who labor and are heavy laden, and I will give you rest. Take My yoke upon you and learn from Me, for I am gentle and lowly in heart, and you will find rest for your souls." -Matthew 11:28-29

"For all that is in the world -- the lust of the flesh, the lust of the eyes, and the pride of life -- is not of the Father but is of the world. And

the world is passing away... but he who does the will of God abides forever." -1 John 2:16-17

"To You, O Lord, I lift up my soul. O my God, I trust in You... Show me Your ways, O Lord; Teach me Your paths. Lead me in Your truth and teach me, for You are the God of my salvation..." -Psalm 25:1-5

"He will wipe every tear from their eyes, and there will be no more death or sorrow or crying or pain. All these things are gone forever." -Revelation 21:4

---

*Seek to Walk in The Ways of the Lord.
Seek Your "Rest" in Jesus.
He Will Never Fail You!*

Have You Received Your Free Gift? If You Haven't, Don't Wait Too Long Because It Just Might Be Too Late!

"As it is written, there is none righteous no, not one"
-Romans 3:10

"For all have sinned and come short of the Glory of God."
-Romans 3:23

Our sins have separated us from a *Righteous* and *Holy God*, but in His *mercy and love* towards us He has made a way of escape for all those who seek it. God loves us so much that He sent His Son to die on the cross for you and me that we might have everlasting life. His love is not based on our performance and it is not something that we can purchase. Christ loves us so much that while we were yet sinners—*He died for us*! In spite of our disobedience, our sin, our weaknesses, and our selfishness…He loves us enough to provide a way to an abundant life. God's love for us is unconditional and it is also undeserved. JESUS WAS GOD'S PROVISION FOR OUR SINFULNESS.

"For God so loved the world, that he gave his only begotten Son, that whosoever believeth

in him should not perish, but have everlasting life." -John 3:16

Eternal life is offered by God as a FREE GIFT. This offer is for all mankind and anyone who desires to receive it by faith in Jesus Christ. Jesus paid for the sins of the whole world with His precious blood on the Cross at Calvary.

Salvation is very simple—we are all sinners and Jesus is the Savior. Christ died, was buried and rose from the dead. Anyone who believes on the name of Jesus for salvation becomes a part of God's family (Romans 10:13). Our part is to acknowledge our guilt of sin and believe the Gospel of the Lord Jesus Christ to be forgiven.

Because of sin we must all die a physical death (Romans 6:23), but Jesus shed His blood and paid the price for our sins so we wouldn't have to die a second death—we are offered eternal life with Him in the Kingdom of God. If you don't *choose* Christ—Revelation 21:8 defines the second death as spending eternity being tormented in a lake of brimstone and fire.

The apostle Paul in Ephesians 2:1 says, *"And you He made alive, who were dead in trespasses and sins"*. To the Romans he wrote, *"For all have sinned and fall short of the glory of God"* (Romans 3:23). Sinners are spiritually "dead". When they receive spiritual life through faith in Christ, the Bible likens it to a rebirth. Only those who are born again have their sins forgiven and have a relationship with God. Jesus said, "Except a man be *born again*, he cannot see the Kingdom of God". Being *born again* is *not* optional. Whether Jew or Gentile, everyone <u>must</u> be born again. Jesus said, *"I tell you the truth, no one can enter the kingdom of God unless he is born of water and the Spirit. Flesh gives birth to flesh, but the Spirit gives birth to spirit"* (John 3:3-6). The phrase "born again" literally means "born from above." We are all in need for a change of heart—a spiritual transformation—a new birth. Being born again is an act of God whereby eternal life is imparted to the person who believes.

All God the Father asks is that we come for salvation by the way of the Cross upon which His Son Jesus died. God is the only one who can do the saving… all we have to do is believe.

> *"Jesus saith unto him, I am the way, the truth, and the life: No man cometh unto the Father, but by me." -John 14:6*

We receive God's free gift of eternal life by receiving Jesus Christ as our Savior…

> *"For by grace ye are saved through faith; and that not of yourselves: it is the gift of God." -Ephesians 2:8*

> *"Every good gift and every perfect gift is from above, and cometh down from the Father of lights…" - James 1:17*

JESUS is the Perfect Gift… accept Him Today!

> *"For whosoever shall call upon the name of the Lord shall be saved" -Romans 10:13*

As the Bible Predicted—
The Churches Are Falling into Apostasy!

"The Spirit clearly says that in later times some will abandon the faith and follow deceiving spirits and things taught by demons."
-1 Timothy 4:1

"...There will be terrible times in the last days. People will be lovers of themselves, lovers of money, boastful, proud, abusive, disobedient to their parents, ungrateful, unholy, without love, unforgiving, slanderous, without self-control lovers of pleasure rather than lovers of God—having a form of godliness but denying its power..."
-2 Timothy 3:1-5

Apostasy means to fall away from the truth. Therefore, an apostate is someone who has once believed and then rejected the truth of God. Apostasy is a rebellion against God because it is a rebellion against truth. In the Old Testament God warned the Jewish people about their idolatry and their lack of trust in Him. In the New Testament the epistles warn us about not falling away from the truth. Apostasy is a very real and dangerous threat.

Paul tells us as to why the end times Church will be weak, vacillating, and full of apostasy. *"..the time will come when they [Christians] will not endure sound doctrine; but wanting to have their ears tickled, they will accumulate for themselves teachers in accordance to their own desires; and will turn away their ears from the truth, and will turn aside to myths"* (2 Timothy 4:3-4).

Paul adds that the basic reason will be due to people *"holding to a form of godliness, although they have denied its power"* (2 Timothy 3:5). There will be no lack of religion, says Paul, but people will deny the true power that is able to transform society for the good—producing peace, righteousness and justice. Paul is talking about the power of the blood of Jesus. It is also the power that comes from *accepting* the Bible as the infallible Word of God. It is the power of believing in a Creator God with whom all things are possible. And certainly it includes a belief in the power of the Holy Spirit.

Apostasy is on the rise in the churches today. It *begins* in our own hearts and minds. It begins when we fall away from the truth of God's Holy Word. The heart and the mind are so closely related that we must guard them both. As Christians, we need to be very sure that we are clinging to the truth of God's word and resisting the inclusion of liberalism, moral relativism, and the oncoming secularism that is all around us. We need to stand on the word of God and never be ashamed of the truth of the Gospel:

> *"For I am not ashamed of the gospel, for it is the power of God for salvation to everyone who believes, to the Jew first and also to the Greek."*
> **-Romans 1:16**

We must focus on the truth of God's word and let our minds be shaped by it. We must seek to have our minds shaped by the love of God as we move not only to learn about Him, but also to carry out His desires.

In these last days, the bible tells us that many false prophets will arise; and that deception will increase in the household of God until there will be little truth remaining. Jesus stated that the deception would be so strong that even the elect would be deceived, if that were possible.

"For false Christs and false prophets will appear and perform great signs and miracles to deceive even the elect--if that were possible. See, I have told you ahead of time." -Matthew 24:24, 25

IT IS HARD TO STAY TRUE TO GOD'S WORD IF YOU DON'T KNOW WHAT IS IN IT!

The *only* way to hold onto the truth is to know God's Word. If we are not living by the Scriptures that were given to us by God, that means we must be living outside the camp of Christ… and that is a dangerous place to be!

We need to stand together believing and striving to follow the true Word of God. Now is the time…READ THE BIBLE! Make it a daily practice to study the Bible. Keep the Gospel at the very center of your heart; love its truth and experience its power and keep sin out of your heart! The bible is the lifeblood of every believer's life. Reading the bible will ground your faith and grow your confidence. Don't be deceived—KNOW in your heart the truth of God's Word!

> **God gave us the Bible because He loves us…so don't you think we owe it to Him to read it?** *"He chose to give us birth through the word of truth, that we might be a kind of firstfruits of all he created." -James 1:18*

Why Are So Many Christians Living A Joyless Life?

"The Joy of the Lord is your strength."
-Nehemiah 8:10

Jesus desires us to understand that He had come, not only to purchase our salvation through His sacrifice on the cross, but also to provide us with an abundant life by the sustaining power of His *joy!*

"Ask using my name, and you will receive, and your cup of joy will overflow." -John 16:24

We know that we have been given the free gift of salvation when we accepted Jesus Christ as our Savior, by *faith.* We also know that we receive the baptism in the Holy Spirit, by *faith!* But many Christians don't realize that Jesus also provided us with His *joy,* again received by *faith!*

Paul told the Corinthians that although he couldn't do much to help their faith, for it was strong already, he wanted to do something about their joy—he wanted them to be happy. *"But that does not mean we want to dominate you by telling you how to put your faith into practice. We want to work together with you so you will be full of joy, for it is by your own faith that you stand firm"* (2 Corinthians 1:24). Paul wanted them to start to practice rejoicing in order to cultivate the joy planted in them by the Holy Spirit. Paul knew that the *outward* circumstances for a strong Christian would be filled with trials and suffering.

The Christian's source of joy was to be *their inward abiding in Christ*. Joy has already been given to us by Jesus. Jesus prayed that His joy would be perfected in us. What He means is that we can't make ourselves joyful any more than we can save ourselves, give ourselves peace, or make ourselves more loving. What we *can* do is *choose* to accept what Jesus has done for us and allow Him to perfect His joy in us. The source of joy was not to be found in happy circumstances, but in knowing Jesus' commandments, obeying them and abiding in Him.

> ***"Just as the Father has loved Me, I have also loved you; abide in My love. If you keep My commandments, you will abide in My love; just as I have kept My Father's commandments and abide in His love. These things I have spoken to you so that My joy may be in you, and that your joy may be made full." -John 15:9-11***

Jesus meant for us to be overflowing with joy. No matter what we are feeling or whatever our circumstances are —we *can* have JOY by praising and rejoicing in the Lord. In reading the book of Psalms you will see that David learned the secret of rejoicing. David's psalms almost always end with a note of joy, expressing cheerful and encouraging words.

> ***"My lips will shout for joy when I sing praise to you— I whom you have delivered." -Psalm 71:23***

> ***"…But he who trusts in the LORD, lovingkindness shall surround him. Be glad in the LORD and rejoice, you righteous ones; And shout for joy, all you who are upright in heart." -Psalm 32:10-11***

The joy of the Lord is our strength. It is *His rejoicing* that gives us a reason to rejoice. It is *His joy* that fills us with hope. It is His joyous wish to save us just as we are—in spite of *all* our sins. It is *God's joy* to stand us back on our feet and strengthen our feeble legs and wobbly knees so that we might discover His joy as our strength. It is truly a sacred day in heaven when a sinner discovers that "the joy of the Lord is his strength!"

"The joy of the Lord" remains our strength today. His faithfulness has continued throughout all generations. For His kingdom extends from generation to generation. He is still the same faithful God. As we look back to Abraham from the cross, we see God's continued faithfulness to the promise He made to Abraham. Today that same God seeks to bless all men through Jesus Christ, the seed of promise to Abraham. He seeks to fulfill the promise He made to Abraham that all the families of the earth would be blessed through His seed. But we *must* commit our lives to Him!

> When you rejoice in the Lord, your joy
> will be filled to overflowing!

> *"You have turned for me my mourning into dancing; You have loosed my sackcloth and girded me with gladness, O LORD my God, I will give thanks to You forever." -Psalm 30:11-12*

In Times Of Trouble... We Need To Know That We Are NOT Alone... Jesus Is ALWAYS With Us!

> **"God is our refuge and strength, a very present help in trouble."**
> *-Psalm 46:1*

All *Children of God* will go through periods of trials, difficulties, pain, and suffering in this life. We may never know the "Why?" until we get to Heaven. Regardless of our age, intellect, responsibilities, or experience, in God's eyes we are still just little children. When we fall into various trials, He wants us to come to Him to seek *His Will* and *His direction* and to quit attempting to carry the burden ourselves. This requires *faith*! Jesus Christ stepped forth from eternity to become a man and He endured much suffering. He has felt the pain of sorrow, rejection, grief, and excruciating physical trauma. He knows how we are feeling. He loves and cares for each of us and promises to help us through the difficult "storms" of life that we will face.

> *"Do not be afraid, nor be dismayed, for the Lord God is with you wherever you go." Joshua 1:9*

NO MATTER HOW ALONE YOU MIGHT FEEL NOW

> *"It is the Lord who goes before you. He will be with you; he will not leave you or forsake you. Do not fear or be dismayed." -Deuteronomy 31:8*

PRAY HONESTLY AND SINCERELY AND SEEK THE LORD FOR DIRECTION

"I will instruct thee and teach thee in the way which thou shalt go: I will guide thee with mine eye." -Psalm 32:8

"The righteous cry out, and the Lord hears and delivers them out of all of their troubles." -Psalm 34:17

FAITH MEANS TRUSTING HIM IN EVERYTHING

"Trust in the LORD with all your heart, and lean not on your own understanding." -Proverbs 3:5

"If any of you lacks wisdom, let him ask of God, who gives to all liberally and with out reproach, and it will be given to him. But let him ask in faith, with NO doubting..." -James 1:5-6

WHEN YOUR HEART AND MIND ARE TROUBLED

"Fix your thoughts on whatever things are true, whatever things are noble, whatever things are just, whatever things are pure, whatever things are lovely, whatever things are of good report, if there is any virtue and if there is anything praiseworthy... meditate on THESE things." -Philippians 4:8

The Bible says the true Child of God will suffer through trials in this life. Each of us will have our faith tested. Jesus waits for us to ask Him into our lives to help, to strengthen, to comfort, and to heal. The Lord promises to see us through *all* of them. His promise is not to take us out of the bitter storms of life, but to safely lead us *through* the storms. No matter how bad the situation might seem now, it will one day be over and behind you. Trust in Him! God answers *all* prayers of those who diligently seek Him. (*The answer is not always "Yes" sometimes the answer is "No," or "Not yet"*). Please remember it is *His Will* we seek, not our will; *His timing*, not our timing; and *His Way*, not our way. *Only* God knows the end from the beginning. Don't be discouraged when prayers aren't answered exactly the way we want or when we want. He truly cares and knows what is best. Remember, the Lord Jesus Christ is the Good Shepherd, for *"The Good Shepherd gives His life for the sheep..."* (John 10:11). He has prepared a narrow path of safety for each of us through this life. Although His path might appear the most difficult, it is the only one which will lead us safely home into His Kingdom of Heaven. It may seem overwhelming at times, but we *must* trust in Him. Without Him we are lost. Seek His direction and then walk in faith!

As we walk with Jesus in these last days, we can expect increased trials and difficulty. Those who love His appearing *are* discerning the times, staying wide awake, and knowing that our time here is short. In the time we have left to live for Him, whether days or decades, it is so important to understand how close Jesus is to us—even when we don't see Him.

Jesus is our ONLY Hope…
He will NEVER leave us nor forsake us!

> *"Do not be anxious about anything, but in every situation, by prayer and petition, with thanksgiving, present your requests to God."* -Philippians 4:6

God Has Promised Us A Great Future! So Why Are You Troubled?

> *"For I know the plans I have for you," declares the LORD, plans to prosper you and not to harm you, plans to give you hope and a future."*
> *-Jeremiah 29:11*

We have all struggled and fretted because our lives weren't going the way *we* wanted. We feel as though our needs and desires are reasonable. After all *we know what would make us happy…* so we pray for it with all our might, asking God to help us to get what *we* want. But if it doesn't come to pass, *we* begin to feel frustrated, disappointed, and even bitter. Sometimes God will let us have exactly what *we* pray for only to discover that it doesn't make us happy after all….just disillusioned. Many Christians spend their entire lives living in this cycle wondering what they are doing wrong! When we live in this cycle, we open the door for the enemy and then depression sets in and all we can think about is *oh woe is me!*

There is a way out— *"Let not your heart be troubled: ye believe in God, believe also in me."* We must learn to trust in God for everything. We want to put our trust in *anything* rather than the Lord. We'll trust in our own abilities--*everyone and everything else* but the Lord? Trusting in the Lord can require that you abandon everything you've ever believed about *what you think that brings happiness and fulfillment.*

Paul lets us know in the Book of Romans that everything that we experience in this life, all the struggles, pain, frustration, heartaches, disappointments, and suffering, that *all things* work together for our good. God rules all things, made all things, is in control of all things, and is working all things together for your good. We don't always understand why bad things happen in our lives but we can have assurance that God has a divine plan. Our God has a master plan for each of us, but it's up to us to surrender to His will. We are more than conqueror's in Christ Jesus. "…If God be for us, who can be against us" (Romans 8:31).

One sure way of defeating the devil is by getting out your Bible and telling him just what God says about your future. We have an opportunity to give glory to God by standing strong on His Word right in the face of all the pressure and lies the devil can bring. We have the opportunity to say, "Go ahead devil, give it your best shot--when you're finished, I will still be standing. I'll still be praising Him—and saying I believe God and His Word and by faith I receive His promises!" We can confidently put the devil under our feet where he belongs, knowing that in Jesus… our bill has been paid…and we'll step boldly into a future full of the promises and provisions of God!

Psalm 145 tells us of God's wonderful love—a love *we cannot even fathom*!

> ***He is gracious and compassionate; slow to anger and rich in love (Vs. 8).***
> ***He is good to all and has compassion on all he has made (Vs. 9).***
> ***He upholds all those who fall and lifts up all who are bowed down (Vs. 14).***
> ***He is loving toward all he has made (Vs. 13, 17).***

The story of Joseph tells us of how God was using all the events of his life to get him where He wanted him to be. Joseph went from the pit to the palace. Sometimes you may have to go through difficult circumstances to get to the place where God ultimately wants you. Sometimes you have to understand that you have to *go through to get through.* "All things work together for the good of *them that love the Lord and are called according to his purpose."*

When you put all of your trust in the Lord… *Peace* will come. After you give your situation over to God in prayer--you don't really have to wait for how He answers or what the outcome because *His peace will fill your heart.* You will be in the *Hands of God…* and in God ALL things will be good!

IF YOU WILL LET HIM,
GOD WILL MAKE SOMETHING BEAUTIFUL OF YOUR LIFE.
but he needs you to trust in him that he will
Do what he says!

> *"Thou wilt keep him in perfect peace, whose mind is stayed on thee: because he trusteth in thee. Trust ye in the LORD forever: for in the LORD JEHOVAH is everlasting strength." -Isaiah 26:3-4*

Not Only is He with you Always... He Will Never Leave You nor Forsake You... and He Will Give You Peace!

> *"Be strong and courageous. Do not be afraid or terrified because Of them, for the Lord your God goes with you, he will never leave You nor forsake you."*
>
> *-Deuteronomy 31:6*

It is essential that we have the presence of the Lord in our everyday lives. His presence is our distinguishing factor. Israel was just another nation without the presence of God. They would have been destroyed without God fighting for them. *Moses wouldn't go without God's presence. Gideon as one man would deliver the nation because of the presence of the Lord. The prophets stood in the presence of the Lord. John's revelation was in the presence of the Lord.*

Everything good is in His presence. Living in God'sthe presence will motivate you to live godly lives and make righteous choices. His presence will help you overcome any challenge that you may be facing. *David didn't have a chance against Goliath, an experienced warrior* (1 Samuel 17:45-47). *But the shepherd boy was aware of God's presence in His life—and he knew that Jehovah God would defend His name and give the victory to Israel. The Lord told Joshua, "Be strong and of good courage; fear not… for the Lord your God is with you wherever you go"* (Joshua 1:9). God's Word is filled with many examples of His faithfulness which should give us peace and confidence in all of our circumstances.

When His presence is upon you, He will clear away all confusion from your mind and give you peace. When you have His presence near you—no power of darkness can stand before you.

> *"This is the message that we have heard from him and declare to you: God is light, and in him there is no darkness—none at all!" -1 John 1:5*

God longs to have this fellowship with us. Sometimes we feel ashamed or unworthy, so we hide from Him. We may feel as though we have no time in our busy schedule to spend time just basking in God's presence. We are easily distracted by things like relationships, work, family, friends, and taking care of our household chores…so we must pray for God to take all these distractions away from us so that we can stay focused on Him. We can get so busy "*doing* that we neglect just *being*" in God's presence. *It is up to us to decide where God is in our lives.* If God is first in our lives, everything else will be less important and He promises to take care of all our needs (Isaiah 43:1-3). He is longing to pour out His favor and blessing upon us. We need to be open to Him and to trust Him. We need, by faith, to receive what He has for us. It is essential that we realize how much He loves us and that He has a good purpose and plan for us.

God wants to speak to us intimately—He wants an intimate relationship with you and me. Only in God's presence can we hear God speak, and there inspiration can flow, creativity can flow and service can flow. If we desire to be used and blessed by God we must take the time to be in His presence, and walk daily in it—before we can experience all that God has for us. When we spend time in God's presence, His character will start changing our attitudes, and the way we think about things, and how we respond to people, and the way we handle situations. In this way we are being transformed. As a result, we are able to take His presence with us wherever we may go. Only when His presence is the center-piece of our lives, can He make our lives His masterpiece.

> *"His presence will empower you to obey—*
> *and obedience brings nothing but blessing."*
> *-Deuteronomy 28:1-2*

Jesus said, *"Come to me...I will give you rest"* (Matthew 11.28). It is the place of hiding *"under the shadow of the Almighty"* (Psalm 91). It is the place of which David said, *"Oh God, My Strength"* (Psalm 18.1). *"You are my hiding place"* (Psalm 32.7).

The only way to true peace and security is being in the presence of God. We can do nothing without Him. *Abiding in God's presence* is where God speaks to us. The closer you move to the Lord...the more of His presence you have!

God never leaves us... but WE do leave Him...

Even so—He is always there waiting for us to return!

> *"In the presence of the Lord is fullness of Joy and pleasure forever more."*
> *-Psalm 16.11*

What Are God's Promises... For Those Who Love Him?

> *"And my God will meet all of your needs according to the riches of His glory in Christ Jesus."*
> *-Philippians 4:19*

According to His Word, there are several things God wants to do for you—good things that we all desire. So what's the catch? The condition is that you must set your love upon Him.

> *"Because he hath set his love upon me, therefore will I deliver him: I will set him on high, because he hath known my name. He shall call upon me, and I will answer him: I will be with him in trouble; I will deliver him, and honour him." -Psalm 91:14-15*

In these two verses there are five things El Shaddai—*the God Who is more than enough*—said He will do for the person who sets his or her love upon Him.

God said, *"Because he hath set his love upon me, therefore I WILL..."*:

- Deliver him
- Set him on high
- Answer him
- Be with him

o   Honor him

God told Abraham that his descendants would be sojourners in a foreign land for four hundred years, but He promised, *"I will bring them out with a strong hand."* God doesn't forget His promises: four hundred-thirty years after Israel's captivity began in Egypt, God raised up Moses and Aaron to lead Israel out of bondage—and He brought them out with a strong hand! He is still the *same* delivering God today!

HE IS... *MORE* THAN ENOUGH!

God has promised us throughout His Word that He hears us and He will answer our call. *"Call unto me, and I will answer thee, and shew thee great and mighty things, which thou knowest not"* (Jeremiah 33:3). Remind God of His promises! Remind Him of His Word! He is faithful to cause it to come to pass in your life.

> ***"Therefore I say unto you, what things soever ye desire, when ye pray, believe that ye receive them and ye shall have them." -Mark 11:24***

God didn't say you weren't going to have trouble just because you've been born again and filled with the Spirit. In fact, He rather infers that you are going to have trouble because you're a Christian. The world is going to persecute you. They're going to talk about you. They're going to speak evil of you. And the devil, who is the god of this world, will put pressure on you at every turn. No, God didn't say we would never have any troubles. But He *did* say, *"Many are the afflictions of the righteous: but the Lord delivereth him out of them all"* (Psalm 34:19). God promises you deliverance! God wants you to know, to believe and to experience abundant life on this earth. He does not want you to go through life unaware of the truth. He went through great pain to make sure that you could know and rest assured in Him.

You *can* believe God will hear and answer your prayers... because He says so! God is the One who is more than enough! He is the All-Sufficient One, the One who never changes and never fails. *"Jesus Christ is the same yesterday, today, and forever"* (Hebrews 13:8). He is just as able today as He ever was, and He's interested in you! He's concerned about you! That's why He said, *"Because he hath set his love upon me, therefore I will answer him."* When you set your love upon God and know His Name, He will honor you and set you on high. I don't know about you, but I want to be set on high where the devil and circumstances and problems of this world can't touch me!

God has given us His Word—all we have to do is BELIEVE, DECLARE, and EXPECT it to be so and He will make it come to pass! If your love is set upon God, begin to thank Him today for His promises that He's given you in His Word. Thank Him and praise Him for delivering you, for setting you on high, for answering you when you call, for being with you in trouble and delivering you, and for honoring you. Thank God for all He is doing in your life!

Faith comes from receiving the Word of God. God's Word is faith food; if you eat it, it will produce faith in your life.

All things are possible with God... IF you have faith!

> *Jesus said to him, "If you can believe, all things are possible to him who believes." -Mark 9:23*

God Is FAITHFUL...
For Those Who BELIEVE And TRUST in Him!

> *"For the Lord is good and his love endures forever; His faithfulness continues through all generations."*
> *-Psalm 100:5*

> *"But blessed is the man who trusts in the LORD, whose confidence is in him."*
> *-Jeremiah 17:7*

By faith Abraham, when called to go to a place he would later receive as his inheritance, obeyed and went, even though he did not know where he was going. And it's very important to note that *if Abraham had not gone where the Lord called him to go he wouldn't have ended up being where he needed to be to receive the inheritance God intended to give him*!

> *"For as the heavens are higher than the earth, so are My ways higher than your ways and My thoughts than your thoughts." -Isaiah 55:9*

The faithfulness of God is true and has been proven many times. In the Holy Scriptures, we can see that God is faithful and His Word is true. The Bible tells us that God cannot lie, nor can He break an unconditional promise that He says He will fulfill. Every covenant He made is kept. Every promise or foretelling has or will come true (Titus 1:2). If we want to receive *all* the promises of God, we must *obey* and *trust* Him!

> *"Whoever has my commands and obeys them, he is the one who loves me. He who loves me will be loved by my Father, and I too will love him and show myself to him." -John 14:21*

We are living in the last of the last days and unrest in our world is increasing rapidly. We are coming into a time when we are going to *need* to know and trust God completely. We *must* have a personal relationship with Jesus. We are commanded to put God first in everything (Mark 12:29-30).

Jesus is coming soon…the time is at hand to *really get serious with God.* God's faithful promise was fulfilled in the New Testament when He sent Jesus to atone for our sins. No matter what sins we have committed, no matter how "bad" we are, GOD IS FAITHFUL to forgive us if we accept Jesus and repent of our sins.

Those who are in Christ have nothing to fear. *"The Lord is faithful, and he will strengthen and protect you from the evil one" (2 Thessalonians 3:3).* When we trust and obey the Lord, we are under the glory spout where the glory pours out! But when we don't trust and obey God, we give the devil power and authority in our lives and as we know, he comes only to steal, kill and destroy. And Jesus very powerfully affirmed God's requirement for obedience in Luke 6:46-49, when He taught that when we OBEY Him and DO what we know His Word tells us to do, our homes will withstand anything and everything that comes against them.

We *can't count on God's blessings, protection and provision* if we don't obey and trust in Him. But when we DO OBEY God and put our trust in Him…He promises that He is always there with us.

> *"God is our refuge and strength, an ever-present help in trouble. Therefore we will not fear, though the earth giveth way and the mountains*

fall into the heart of the sea, though its waters roar and foam and the mountains quake with their surging" -Psalm 46:1-3

God is *so* faithful that anyone who seeks Him can find Him. Faith is a gift, but even a gift must be opened to be enjoyed. As we implement our faith, we begin to realize more and more about God's faithfulness to us. If we live up to the conditions he has expressed or implied, God is faithful to keep his promises. We *can* count on him. We may fail him, but if we remain true, he will not fail us. God promises *"Never will I leave you, never will I forsake you"* (Hebrews 13:5).

"For this is the love of God, that we keep His commandments; and His commandments are not burdensome. For whatever is born of God overcomes the world; and this is the victory that has overcome the world- our faith." -1 John 5:3-4

FAITH is simply… BELIEVING GOD'S WORD!

"May the God of hope fill you with all joy and peace as you trust in him, so that you may overflow with hope by the power of the Holy Spirit." -Romans 15:13

Living Out Our Faith through The Teachings of the Beatitudes!

> *"All Scripture is inspired by God and profitable for teaching, for reproof, for correction, for training in righteousness;"*
> *-2 Timothy 3:16*

The teachings of Jesus called *The Beatitudes* are an invitation to a way of life. The beatitudes call us to a new way of *being* and *doing* that can radically transform our lives. They bring true happiness and the deepest of joy as we find our true identity in our relationship with God. To live the Beatitudes is to *be centered on God and God's desires for our life!*

> **"Blessed are those who hunger and thirst for righteousness, for they will be filled."**
> **-Matthew 5:6**

One of the keys to the Kingdom is to hunger and thirst for it. You must desire for it to *become* thirst in your life. When God becomes the very center of our thinking, our affection, and our feelings, we shall possess and *be* possessed by God. The word "righteousness" refers to living in accordance with God's desires for us, in right relationship with God and with others. Turn away all your own ambitions for the things of God!

TURN FROM YOUR OWN AMBITIONS AND FOLLOW GOD'S DESIRES!

"Blessed are the poor in spirit, for theirs is the kingdom of Heaven." -Matthew 5:1

Blessed are those who know they need God more than they need anything else and they *utterly depend* on God for their very existence. Jesus calls us to realize our own spiritual helplessness and to put our whole trust in God. Being poor in spirit leads us to humbleness before God.

GIVE UP YOUR PRIDE!

"Blessed are those who mourn for they will be comforted." -Matthew 5:4

We should be so grieved over our moral and spiritual shortcomings that we can not rest until we find God. You will never be comfortable as long as you have sin in your life. When you begin to mourn and to cry out to God for deliverance and mercy, He *will* remove the cause for mourning and comfort you. Jesus promises that each of us will be comforted by the presence of the Living Christ, who walks with us in our pain. He will lead us through our pain to help us compassionately reach out in love and comfort others.

GIVE UP YOUR SIN!

"Blessed are the pure in heart, for they will see God." -Matthew 5:8

In Jesus, we see what it is like to be pure in heart. He took on human nature and modeled a life centered on God. He was constantly in touch with God and did God's will in all things. He accepted lowliness and poverty. He had a particular regard for those rejected by others; the ones that others rejected and did not love – the poor, the prisoners, the sick, and the women and children. To become pure of heart is to have all aspects of our lives centered on God, our thoughts, desires, and actions.

GIVE UP ALL THINGS THAT ARE IMPURE!

"Blessed are the meek for they will inherit the earth." -Matthew 5:5

Meekness arises from being centered on God. It is a fruit of being pure in heart, of living out God's will in all aspects of our daily life. We must completely yield our lives to His purposes. Meekness helps us live in true humility and makes us "teachable". The more we grow spiritually, the more we realize how little we do know, and that in our spiritual life it is not possible or important to know everything. In meekness, we come to trust in God, that what we do need to know *will* be revealed to us, as we need it, and that walking with God is taking only one step at a time in faith.

SURRENDER YOUR ALL TO GOD!

"Blessed are the merciful, for they shall obtain mercy." -Matthew 5:7

The key to God's mercy toward us, is the mercy we have toward others.

RETURN GOOD FOR EVIL!

"Blessed are the peacemakers, for they will be called children of God." -Matthew 5:9

When one is at peace, one is in a perfect state of well-being within one's self and with others and is in perfect harmony with God. Accept God's peace! We are given purity of heart when our whole heart and life is given over to God. From this overwhelming experience of the abundance of God's love, we are led to be loving to others.

MAKE PEACE WITH GOD AND OTHERS!

"Blessed are those who are persecuted for righteousness sake, for theirs is the Kingdom of Heaven." Matthew 5:10

We must be willing to die for the cause of Christ. Jesus tells us, *"Be thou faithful until death and I will give thee a crown of life"* (Revelation 2:10). We are called to be meek and respond to persecution with loving-kindness.

Be willing to give your life for Christ!

> *"Thou wilt keep him in perfect peace, whose mind is stayed on thee: because he trusteth in thee." -Isaiah 26:3*

Jesus Gives Us Strength in All Things— Not SOME but ALL Things!

> *"I can do all things through Christ who strengthens me."*
> *-Philippians 4:13*

In 2 Timothy 4:16-17 Paul describes one of his most difficult emotional times. He said, *"At my first defense no man stood with me, but all men forsook me."* The great apostle felt abandoned and all alone. Have you ever felt that no one else in the whole world understood you or was willing to stand by you? It's during those times that we must learn (like Paul) to draw on the strength of Jesus Christ alone. Paul went on to say, *"However, the Lord stood with me and strengthened me."* Paul had learned the secret of drawing on the strength of Christ. He had learned to exchange his *inability* for God's *ability*. Paul wrote these words while facing some of the worst trials of his life. Despite the threat of pain and death, he realized that God gives us strength in ways that go beyond the good times and the everything-is-okay moments. The strength of Christ reaches right down into our turmoil and pain. And it's there that we can truly do "all things."

Christ gives us the strength to not only endure the tough times, but also to *grow* during them. We aren't meant to just struggle through our pain; we're meant to see our faith blossom right in the face of our battles. God equips us with the armor that we need to stand firm.

> *"Therefore put on the full armor of God, so that when the day of evil comes, you may be*

***able to stand your ground, and after you have
done everything, to stand." -Ephesians 6:13***

Because of our lack of contentment, we allow disappointments, setbacks, and delays to keep hammering away at us. Apart from Christ, we'd quickly trip and stumble our way into bitterness and entitlement. But in Christ, we move our eyes off the things we don't have, the frustrations that surround us, and we put them where they need to be. Paul's words from prison show this spiritual truth in action: *"I know what it is to be in need, and I know what it is to have plenty. I have learned the secret of being content in any and every situation, whether well fed or hungry, whether living in plenty or in want"* (Philippians. 4:12).

The good news is we *can* have contentment by turning our attention from what we think we need—to the *only* thing that matters. *"For the pagans run after all these things, and your heavenly Father knows that you need them. But seek first his kingdom and his righteousness, and all these things will be given to you as well"* (Matthew 6:32–33). Our hope is in Christ: *"But godliness with contentment is great gain. For we brought nothing into the world, and we can take nothing out of it"* (1 Timothy 6:6–7). Jesus gives us the strength to see beyond our present circumstances and to trust in Him to provide everything we truly need.

If you *truly* believe that God loves you and cares for you, then there is no need to worry. If you are *truly* convinced that God loves you, then you don't need to worry about others who may let you down or betray you. You know that God will watch over you and show you what to do and how to respond. For He is more powerful than any plot that the enemy may have against you! It is most important that you know just how much God truly loves you and how you *can* trust Him in every situation. So, when you sense that tormenting "feeling" that something may not work out, learn to pause and THANK GOD FOR HIS GREAT LOVE!

***"What shall we say to these things? If God be
for us, who can be against us? He that spared***

not His own Son, but delivered Him up for us, how shall He not with Him also freely give us all things." -Romans 8:32-33

The secret of your success is all in THE DIVINE EXCHANGE. In truth, we can learn to live an EXCHANGED LIFE where we can actually exchange our weakness for *His strength*; our discouragement for *His encouragement*; our lack of provision for *His provisions*; our inability for *His ability*; and our impending defeats for *His victories!*

"He gives power to the faint; and to them that have no might, he increases strength. Even the youths shall faint and be weary, and the young men shall utterly fall. But they that wait upon the Lord shall renew their strength; they shall mount up with wings as eagles; they shall run and not be weary; and they shall walk and not faint." -Isaiah 40:29-31

He won the Victory and we can share the prize!

> *"And He said unto me, "My grace is sufficient for thee; for my strength is made perfect in weakness."" -2 Corinthians 12:9-10*

Trust in the Lord
He Makes Everything Beautiful In His Time!

Each and every one of us has broken the laws of God and in that sense… we are all unworthy. *"All of us have sinned and fallen short of God's glory"* (Romans 3:23). But not *one* is worthless because our Almighty God created each and every one of us in His image. We are all are valued by God and may be redeemed if we will put our trust in Jesus. The wonderful message of God's amazing grace is that once we have repented, turned to Christ, and received his total forgiveness that was purchased for us by his death on the cross; we are both fully accepted and unconditionally loved.

We are all God's masterpiece in the making. He has a *specific and unique purpose for our lives.* But in order to accomplish those works and fulfill His purpose and goal for our life, we need to know *who we are* in Christ. When we receive Christ into our lives, the Bible says we become a "new creation" and we have a *new identity* in Christ. We receive a spiritual inheritance as God's adopted sons or daughters, and we are fully loved and accepted by God.

There is nothing we can do to earn this. It's solely by His grace that we are saved. And as God's children, we are expected *"…to walk in a manner worthy of our calling that we've received, completely humble and gentle; being patient, bearing with one another in love* (Ephesians. 4:1-2). God's Word tells us that He has a unique and custom-designed plan for those who have put their trust in Jesus Christ. God selected you and chose you so that in the ages to come He might show the exceeding riches of His grace.

God has a calling for you to accomplish the "good works" that He prepared for *you* to do that *no one else* could do. *"For we are*

God's masterpiece; He has created us anew in Christ Jesus, so we can do the good things he planned for us long ago (Ephesians 2:10). God has an assignment for each of us on earth with our name on it! *PRAISE HIM!*

When God created you, He went to great length to make you exactly the way He wanted you. You're not meant to be like everyone else; God designed you the way you are for a purpose. Everything about you is unique and everything about you matters. You may feel like your life looks ordinary today, but when you understand—not only *who* you are, but also, *whose* you are—only then you will love yourself more, and you will also love those people around you in a greater way. You are God's special treasure, selected *by* Him and *for* Him. You are created in the image of Almighty God and He has equipped you with everything you need.

He will give you the strength to stand strong in the midst of difficult situations, and the wisdom it takes to make good decisions. Know how important you are to God and out of your importance, know that you are called to add value to those around you. No matter where you are in life today, you have potential to increase, grow, to be strengthened, and to move forward. When we think about ourselves and our failings, it is hard for us to believe that we have been made perfectly righteous in Christ.

"The gift of righteousness" is one of the most amazing and wonderful gifts that God could possibly give to us. This righteousness which God gives us is… *perfect righteousness*. It cannot be improved upon. We are made *"the righteousness of God"* in Christ. Nothing can be added to His perfection, nor can anything be taken from it. Regardless of how many times we fail, Christ is always our righteousness.

The glorious message of the gospel is that whatever your past may have been, or however many negative thoughts you may think about yourself, Jesus can change all that. He *offers* total forgiveness and a fresh start. He will give you the *assurance* that one day his work in you will be *complete* and that you *will know* the greatest joy possible as you serve and worship him in his eternal kingdom. *God has a beautiful plan for your life,* so don't try to alter His plan. Patiently *wait* and *trust* in Him!

> *"Commit your way to the Lord; trust in Him, and He shall bring it to pass." -Psalm 37:5*

> *You have been fearfully and wonderfully made ...*
> **YOU ARE TRULY... HIS MASTERPIECE!**
> *This should cause your heart to* **REJOICE!**

If You Knew How Much Jesus Cares For You... You Would Not Worry!

> *"Cast your cares on the Lord and He will sustain you; He will never let the righteous fall.*
> *- Psalm 55:22*

Sometimes we take things to the Lord and leave them at the foot of the cross only—to take them back again. Just because we don't see the air that we breathe does not mean we stop breathing; and just because we don't see the answer to our prayers right away—does not mean we stop believing. Keep your faith and trust in the Lord-- for He is the God of the breakthrough and the God of miracles. God delights in answering our prayers!

We all face many trials, but we must remember Jesus will always bring us through. He will always be our anchor through the storms of life and our Rock in times of trouble. If we ever feel that things are getting too much, and we feel like we are sinking...His gentle loving hand is there to lift us up and bring us out. The Bible says in Matthew 11:28-29: *"Come unto me all who are weary and heavy burdened, and I will give you rest. Take my yoke upon you and learn from me, for I am gentle and humble of heart, and you will find rest for your souls."*

The Bible also says in Isaiah 40:29-31: *"He gives strength to the weary and increases the power of the weak. Even youths grow tired and weary, and even young men stumble and fall; but those who hope in the Lord will renew their strength. They will soar on wings like eagles; they will run and not grow weary, they will walk and not grow faint."*

So throw your pain, your disappointment, your broken dreams and your heartache on to the Lord for HE CARES FOR YOU! Allow Jesus to carry you and bring you through whatever life may throw at you. The bible tells us we *must* expect many tribulations *to enter* into the Kingdom of God. During those trials, if you put your trust in God's loving care, it will enable you *to experience* God in the midst of all your troubles. There is nothing that is happening to you that He is *not* ultimately in control of. Be assured that God has a tender affection for his church and people… *He would not have you to be discouraged.* Jesus will never leave you nor forsake you. Come to Him in prayer for every detail of your life and let the Lord lift you up once more. Let Jesus *heal* you and *bring* you *peace*.

If you've given your life to Jesus and made Him your Lord and Savior, then He is talking to you. *"Fear not, therefore; you are of more value than many sparrows"* (Matthew 10:31). God says that He will make a man (*that is you and me*) more precious than fine gold (Isaiah 13:12). When we look at the greatness of the price He paid to save us—it is so much more precious than gold! If the Lord God Almighty, who is in absolute and total control of every nanosecond of every event in the entire universe, takes the time to care for the lowly little sparrows, then how much more will He listen to, and respond to, His precious sons and daughters that Jesus engraved on His palms at His crucifixion!

Jesus tells us how important His children are to Him by referring back to the lowly sparrow—a small bird that his audience deemed quite unimportant. God loves us so much more than we can even imagine!

> *"Are not two sparrows sold for a penny? And not one of them will fall to the ground apart from your Father. But even the hairs of your head are all numbered. Fear not, therefore; you are of morevalue than many sparrows."*
> *-Matthew 10:29-31*

Let the Lord put a new song in your heart. Let the Lord give you a new hope. Let the Lord give you a new beginning on this new day. Always remember that The Creator of the heavens and the earth knows you by name and loves you!

JESUS LOVES YOU! ...so there is no need to be discouraged with all the things of this world!

> *"Trust in the LORD with all your heart And lean not on your own understanding."*
> *-Proverbs 3:5*

Why It Is So Important to Have Unity in The Church?

> *For as in one body we have many members, and the members do not all have the same function, so we, though many, are one body in Christ, and individually members one of another."*
> *-Romans 12:4-5*

The Bible is clear that the best place for us to thrive is in fellowship with other believers. We are all *"one body in Christ."* Hebrews 10:24-25 says, *"And let us consider how to stir up one another to love and good works, not neglecting to meet together, as is the habit of some, but encouraging one another, and all the more as you see the Day drawing near."*

In order to make the soil of your heart soft and receptive to God, you must have help from those God has placed around you. We are created to worship with the body of Christ for all eternity. The Church is *God's Bride.* He loves to pour out his presence in different ways as we gather together in the presence of fellow believers. These blessings can *only* be received when you *open your heart* to the family of God. We all *need* grace and we all *need* each other. One of the most useful tools God has given us for making our hearts receptive to him is *each other.*

The church is both a beautiful and broken group of people—beautiful because of the grace of God working in each of us making us more like Jesus—broken because we have yet to walk in the fullness of what Christ did for us on the cross. But if we are to walk in the fullness of what God intends for us here on earth, we must continually forgive and ask forgiveness from each other and share life with believers in accordance with God's word. We aren't meant to live and love out of our own strength. Instead, we are to seek God's heart for his people and align ourselves with Him. God's desire for the church is so vast and powerful. He loves us in His perfect faithfulness despite all of our transgressions.

The church is to be a place of fellowship, where Christians can be *devoted* to one another and *honor* one another (Romans 12:10), *instruct* one another (Romans 15:14), *be kind and compassionate* to one another (Ephesians 4:32), *encourage* one another (1 Thessalonians 5:11), and most importantly, *love* one another. (1 John 3:11) The Bible tells us we must exercise humility and lowliness of mind, and "be completely humble and gentle; be patient, bearing with one another in love" (Ephesians 4:2). A church filled with such people cannot help but have *peace, unity and harmony.*

Each one of us is given the commission to proclaim the Gospel of Salvation through Jesus Christ. The church is called to be faithful in sharing the gospel through word and deed. The church is to be a "lighthouse" in the community, pointing people toward our Lord and Savior Jesus Christ. The church is to both promote the gospel and prepare its members to proclaim the gospel (1 Peter 3:15).

The glory of the Lord dwelt right in the middle of the two cherubim. This tells us that the Lord's glory dwells where there is unity in the Spirit, and intimacy of fellowship. The Lord wants us to see His glory! He has created an incredibly beautiful and marvelous universe to proclaim His glory and omnipotence! He has given us Jesus Christ to reveal Himself to us.

God is teaching us to move in the heavenly realm. When His glory is revealed in full-- we will see the glory of God's redemption, love, and mercy for all eternity. We have been called to share and manifest His glory! His glory initiates true worship in us, for we see that He is worthy of all honor, praise and worship. We recognize that He alone is truth, and therefore we can trust Him in every situation that comes our way. In worship, we submit all we are and have to our Lord and Savior Jesus Christ, and stand in awe at His power and love to change us into heavenly beings. Our unity *needs to be* like that which exists between God and Christ (John 17:20).

When we are perfected in unity… the world will marvel!

> *The HOLY SPIRIT moves in a church where the BODY OF CHRIST is in UNITY!*

Are You Stumbling Around in Darkness... Living in the World... Or is Jesus The Light of Your Life?

> *"When Jesus spoke again to the people he said, "I am the light of the world. Whoever follows me will never walk in darkness, but will have the light of life."*
>
> *- John 8:12*

If you are living "in" and "for" THE WORLD, you are living in darkness. There are those who trade God's wonderful plan for their life for drugs, alcohol, and other things of the world. Many in our midst believe themselves to be useless; rather than the treasured sons or daughters of The King. Many grope around in a black fog of failure and shame, with many regrets haunting them and causing their dreams to fade away. We allow the things of the world to keep us in bondage and live in fear... without any hope. WITHOUT JESUS these things leave us sitting in the dark, never satisfied, weary, overwhelmed, troubled and depressed... BUT THERE IS REALLY GOOD NEWS!

It was into this dark world... that Jesus arrived.

> *"In him was life, and the life was the light of men. The light shines in the darkness, and the darkness has not overcome it. The true light,*

> *which enlightens everyone, was coming into the world." -John 1:4-5, 9*

In the midst of the blackness of our lives, Jesus has come, piercing the darkness, shining a light that will never go out.

AS THE LIGHT OF THE WORLD
He causes our shame to fade away, *replacing shame with honor*

AS THE LIGHT OF THE WORLD
He causes our deepest fears to melt, *replacing our fears with power.*

AS THE LIGHT OF THE WORLD
He causes our sin and guilt to fall away from us, and he *replaces our sin and guilt with forgiveness and righteousness.*

AS THE LIGHT OF THE WORLD
He opens up our empty places within, and *He fills them with meaning and purpose, hope and joy.*

Jesus' death on the cross purchased for us… passage from death to life, from darkness to light. What he asks of us is not that we work harder or continue scrambling to find our way. What he asks is that we call on him for salvation, that we trust him, confessing to Him our sin and shame, and our need for a Savior and believe that He is God's provision for our salvation.

> *"For God so loved the world that he gave his only begotten Son, that whosoever believes in him will not perish but have everlasting life."*
> *- John 3:16*

JESUS CHRIST IS THE LIGHT THAT WILL NEVER GO OUT, illuminating our pathway through the blessings and burdens of this old world in which we find ourselves, causing all of our sin and shame to take flight under the burning light which is his love and grace and mercy and goodness. In His light there is great freedom for our souls freeing us from any bondage. ***JESUS IS OUR ONLY HOPE that will never fade.***

Is there anything that is keeping you from basking in the Light which is Jesus Christ? Ask yourself, "Is there anything in my life that keeps me from living in the liberating light of Jesus?" He wants to fill you with His light and have all the darkness around you flee. Ask Him to shine His light within you and around you, and tell Him that you desire to believe Him for your salvation and hope. Accept Jesus as your personal Savior and receive His Light...

JESUS IS THE TRUE LIGHT...

Come out of the darkness... before it is too late...

JESUS IS COMING BACK SOON!

> *"For everyone who calls on the name Of the Lord will be saved." -Romans 10:13*

If God Were to Look at Your Heart Right Now... Would He See a Pure Heart?

> *"The eyes of the Lord run to and fro over the whole earth to show Himself strong on the behalf of those whose heart is perfect toward Him."*
>
> *- 2 Chronicles 16:9*

God isn't looking for someone who is perfect for there is none, but for someone whose *heart* is perfect. He is looking for those who hunger and are open-minded towards Him and the realm of the Spirit.

> *"Draw nigh unto me and I will draw nigh unto you." -James 4:8*

> *"If you delight yourself in the Lord, He will give you the desires of your heart."- Psalm 37:4*

When Jesus speaks, His Words are *alive and forevermore*. The *only* way His Words can continue to grow in us is by meditating, thinking and giving those words a place in our lives. Jesus has instructed us to pray with our whole heart. *"Blessed are the pure in heart; for they shall see God" (Matthew 5:8)*. If you are born again, allow that Christ-like spirit that is within you to have its way, for your spirit is always willing and wanting to see God. The things of God are of the Spirit world.

> *"Let us draw near to God with a sincere heart and with the full assurance that faith brings, having our hearts sprinkled to cleanse us from a guilty conscience and having our bodies washed with pure water."- Hebrews 10: 22*

God invites all of us to live in His presence. If you can learn to pray with your *whole* heart, you will enter into the very presence of God. In His presence, you will be shown the path of life. You will receive direction from God himself, into an abundant life and fullness of joy. *"As a person thinks in their heart so are they"* (Proverb 23:7). Your heart is your spirit, and the only way to think spiritually is with spiritual substance. There is nothing more pure and more perfect in spiritual substance than the *eternal* Word of God.

God's treasures will be given to *all* who read His Word, believe it and act as if it were the truth. *"But if from there you seek the LORD your God, you will find him if you seek him with all your heart and with all your soul"* (Deuteronomy 4:29).

If you make God a requirement in your life—if He becomes as much of a requirement as food, water or air, then you will find Him. When you get serious with God…He *will* get serious with you. Jesus tells us: *"If you hunger and thirst you will be filled"* (Matthew 5:6).

People, today, have their lives so full of junk of this temporal world, that they do not have any room for the things of God. When you allow other things in your life to become more important than the things of God—it becomes difficult and often impossible to pray with your *whole* heart. *"And the cares of this world, deceitfulness of riches, and lust of other things entering in, choke the Word, and it becometh unfruitful"* (Mark 4:19). If we, as Christians, will begin starving out some of the things of this world, the eternal, supernatural, life-changing *WORD OF GOD* will become exciting to read and mediate upon.

> *"And in every work that he began in the service of the house of God, and in the law, and in the commandments, to seek his God, he did it with*

all his heart, and prospered." -2 Chronicles 31:21

The Word promises to those who seek the Lord that... He will be found. *"If you seek him, he will be found by you"* (1 Chronicles 28:9). And when He is found...there is great reward. *"Whoever would draw near to God must believe that he exists and that he rewards those who seek him"* (Hebrews 11:6).

God himself is our *greatest* reward. And when you have Him—you have everything. Therefore, "Seek the Lord and his strength; seek his presence continually!" *"Call to me and I will answer you and show you great and mighty things thou knowest not"* (Jeremiah 33:3). God wants to show you things that are just for you and prepared for you, and that no one else has ever seen or heard. He will show you things that have never entered into the heart of man.

Simply call out to Him in love and live for Him with your *whole* heart.

> *Jesus wants to be found!*
> *In His Presence... Your life will be changed*
> *forevermore!*

Don't Worry... Pray about Everything and Trust God to Deliver!

> *The Sovereign Lord, The Holy One of Israel says: "In repentance and in rest is your salvation, in quietness and trust is your strength."*
> *- Isaiah 30:15*

Worry is misplaced faith…a faith in fear….a lack of faith in God's ability. Far too many Christians today are filled with worry. They worry about money, job security, their safety, health and their future. God never intended you to live a life of worry and stress. He wants you to walk in faith and liberty! The secret of a worry-free life is seeking God's kingdom and His righteousness.

> *"But seek ye first the kingdom of God and His righteousness and all these things will be given to you…"- Matthew 6:33*

Abraham sought God's Kingdom! Abraham was a man who refused to worry. Hebrews 11:8 tells us, *"By faith, Abraham when he was called to go out into a place which he would later receive for an inheritance, obeyed; and he went out."* He had no idea where he was going, but he refused to worry. God had promised to bless him and his family—and that was enough!

> *"Don't worry about anything; instead, pray about everything. Tell God what you need, and thank him for all he has done." -Philippians 4:6*

God wants us to enter into *HIS REST!* He is the only one who can remove our heavy burdens that man has placed upon us, as we follow His leadership in our daily lives. The Holy Spirit in you will reveal within your heart on which way He will have you go.

> *"For my thoughts are not your thoughts, neither are your ways my ways, declares the Lord. As the heavens are higher than the earth, so are my ways higher than your ways and my thoughts than your thoughts."- Isaiah 55:8-9*

God is the only One that knows the perfect path that we should follow… a place that will bring us *BLESSED REST.* Jesus said, "Come unto me." We will never find rest until we come unto Him and make Him the Lord and Master of our life! In Him we find His rest for us, and His yoke that is easy and His burden that is light.

> *"Come to me all you who are burdened, and I will give you rest. Take my yoke upon you and learn from me, for I am gentle and humble in heart, and you will find rest for your souls. For my yoke is easy and my burden is light." - Matthew 11:28-30*

As we rest in His love and care, He will give us His joy and His peace to help us to live in this anxious and troubled world. IF WE WILL ONLY LET HIM, He will show us the way. We will find rest when the Master is allowed to have complete control—as we develop a personal and intimate relationship with Him! TRUSTING HIM in every way and allowing His precious Holy Spirit to lead and direct our path each and every day!

> *"My soul finds rest in God alone; my salvation comes from Him. He alone is my rock and my salvation; He is my fortress and I will never be shaken."- Psalm 62:1-2*

When you experience upheavals in your life, look to the Lord and know there is peace in the midst of the storm. ---*"And the peace of God, which transcends all understanding, will guard your hearts and your minds in Christ Jesus"* (Philippians 4:7).

The Holy Spirit *clothes* the *one* who believes God's promises with Himself, and then He works through him. *"Those who live in the shelter of the Most High will find rest in the shadow of the Almighty"* (Psalm 91:1). God's rest is available to every born-again believer. We can *only* enter God's rest by obtaining the faith that truly believes *all* God's promises. In the midst of *great spiritual conflict*, we can rest inwardly and have perfect PEACE! God has provided for us to live the Christian life by believing His promises.

> *"We live by faith and not by sight." - 2 Corinthians 5:7*

Be diligent to enter into God's rest. *It is only in His rest* where we will find *His peace*. Let the Holy Spirit be your guide and experience Heaven on earth!

God will deliver... if you will have FAITH and TRUST in His Promises!

Do not let your hearts be troubled!

"Delight thyself in the Lord and He will give you the desires of your heart." - Psalm 37:4

Christ-Focused Living

*"I have set the Lord continually before me;
Because he is at my right hand, I shall not be shaken."*

-Psalm 16:8

Before Salvation, we were blinded by sin. Now, as a Christian, our eyes are made to see by the light of God's Word so that we may daily walk in faith and not stumble. Daily devotion to Christ is spending time in His Word daily. In our lost condition we were led astray by the many kinds of voices in the world. We were deaf to the voice of God and doomed to be devoured like a lone sheep among ravenous wolves.

Thankfully, we have been found, restored, redeemed, and reborn by the "Good Shepherd" which is Christ. In John 10:4, *Jesus said that, "He putteth forth his own sheep, He goeth before them, and the sheep follow him...FOR THEY KNOW HIS VOICE."* We hear and recognize the voice of our Good Shepherd leading us each day as we listen to his commands. He speaks to us in the garden of prayer as we fellowship together. We receive Godly guidance, council and wisdom. In our sinful state we lived according to the lusts and desires of our flesh being dead in sins and trespasses.

Currently we have been spiritually resurrected to walk in the Spirit of power, love and a sound mind. Like Paul, we have to die *daily* to our forever fleshly wicked ways and works. *Daily,* we must put on the mind of Christ and the whole armor of God. We do this by taking our authority as warriors and submitting to the leadership of the "Captain of the Host."

As Christians we are required by God to be consistent and faithful in our service to Him. Sincere and genuine ministry as a blood-bought believer in Jesus Christ demands more than mere self-sacrifice and good works. It demands total surrender to God and a willingness to obey His commandments.

> *"...Behold, to obey is better than sacrifice and to harken (listen) than the fat of rams." - 1 Samuel 15:22*

> *"Be not deceived; God is not mocked: for whatsoever a man soweth, that shall he also reap. For he that soweth to his flesh shall of the flesh reap corruption; but he that soweth to the Spirit shall of the Spirit reap lifeeverlasting. And let us not be weary in well doing: for in due season we shall reap, if we faint not." - Galatians 6:7-9*

Faithfulness to Christ is necessary to victorious living. We must remain spiritually alert, devoted to Him, discerning the truth and free from deception, serving Him faithfully until He comes again. Having put our trust in Christ as our Savior and Lord, we can truthfully say, "I was saved, I am being saved, and will be saved by Jesus Christ." If we remain committed to Christ to the end, according to His own word, His own promise, we will be saved eternally.

The WORD "DAILY" is very important here. And if we really want to see God working in our lives and seeing miracles happen… We all need to read this lesson over and over again… every day… until you have these things imprinted upon your heart. We need to know and hear our "Good Shepherd's" voice IN THE COMING DAYS … YOUR ONLY HOPE MAY DEPEND ON YOUR KNOWING and HEARING OUR SAVIOR JESUS' VOICE!

My question to you is, "Are you living Christ-focused?"

WALK CLOSER WITH THE LORD AND... PLACE ALL YOUR TRUST AND FAITH IN HIM!

If you don't do this... you might find yourself DECEIVED!

> *"For me to live is Christ, and to die is gain." -Philippians 1:21*

Can You Help God's Judgment Not Come to America?

> *"If My people, who are called by My name, shall humble themselves and pray, and seek my face and turn from their wicked ways, then I will hear from heaven, and will forgive their sin and will heal their land."*
> *-2 Chronicles 7:14*

Why is there such an increase of trouble for America? Moses warned Israel that if she served God she would be the most blessed of all nations, but if she disobeyed God, terrifying judgment would come. Moses warned: *"And among those nations you shall find no rest, nor shall the sole of your foot have a resting place; but there the Lord will give you a trembling heart, failing eyes, and anguish of soul. Your life shall hang in doubt before you; you shall fear day and night, and have no assurance of life."* (Deuteronomy 28:65-66).

Today America is heading down a dangerous path. We have already started experiencing major problems in our Country. We are a nation divided morally, spiritually, intellectually, and politically. Jesus Himself said in Luke 11:17, *"Any kingdom divided against itself is laid waste; and a house divided against itself falls."* Many churches have fallen asleep and it is time to wake.

If ever there has been a nation who has enjoyed prosperity, God has really blessed America; but instead of giving thanks to God, we have offered our reverence and worship to the things of man.

The Apostle Paul said, "They boast of their wisdom, but they have made fools of themselves." Then comes awful judgment—*"For this reason God has given them up to the vileness of their own desires"* (Romans 1:21-24). The Bible tells us there will come a day…when a nation sins so much against God that God will give them up. He will allow them to go on for a time in pleasure, worldliness, idolatry, wickedness and immorality. The pleasure in this sin will be for a season, but God warns that it will be extremely short-lived and that judgment will follow.

From the beginning of the Bible to the end, God warns that any nation that departs from Him is going to suffer judgment. America has been given more spiritual and moral light than any nation in all history. How long will God withhold His hand of judgment? Unless we as a nation repent and turn to God, we are going to suffer a judgment such as no nation has ever endured. This day---God is speaking to our nation but He is also speaking to us individually urging us to repent of our sins and to turn to Him…Turn back to God before it is too late. I urge you to take this message very seriously and if you are not right with God, don't hesitate…DO IT NOW!

The Prophet Joel preached to God's people in Judah just before the Babylonian armies came and destroyed Jerusalem and took God's people into exile. He cried out for them to repent so that God could spare the land from the coming invasion. HIS WORDS OF WARNING ARE VERY PERTINET FOR US TODAY. I personally believe that if America does not repent, she is headed for national disaster. In Joel 2:12, the Lord says: *"Yet even now," declares the LORD, "Return to Me with all your heart, and with fasting, weeping and mourning; and rend your heart and not your garments." Now return to the LORD your God for He is gracious and compassionate, slow to anger, abounding in loving-kindness…"* God desires to send spiritual awakening. He is sounding an alarm and crying out to His people in America, saying:

IT IS TIME! *Repent before it's too late!*

God is gracious, compassionate, slow to anger, and abundant in loving-kindness. He promises He will relent of evil if we will turn back to him and He will forgive us. God is graciously giving us a warning. If only we will allow Him to get a hold on our hearts; if we would rend our hearts and not our garments; if we would weep and fast and pray and say, *"O God, spare Thy people."* If we come together and pray HE WILL DO IT!

Please repent and pray for our nation to repent!

> *Then they cried to the LORD in their trouble, and he delivered them from their distress. He made the storm be still, and the waves of the sea were hushed. Then they were glad that the waters were quiet, and he brought them to their desired haven." - Psalm 107:28-30*

Does GOOD WORKS...
Give You a Free Ticket to Heaven?

"He saved us, not because of righteous things we have done, but BECAUSE OF HIS MERCY..."
- Titus 3:5

"For by grace are ye saved through faith; and that not of yourselves: it is the gift of God: NOT OF WORKS, lest any man should boast."
- Ephesians 2:8-9

"Knowing that a man is not justified by the works of the law, but by the faith of Jesus Christ, even we have believed in Jesus Christ, that we might be justified by the faith of Christ, and not by the works of the law: for BY THE WORKS OF THE LAW SHALL NO FLESH BE JUSTIFIED?"
- Galatians 2:16

Examine your life...and ask yourself... Are you truly saved?

Salvation is of God and not dependent upon man's works. Over and over the Bible tells us that good deeds cannot merit us salvation. If salvation came by works, then it would not be by God's grace anymore. The whole reason that Jesus died on the cross is because we cannot do enough good works to get saved. There is no amount of good deeds that can reconcile us to God. Only through Jesus Christ can anyone be saved. If it is possible for us to get to Heaven by living a good and upright life, then Jesus died for nothing—Jesus paid a debt He did not owe, because we owed a debt we could not pay. HE DID IT... BECAUSE HE LOVES US!

Because we cannot earn our way into Heaven, God had to provide a way of escape for humanity. This way of escape has been provided through the blood sacrifice of Jesus Christ.

> *"This is how we know what love is: Jesus Christ laid down his life for us. And we ought to lay down our lives for our brothers." - 1 John 3:16.*

> *"But we are all as an unclean thing, and ALL OUR RIGHTEOUSNESSES ARE AS FILTHY RAGS; and we all do fade as a leaf; and our iniquities, like the wind, have taken us away" - Isaiah 64:6.*

Your money, kindness, sincerity, generosity and commitment mean nothing to God if you are relying upon your own self-righteousness. If you are trusting in the righteousness of Jesus Christ (realizing that you have no righteousness of your own), then all the good things you do as a Child of God are well pleasing unto the Lord.

"But by THE GRACE OF GOD I am what I am" (1 Corin. 15:10). God's grace is God's goodness, His doing for us what we certainly don't deserve. God's grace is everything that God has ever done, is doing, or ever will do for us. THE GRACE OF GOD DOES FOR US... WHAT WE CANNOT DO FOR OURSELVES, if we could save ourselves, we wouldn't need the grace of God or a Savior.

The grace of God is available to help each believer through every trial and problem in life because we can't make it on our own. God wants to help us through the tough times. It is our privilege and God-given right to approach God's throne of grace in times of trouble, *"Let us therefore come boldly unto the throne of grace, that we may obtain mercy, and find GRACE TO HELP in time of need" (Hebrews 4:16).* This is only made possible by the blood sacrifice of Jesus Christ. Even though good works can't save you, knowing Jesus Christ as your personal Savior and the Holy Spirit that lives in you will continually inspire you to do good.

> *He refreshes and restores my life (my self); He leads me in the paths of righteousness [uprightness and right standing with Him--not for my earning it, but] for His name's sake. - Psalm 23: 3(Amplified)*

Have you opened your heart to Jesus Christ? If not, turn to Him with a simple prayer of repentance and faith, and thank Him for what He has done for you. And if you do know Christ, how long has it been since you thanked God for your salvation? We should not let a day go by without thanking God… for His mercy … and His grace to us in Jesus Christ.

Don't miss your flight… GET RIGHT… GET JESUS!

ARE YOU LIVING THE TRUE CHRISTIAN LIFE:

"But the fruit of the Spirit is love, joy, peace, long-suffering, kindness, goodness, faithfulness, gentleness and self-control." -Galatians 5:22

Sometimes When the Things of This World Go Dim... Only Then Can We See God in All of His Fullness!

> *But now the Lord who created you says: "Do not be afraid, for I have ransomed you. I have called you by name; you are mine. When you go through deep waters and great trouble, I will be with you. When you go through rivers of difficulty, you will not drown! When you walk through the fire of oppression, you will not be burned up; the flames will not consume you. For I am the Lord, your God, the Holy One of Israel, your Savior..."*
> *-Isaiah 43:1-3*

In life, we are bound to face problems of many kinds. How we respond to our problems reveals our character. It's a testament of our faith. Remember dear friends, God is in control.

> *"I have told you these things, so that in me you may have peace. In this world you will have trouble. But take heart! I have overcome the world." -John 16:33*

In the Book of Daniel we read the story of the three heroic men who did not waiver in their faith or trust in the one true God. We cannot help but be astonished by Shadrach, Meshach, and Abednego's unswerving conviction of the God of the Bible; their confidence in the God who is who He says He is and will do what He says He will do—and their faith as revealed by their reliance upon the *only* One who had the power to deliver them from evil. For their refusal to obey the king's decree to bow down to an idol, they were thrown into a fiery furnace.

> *"O Nebuchadnezzar...If we are thrown into the blazing furnace, the God we serve is able to save us from it, and he will rescue us from your hand, O king. But even if he does not, we want you to know, O king that we will not serve your gods or worship the image of gold you have set up" -Daniel 3:15-18*

King Nebuchadnezzar was astonished that the fire did not consume Shadrach, Meshach, and Abednego. He was even more amazed when he saw not three, but a *fourth* person with them: *"Look!" he answered, "I see four men loose, walking in the midst of the fire; and they are not hurt, and the form of the fourth is like the Son of God"* (Daniel 3:25). The point here is that, when we *walk* by faith (2 Corinthians 5:7), there may be those times of fiery persecution, but we *can* be assured that He *is* with us (Matthew 28:20). He *will* sustain us (Psalm 55:22; Psalms 147:6). He *will* ultimately deliver us. He *will* save us eternally (Matthew 25:41, 46).

As believers, we know that God is *able* to deliver. However, we also know that He does not always do so. God may allow trials and difficulties in our lives to build our character, strengthen our faith or for other reasons unknown to us. We may not always understand the purpose of our trials, but God simply asks that we *trust* Him—even when it is *not* easy. We also know that God does not always guarantee that we will never suffer or experience death, but He does promise to be with us always. We should learn that in times of trial and persecution our attitude should reflect that of these three young men: *"But even if he does not, we want you to know, O king, that we will not serve your gods or worship the image of gold you have set up."* (Daniel 3:18). Without question, these are some of the most courageous words ever spoken.

The lesson from the story of Shadrach, Meshach, and Abednego is that, as Christians if we are put before the fiery furnace, we *can* reveal the One who can deliver us from it. Remember the powerful, yet comforting words, of the apostle Paul: *"Therefore we do not lose heart. Though outwardly we are wasting away, yet inwardly we are being renewed day by day. For our light and momentary troubles are achieving for us an eternal glory that far outweighs them all, so we fix our eyes not on what is seen, but on what is unseen. For what is seen is temporary, but what is unseen is eternal"* (2 Corinthians 4:16-18).

GOD NEVER CHANGES! What God says—He *will* do! Let God fulfill His purpose in your life which is to love you unconditionally. Allow Him to work in your life so you may be a vessel of His awesome power and love.

When you are walking in FAITH
you can be assured GOD is with you!

> *"Have not I commanded you? Be strong and courageous. Do not be terrified; do not be discouraged, for the Lord your God will be with you wherever you go." - Joshua 1:9*

Are Your Wedding Garments Ready? The Bridegroom Is Coming for His Bride! What a Glorious Day That Will Be!

> ***"Then he said to his servants, 'The wedding is ready, but those invited were not worthy. Go therefore to the thoroughfares, and invite to the marriage feast as many as you find.' And those servants went out into the streets and gathered all whom they found, both bad and good; so the wedding hall was filled with guests."***
> ***- Matthew 22:8-10***

The Lord has sent an invitation to the world—*The Gospel*. This invitation goes out to all who would hear and want eternal life. No matter who you are, if you have a need, if you want eternal life, whether you feel you are of good reputation or not—**YOU are invited!** The gospel has gone out to all of the world, and it has been *"whosoever will may come"* (Revelation 22:17). God has invited all to a joyful feast in fellowship with His son...Jesus Christ! This joyous celebration with be the Wedding Feast of the Lamb of God. When God offers to us this marvelous gift of life in Jesus Christ, he does not threaten us. He does not try to coerce or compel us to come; He *offers* it as an invitation which we are free to accept, or reject, if we want to (Matthew 11:28).

Many don't heed the warning of the King and they turn a deaf ear to His message. They are willing to come... but *without* a wedding garment. Those who come and refuse to wear the garment are refusing to accept the gift of the righteousness of Jesus Christ. Instead they cling to something in themselves upon which they are depending for favor before God. Therefore, they will not be allowed to enter in.

> *"But when the king came in to look at the guests, he saw there a man who had no wedding garment; and he said to him, 'Friend, how did you get in here without a wedding garment?' And he was speechless. Then the king said to the attendants, 'Bind him hand and foot, and cast him into the outer darkness...'" -Matthew 22:11-14*

> *"Now Joshua was dressed in filthy clothes as he stood before the angel. The angel said to those who were standing before him, "Take off his filthy clothes." Then he said to Joshua, "See, I have taken away your sin," and I will put rich garments on you." "This is what the Lord Almighty says: 'If you will walk in my ways and keep my requirements, then you will govern my house and have charge of my courts..."*
-Zechariah 3:3-7

God wants to remove your filthy clothes (sins), and provide you with new clean rich garments... *The Righteousness and The Holiness of God.* All you need to do is repent of your sins and ask God to forgive you. God is looking at your heart to see if you have genuinely accepted His gift of eternal life and He is focusing on your relationship with His Son. It is not the will of God to cast any one out. He has made full provision for a wedding garment for us all. But *only* those who actually put it on will enter into the Kingdom of Heaven. Be prepared for that glorious day of Jesus' return. Ask God to remove your clothing of sin and dress you with His goodness.

Once you have *received* Jesus as your Savior, you are given your own personal wedding garment and will be robed in His righteousness. This is *not* a righteousness *we earn* but receive through the Blood of Christ. These wedding garments have been created out of the love of Christ to prepare us to dance in Glory in Heaven worshiping God in truth and in Spirit. The Christian's clothes or garments symbolize flawless, beautiful, untainted, pure, perfect and without blemish— *The Righteousness of Christ*. We cannot possess this gift through *our own works* but *only by being washed in the Blood of Christ*.

There will be a *bride in heaven* and that bride will be *all* believers who by faith were saved by the grace of God and who the Bible says are the bride and body of Jesus Christ. This betrothal is a picture of salvation.

> *Jesus answered and said unto him, "Verily, verily, I say unto thee, except a man be born again, he cannot see the Kingdom of God." -John 3:3*

If you want to enter into this glorious celebration…
The Wedding Feast, you <u>must</u> accept Jesus
Christ as your Personal Savior.

> *"If we confess our sins, He is faithful and just to forgive us our sins, and to cleanse us from all unrighteousness." -1 John 1:9*

Have You Become So Busy With the Concerns of This Life That You Have Left the Work of God Undone?

> *"Now this is what the* Lord *Almighty says: "Give careful thought to your ways. You have planted much, but harvested little. You eat, but never have enough. You drink, but never have your fill. You put on clothes, but are not warm. You earn wages, only to put them in a purse with holes in it." This is what the Lord Almighty says: "Give careful thought to your ways."*
> *-Haggai 1:5-7*

Judah started building a temple for God as He had instructed them. But once they had the foundation done they had become double-minded and left their directive to build the temple. God watched them building their own lavish houses and being so busy with their own concerns that they allowed the work of God to go undone. Israel was chastised many times by the Lord because they strayed away from His ways and began to walk in their own ways.

> *"You expected much, but see, it turned out to be little. What you brought home, I blew away. Why?" declares the* Lord *Almighty. "Because of my house,* **which remains a ruin, while each of you is busy with your own house.** *Therefore,*

> *because of you the heavens have withheld their dew and the earth its crops. I called for a drought on the fields and the mountains, on the grain, the new wine, the olive oil and everything else the ground produces, on people and livestock, and on all the labor of your hands."*
> *- Haggai 1:9-11*

Are we living in the same cycle as the people in Judah—where simple blessings are gone? Are we neglecting God by being too busy pursuing our own personal concerns to have time for Him? Are we more interested in our house than God's House?

As a nation, we are no longer focused on God. Instead—we allow meaningless things of this world to replace Him in our daily lives. Many are worshiping the god of *self* and not the God of the Bible. God tells us in the Bible, *"Remember and forget not"* because as long as we remember —*we will obey.*

When we do *not* seek God first, and are *busy* with our own interests, we get to the end of it all and find that what we worked hard for is empty and we missed God, the one and only thing that *is* really important. Where do your priorities lie? Do you have a *longing* for the things of God as King David did?

> *"O God, you are my God, earnestly I seek you; my soul thirsts for you, my body longs for you, in a dry and weary land where there is no water. I have seen you in the sanctuary and beheld your power and your glory. Because your love is better than life, my lips will glorify you." - Psalm 63:1-3*

When we set the Lord aside there are consequences. We were not created and saved merely to survive our time on earth. If we do NOT truly, in word and deed, find our satisfaction in God and God alone, we cannot know the joy of HIS pleasure. If our heart's desire is not to honor Him and to bring Him pleasure, then HIS House is not in OUR house. Have we forgotten that we have been created for God, by God? His desire is that we rule over this earth in love and partnership with Him. We need to start living our lives with one purpose: to glorify Him. We must not forget that He is the one who created us with His own hands, with this goal: *"to love and enjoy us."*

The house that lets the House of God IN takes His yoke up and finds rest and peace in God. If you truly want godliness and eternal results you must turn to the Lord and set your hearts and homes on HIM. You *must* become hungry to be in the presence of God and to know Him for yourselves if you are ever to become the house where God's glory abides. If you truly desire to please your heavenly Father and have His glory abide in you, then you will seek Him with your whole heart. God will bless you if you spend time with Him in prayer and His Word. Ask Him to teach and guide you so that you will become even more faithful in following Him. *God desires to have a personal and intimate relationship with every one of you—so* **MAKE YOUR HOUSE... GOD'S HOUSE!**

HOW CAN WE PRESENT OURSELVES APPROVED BEFORE GOD?

We need to diligently study His Word so that we acquire an accurate understanding of it and then faithfully act upon the truth. **-2 Timothy 2:15**

Do You Have a Thankful Heart Or Do You Find Yourself Always Looking For Something to Grumble About?

In the book of Numbers, we read about the Israelites' experience in the wilderness. They were constantly grumbling against God instead of trusting Him. They had seen His awesome wonders and grace. He sent manna from heaven and provided water from a rock. God had miraculously delivered them from slavery in Egypt, but their hearts were turning back. Here they were experiencing God's miraculous provision, but they seem to have taken it for granted. As soon as God had done one thing for them, they were wanting something else and finding another reason to grumble. Their faith and focus were not where they should have been.

It's easy for us to judge the Israelites as unthankful complainers, but are we not really doing the same things? Are we taking God for granted instead of thanking Him for His blessings? How many times have you experienced God's great blessings in your life, but then turn around and look at another situation and start complaining about that *instead of* praising and thanking God for His goodness? How many times do you focus your attention on your problems and needs instead of on Jesus and His love?

We should have thankful hearts toward God even when we do not feel thankful for the circumstance. We can grieve and still be thankful. We can hurt and still be thankful. We can be angry at sin and still be thankful toward God. That is what the Bible calls a "sacrifice of praise" (Hebrews 13:15). Giving thanks to God keeps our hearts in right relationship with Him and saves us from a host of harmful emotions and attitudes that will rob us of the peace God wants us to experience (Philippians 4:6–7). We tend to focus on what we *don't* have. By giving thanks continually we are reminded of how much we *do* have. When we focus on blessings rather than wants, we are happier. When we start thanking God for the things we usually take for granted, our perspective changes. We realize that we could not even exist without the merciful blessings of God.

We should be thankful because God is worthy of our thanksgiving. It is only right to credit Him for "every good and perfect gift" He gives. (James 1:17) When we are thankful, our focus moves *off* selfish desires and *off* the pain of current circumstances. Expressing thankfulness helps us remember that God is in control. Thankfulness, then, is not only appropriate; it is actually healthy and beneficial to us. It reminds us of the bigger picture, that we belong to God, and that we have been blessed with every spiritual blessing (Ephesians 1:3).

If we look at the things that are truly important to us we would find that we have much more to be thankful for other than our material possessions. The most important thing that we should be thankful for is our salvation, our church family and the mercy that God showers on us each day. In Jesus, we have His presence, His promises and His power available every single day that we live. He is faithful and He is true. We can count on Him. He is our refuge and our strength, a very present help in time of trouble. He is our high tower; He is alpha and omega, the beginning and the end, the first and the last, the one who was and is and evermore shall be. He is our everything!

We can be thankful for God's constant goodness and His steadfast love. When we recognize the nature of our depravity and understand that, apart from God, there is *only* death *(John 10:10; Romans 7:5).* The Bible tells us to live a life of thanksgiving each day. *"In everything give thanks; for this is God's will for you in Christ Jesus"* (1 Thess. 5:18). *Choose* thankfulness as your way of life and let it flow from your hearts and mouths. Be thankful for all of His blessings!

JULIA BROWN

"Give thanks to the Lord, for He is good. His love endures forever." -Psalm 136:6

> *Thank God especially for His free gift of Salvation through His Son—Jesus Christ!*
>
> *"Give thanks to the Lord, call on his name; make known among the nations what He has done." -1 Chronicles 16:8*

Praising God Will Fill You with Peace And Contentment and Transform Your Life! TRY IT!

> *"Then a voice came from the throne, saying: 'Praise our God, all you His servants, you who fear him, both great and small!' Then I heard what sounded like a great multitude, like the roar of rushing waters and like loud peals of thunder, shouting: "Hallelujah! For our Lord God Almighty reigns. Let us rejoice and be glad and give him glory!"*
>
> *-Revelation 19:5-7*

One of the most important keys that will make it possible for us to walk in kingdom living is our expression of praise. The Lord's Prayer begins in an attitude of worship and praise: *"Our Father which art in heaven, Hallowed be thy name. Thy kingdom come. Thy will be done, as in heaven, so in earth"* (Luke 11:2). Praise is the *will of God*, and heaven overflows with it. Our voices should also be lifted up in praise to our Lord.

> *"Rejoice evermore. Pray without ceasing. In everything give thanks: for this is the will of God in Christ Jesus concerning you."* *-1 Thessalonians 5:16-18*

Praise, according to the Scriptures, is an act of our will that flows out of an awe and reverence for our Creator. Praise gives glory to God and opens us up to a deeper union with Him. It turns our attention off of our problems and on the nature and character of God Himself. So our number one priority must be to love God personally. Praise is giving of yourself to God — an intimate communion with Him. If we would praise and seek God first, during our prayer time, other things would be added unto us (Matthew 6:33). As you are praising Him your faith will be increased.

Praise is a wonderful method we can use to bring healing and deliverance to our souls and bodies! We must make our souls bless the Lord when we are not feeling well. It will bring liberation and healing. We receive many benefits from praising the Lord: He forgives our sins, heals all our diseases, shows us His loving kindness, is merciful toward us, gives us good things to eat, restores our youth and strength, and He delivers us from oppression and judges us righteously. Praising God helps restore us to that right relationship, for God actually dwells in the praises of His people (Psalm 22:3). Praise is the way to begin a love relationship with God.

Another reason to praise God is simple obedience. The Bible says God is a "jealous" God who demands and desires our praise. *"You shall have no other gods before Me"* (Deuteronomy. 6:7). As the psalmist said, *"Let everything that has breath praise the Lord"* (Psalm 150:6). Very simply, we praise God because He is worthy of our praise (1 Chronicles 16:25; Revelation 5:11-14). He is the Alpha and Omega, the Beginning and the End, the King of Kings and Lord of Lords. He is our Creator, Provider, Healer, Redeemer, Judge, Defender and much more.

Praise is both important and powerful. God gives us assurances of additional blessings as we praise Him. When we praise God, He honors us as His children, and provides His loving protection (2 Samuel 22:47-51). Failure to praise God, however, leaves us out of fellowship with God and out of His divine protection (1 Samuel 2:27-32). Our praise can also serve as a powerful witness to those who do not know the Lord (1 Peter 2:9). Also, God can work miraculously through our praises—The ancient walls of Jericho came crashing down, giving victory to God's people, as a result of shouts of praise (Joshua 6:1-21). The prison doors shook open when Paul and

Silas praised God (Acts 16:25-26). We were created by God to praise Him! (Isaiah 43:7).

> *"I will bless the Lord at all times: his praise shall continually be in my mouth. My soul shall make her boast in the Lord: the humble shall hear thereof, and be glad. O magnify the Lord with me, and let us exalt his name together. I sought the Lord, and he heard me, and delivered me from all my fears." -Psalm 34:1-4*

PRAISE HIM! PRAISE HIM! PRAISE HIM!

Praise should be a natural expression of our love for Our Heavenly Father.

Are We Being Obedient in Witnessing for Jesus Christ?

> *"Ye are my witnesses, saith the Lord, and my servant whom I have chosen; that ye may know and believe me, and understand that I am He; before me there was no God formed, neither shall there be after me."*
> *-Isaiah 43:10*

As born again believers we desire to witness for Jesus, but we don't really understand that our Lord has commanded and commissioned each of us to share the Good News and to seek the lost. He said, *"Go and make disciples of all nations"; and "Go into all the world and preach the good news to all creation"* (Matthew 28:19; Mark 16:15). It is our greatest calling, then, to share the love and forgiveness God has given us with those who have never received Jesus as their Savior and Lord. In fact, the need for people to hear the Good News of God's love and forgiveness is a matter of life and death.

> *"Death is the destiny of every man; the living should take this to heart."-Ecclesiastes 7:2.*

Man's self-will is characterized by an attitude of active rebellion or passive indifference. Because of sin, he is by nature degenerate and corrupt, and destitute of God's love, undeserving of His forgiveness, and so destined to death - eternal separation from God. But Christ does... *not want anyone to perish, but wants everyone to come to repen-*

tance (2 Peter 3:9). Jesus placed such a high value on the human soul that He personally and gladly exchanged the perfection of Heaven for a life of poverty, suffering, shame, and death to seek and to save what was lost.

From His earliest youth and Throughout His life, Jesus clearly understood His mission and purpose. His concern for the lost was so deep that at times the flood of compassionate tears rolled down His face. Christ has given a clear command to every Christian. Jesus Christ's last command to the Christian community was to make disciples. This command, which the Church calls the Great Commission, was not intended merely for the eleven remaining disciples, or just for the apostles, or for those in present times who may have the gift of evangelism. This command is the responsibility of every man and woman who professes faith in Christ as Lord.

Men and women are lost without Jesus Christ. Jesus said, *"I am the way and the truth and the life. No one comes to the Father, except through me"* (John 14:6). God's Word also reminds us, *"There is salvation in no one else! Under all heaven there is no other name for men to call upon to save them"* (Acts 4:12). All men and women are truly lost without Jesus Christ. He is the only way to bridge the gap between man and God. Without Him, people cannot know God and have no hope of eternal life.

Jesus said, *"The fields are ripe unto harvest."* Can we afford to be selfish with the gospel when such overwhelming evidence shows that so many people are hungry for God? *"For the message of the cross is foolishness to those who are perishing, but to us who are being saved it is the power of God"* (1 Corinthians 1:18). We Christians have in our possession the greatest gift available to mankind: God's gift of eternal life, which we received with Jesus Christ at our spiritual birth. (John 3:16) Helping to fulfill the Great Commission is both a duty and a privilege. We witness because we love Christ. We witness because He loves us. We witness because we want to honor and obey Him.

We witness because He gives us a special love for others. Jesus said, *"The one who obeys me is the one who loves me…"* (John 14:21). In other words, He measures our love for Him by the extent and genuineness of our obedience to Him. As we obey, He promises He will reveal Himself to us.

> *"Because he loves me, my Father will love him; and I will too, and I will reveal myself to him"*
> *-John 14:21*

> *"..And pray for us, too, that God may open a door for our message, so that we may proclaim the mystery of Christ..." -Colossians 4:3*

SUCCESS IN WITNESSING....is simply TAKING THE INITIATIVE... sharing Christ in the power of the Holy Spirit .... and LEAVING THE RESULTS TO GOD.

Only Your Faith in Jesus...
Can Truly Restore Your Joy!

> *"Consider it pure joy, my brothers, whenever you face trials of many kinds, because you know that the testing of your faith develops perseverance. Perseverance must finish its work so that you may be mature and complete, not lacking anything."*
>
> *- James 1:2-4*

Many Christians think once they've made that decision for Christ that everything will fall into place and life will be that proverbial bowl of cherries. And when trials and tough times come upon them or continue, they begin to question, "Why?" wondering how they could possibly endure horrible circumstances and considers it joy.

> *"In this you greatly rejoice, though now for a little while you may have had to suffer grief in all kinds of trials. These have come so that your faith of greater worth than gold, which perishes even though refined by fire, may be proved genuine and may result in praise, glory and honor when Jesus Christ is revealed. Though you have not seen him, you love him; and even though you do not see him now, you believe in him and are filled with an inexpressible and glorious*

> *joy, for you are receiving the goal of your faith, the salvation of your souls" -1 Peter 1:6-9.*

In these passages, we see the instruction of what we *should* do. "Consider it pure joy…In this you greatly rejoice…" because in our trials, we will become much stronger. Our faith, which is priceless, will be proved genuine and result in praise to God. We can find joy in the midst of all the junk, hardships, and painful circumstances.

We need to understand that joy is not the same as happiness. Happiness comes and goes sometimes as often as waves hitting the shore. Happiness isn't something you can cling to when trials come. Joy, on the other hand can stay with you because real joy is from God. For the believer, it is like a bottomless well of water—always an abundant supply. Even in the darkest days, when sadness, grief, and loss may threaten to overwhelm you—God's joy is there. As believers, we are promised His joy in the presence of the Holy Spirit, just as our salvation is assured through Jesus' one-time sacrifice for all. Jesus said, *"I have told you this so that my joy may be in you and that your joy may be complete"* (John 15:11).

You can choose joy over bitterness, anger, and sorrow. Make a decision to choose joy every day.

> *"Let us fix our eyes on Jesus, the author and perfecter of our faith, who for the joy set before him endured the cross, scorning its shame, and sat down at the right hand of the throne of God." -Hebrews 12:2*

Many of us have and will suffer many trials, but we can call it pure joy unto the Lord Jesus Christ. Even though our problems can seem insurmountable with each trial we can greatly rejoice with joy inexpressible and full of glory even if you feel like you have fallen face first in the mud. With Jesus Christ on your side you can endure whatever circumstances come your way. If you have been saved through faith in Jesus Christ—you have all you need—and YOU ALREADY HAVE VICTORY!

"...In your presence is fullness of joy..." -Psalm 16:11

HOLD ON TIGHT to the HAND OF JESUS and...
Satan can never snatch you away!

> *"...This day is Holy to our Lord. Do not grieve, for the Joy of the LORD is your strength." -Nehemiah 8-10*

Can You Really Grasp the Love...
Our Almighty God...has for You?

"Behold, I have engraved you on the palms of my hands."
                                              -Isaiah 49:15

Do you really understand what this means? Why do we have so many unfounded doubts and fears of God's love for us? The Lord's loving word of rebuke should make us feel ashamed, as he cries, *"How can I have forgotten you, when I have engraved you on the palms of my hands?"* Can you really doubt his constant remembrance for you, when *He has set a memorial upon His very flesh?"*

"I have engraved you..." Understand the fullness of these words: *I have engraved your person, your image, your case, your circumstances, your sins, your temptations, your weaknesses, your wants, your works. I have engraved you, everything about you, all that concerns you. I have put you altogether there.* What a powerful image this is and what an expression of love and commitment. And it's a beautiful reminder of God's commitment to us. His hands bear the marks of the lengths to which he has gone to show us his love. The ultimate proof of his love for you is found in those engraved hands. If you start feeling any doubt of His love for you and find yourself feeling forgotten and forsaken, REMEMBER HIS SCARRED HANDS!

God always keeps His promises...so don't let the next trial that comes along make you doubt him once again. Place all your trust in the Lord. He never fails. Jesus will give living water to provide all your needs. He will never leave nor forsake you in your trials. *He is right in the middle of it all*—and yet we are as continually vexed with anxieties, bothered with suspicions, and disturbed with fears, as if our God were the mirage of the desert.

Can you see Jesus before the throne of God with His hands open in prayer, saying to the God of all the ages…. Look at "this one" engraved on my palm—I love them, and I am praying to you ABBA Father for them, keep them safe, and bless them. Heal them, prosper them, and let them know your bountiful abundance. The LORD is interested in every detail of our lives. If you have accepted Jesus into your heart and have the faith to trust Him, He will never let go of you. He promises that *"Your name is engraved on the palms of His hands and the wall of your life is ever before Him."* He loves you and is constantly praying for you and thinking of you. Listen to these tender words of love:

> ***"How precious to me are your thoughts, O God!***
> ***How vast is the sum of them!" Psalm 139:17***

You can ignore His love for you, you can reject it and you can deny it—but you can't make Him stop loving you. When we try living without Jesus, we make a mess of our lives. Our only hope is found in God's Word. It is there that we find out how much He loves us. It is there that we see Christ and what He has done for us. He died for your sins on the cross. All that remains is for you to… BELIEVE IT and then SOAK IN IT. You can drink in doubt, or you can drink the living water of God's love. The river of God's love has more than enough water for everyone who would like to receive it. Go ahead and *take the leap of faith and receive the love that will change your life forever.*

> ***"You have searched me, LORD, and you know me. You know when I sit and when I rise; you perceive my thoughts from afar. You discern my going out and my lying down; you are familiar with all my ways. Before a word is on my tongue, you LORD, know it completely. You hem***

me in behind and before, and you lay your hand upon me." -Psalm 139:1-5

TRUST IN THE ONE WHO DIED… FOR YOU!

God really loves you and cares about every detail of your life. If you don't believe that… PRAY that He will increase your faith and remove all disbelief. He loves YOU with an everlasting LOVE!

Do You Rejoice in the Lord—
In ALL Your Circumstances? You Can Always Rejoice... If You Live on the Promises of God!

> *"I delight greatly in the Lord; my soul rejoices in my God. For He has clothed me with garments of salvation and arrayed me in a robe of His righteousness, as a bridegroom adorns his head like a priest, and as a bride adorns herself with her jewels."*
> *-Isaiah 61:10*

It is not merely a suggestion and it is not optional. *Rejoicing in the Lord is commanded* by God in the Bible:

> ***Rejoice in the Lord always; again I say, Rejoice.***
> *-Philippians 4:4*

An obedient follower of Christ will always rejoice in the Lord! It is having a relationship with the Lord that brings the joy that one feels in his spirit. The rejoicing just flows from his heart and mouth. If we are rejoicing *in the Lord* we are living in obedience to God's Word. If we are not rejoicing *in the Lord* we are disobeying the Word of God.

Rejoicing in the Lord is not dependent on our circumstances or our surroundings—it is dependent on our relationship with Jesus Christ. We can be facing the greatest difficulties and challenges in our lives but if we have trusted Christ, regardless of how bad things are for us, we can rejoice. How encouraging it is to know that we can rejoice in the Lord in spite of situations that we feel are seemingly hopeless. And if you can't rejoice in difficult circumstances, then rejoice in the fact that God is ultimately in control and He knows what's best for us.

If we are complaining and not satisfied instead of rejoicing, we're going to be vulnerable to sin. *Rejoicing in the Lord* keeps our focus on the goodness of God, where it should be and off of ourselves. When we take our eyes off of Jesus, it's easy for us to be selfish and chase the things that please us instead of choosing those things that please the Lord. Are we showing contentment by seeking to do all things, "without complaining and grumbling?" Lack of prayer and the wrong kind of thinking will keep us from where we ought to be in the Lord. When you are feeling troubled about your situation—don't take your eyes off of Jesus or you will open the door for Satan to steal your joy.

When you trust God and place all of your confidence in His power and goodness, your heart will be filled with joy and praises and then rejoicing will flow out of your mouth.

> ***"Let us hold fast the profession of our faith without wavering; for He is faithful that promised." -Hebrews 10:23***

We are to rejoice in the Lord because of our obedient faith regardless of the circumstances in which we find ourselves. If you can do this… you will never lack—*love* and *contentment* within your heart. You must really believe that God is working through you when you are seeking to do His will. *Rejoicing in the Lord* is a matter of looking for God's presence in every situation. *"Rejoice in the LORD, O you righteous! For praise from the upright is beautiful"* (Psalm 33:1). Rejoicing is the way to success in the Christian life.

> ***"He destined us in love to be His sons through Jesus Christ, according to the purpose of His***

will, to the praise of His glorious grace which He freely bestowed on us in the Beloved. In Him we have redemption through His blood, the forgiveness of our trespasses, according to the riches of His grace which He lavished upon us." -Ephesians 1:5-8

We have so many reasons to rejoice—*"Praise Him!"*

> *There is no greater blessing than to be called the Sons and Daughters of The Mighty King! When you are feeling down... LOOK UP... PRAISE HIM... Trust in the promises of God!!*

Lord, Please Teach Me to Do Your Will... Let Me Do unto Others In The NAME OF JESUS!

> *"Love the Lord your God with all your heart and with all your soul and with all your mind and with all your strength. The second is this, "Love you neighbor as yourself. There is no commandment Greater then these."*
> *-Mark 12:30-31*

Those who hunger and thirst for righteousness who desire its' fruit which is that of peace; to those poor in spirit, who seek a much closer relationship with God and Christ; to those who know *there has to be something more*; to those who mourn under the burden of sin and want to be truly clean in thought, word, and deed; to those who long to serve the Lord, according to His direction and will; to them who heeded Him and heard His call; to those who have been searching for their Beloved—BELIEVE IN JESUS!

In Jesus, you will find the living water so that you will never thirst again. You will find the Bread from heaven and you will receive the fullness and completeness in Christ. You will hear, see and know your Beloved—CHRIST IN YOU, THE HOPE OF GLORY

We need unity and maturity in the Body of Christ.

> *"...I urge you to live a life worthy of the calling you have received. Be completely humble and gentle; be patient, bearing with one another in love. Make every effort to keep the unity of*

> *the Spirit through the bond of peace. There is one body and one Spirit, just as you were called to one hope when you were called; one Lord, one faith, one baptism; one God and Father of all, who is over all and through all and in all."*
> *-Ephesians 4:1-5*

We have all been called to build unity and mature in the knowledge of the Son of God to attain the measure of the fullness of Christ. God's Word tells us that we must put off our former way of life, which is being corrupted by its deceitful desires. We must be made new and put on the new self, created to be like God in true righteousness and holiness.

> *"Therefore each of you should put off falsehood and speak truthfully to your neighbor.....In your anger do not sin. Do not let the sun go down while you are still angry, and do not give the devil a foothold. Anyone who has been stealing must steal no longer, but must work, doing something useful with their own hands, that they may have something to share with those in need. Do not let unwholesome talk come out of your mouths, but only what is helpful for building others up according to their needs.....Do not grieve the Holy Spirit of God, with whom you are sealed for the day of redemption. Get rid of all bitterness, rage and anger, brawling and slander, along with every form of malice. Be kind and compassionate to one another, forgive each other, just as in Christ God forgave you." -Ephesians 4:25-32*

This is all we need to do! It sounds so simple, yet we fall so short of all these things. If you truly seek God and truly want Him to make these changes in you, GOD WILL DO THIS FOR YOU!

"For everyone who asks receives; the one who seeks finds; and to the one who knocks, the door will be opened." -Luke 11:10

"For this is the will of God, that everyone who sees the Son and believes in him should have eternal life; and I will raise him up at the last day." -John 6:40

"Teacher, which is the greatest commandment in the Law?" Jesus replied: "'Love the Lord your God with all your heart and with all your soul and with all your mind. This is the first and greatest commandment. And the second is like it: 'Love your neighbor as yourself.'" -Matthew 22:36-40

God will judge us one day on how much we loved! Love your neighbor more than yourselves and treat your neighbor better than you would like to be treated.
BE HOLY... AS HE IS HOLY!

The Wages of Sin Is DEATH! Do You Take The Dreadful Effects of Sin Seriously? There Is a Hell to Shun, and a Heaven to Gain!

"Do not be deceived, God cannot be mocked. A man reaps what he sows."
-Galatians 6:7

Unless we come to grasp the exceedingly sinfulness of sin, few of us will enter into the narrow Gate of Heaven. The issue is important, in fact it is vital! If we are wrong about the effects that sin has upon us, we could be fooling ourselves about our relationship to God. A true relationship with God must be based upon the fruit of Christ working in and through us. The question is—Can one be "saved" and refuse to forsake sin?

If we deaden our minds to the seriousness of sin, and convince ourselves through mental trickery that we are safe in the arms of Jesus while we willfully continue in rebellion towards God, we lie, and the truth is not in us! Sin separates us from God. It has caused all the trouble, sorrow, suffering, sickness, death, destruction, either directly or indirectly, since the fall of man. *"Fear not them that can kill the body, and are not able to kill the soul, but rather fear Him which is able to destroy both soul and body in hell"* (Matthew 10:28).

"For God so loved the world that he gave his one and only Son, that whosoever believes in

Him shall not perish but have eternal life."
-John 3:16

We have been given a way of escape from our sins through Jesus Christ's death on the cross. Now we have the opportunity to come directly to the Lord to ask and receive forgiveness. *"Repent and be baptized, every one of you, in the name of Jesus Christ for the forgiveness of your sins"* (Acts 2:38). But it doesn't stop here...the Bible also says *"Say to them, 'As surely as I live, declares the Sovereign Lord, I take no pleasure in the death of the wicked, but rather that they turn from their ways and live. Turn! Turn from your evil ways!"* (Ezekiel 33:11).

"For God will bring every deed into judgment, including every hidden thing whether it is good or evil." -Ecclesiastes 12:14

"...and you may be sure that your sin will find you out." -Numbers 32:23

Only God knows your true thoughts and intent. You cannot run and hide. *"...and you may be sure that your sin will find you out"* (Numbers 32:23). You will one day stand before Almighty God! So repent now! Turn from your sin and live! If you truly believe God's Word is true, read and study the Bible and see for yourself what God has to say about sin.

If you read God's Word and follow Jesus Christ, He *will* change your heart. He *will* help you break the chains of sin.

"For if you live according to the flesh, you will die; but if by the Spirit you put to death the misdeeds of the body, you will live. For those who are led by the Spirit of God are the children of God." - Romans 8:13-14

Satan's greatest threat to any of us is a permanent separation from God because of our own sin. Satan sets the trap, and hopes we'll fall into it. Because of His love for us, God sacrificed his son for our sins. When Jesus gave his life at Calvary, the ultimate power of sin was defeated once and for all. *"For all have sinned and fallen short of the glory of God, and all are justified freely by His grace through the redemption that came by Jesus Christ"* (Romans 3:23-24).

When we accept the gift of God's grace we can still experience God's glory as if we had never sinned at all. This is great news for all that have accepted Jesus as their Personal Savior. WE HAVE A MERCIFUL GOD who is willing to forgive ALL of our sins, but He also tells us to turn from our wicked ways.

TAKE SIN SERIOUSLY.....
AND ASK GOD TO REVEAL TO YOU
WHATEVER YOU MAY BE DOING
THAT IS NOT PLEASING IN HIS SIGHT ...
REPENT AND CHANGE YOUR WAYS!

"We are more than conquerors through Him that loved us." -Romans 8:37

If you should lose your life unexpectedly, DO YOU KNOW FOR SURE in your heart *YOU will be with Jesus?*

We May not know the Day nor the Hour. But God Says 'His Children' Will Not be Caught off Guard and Will See THE SIGNS OF HIS COMING!

> *"Now, brothers and sisters, about times and dates we do not need to write to you, for you know very well that the Day of the Lord will come like a thief in the night. While people are saying, "Peace and safety," destruction will come on them suddenly, as labor pains on a pregnant woman, and they will not escape. But you, brothers and sisters, are not in darkness so that this day should surprise you like a thief. You are all children of the light and children of the day. We do not belongto the night or to the darkness. So then, let us not be like others, who are asleep, but let us be awake and sober...For God did not appoint us to suffer wrath but to receive salvation through our Lord Jesus Christ..."*
>
> *-1 Thessalonians 5:1-9*

Jesus criticized the religious leaders of His day because they could not discern the signs of the times. "*.... You know how to interpret the appearance of the sky, but you cannot interpret the signs of the times*" (Matthew 16:1-3).

In some respect, the coming of Jesus will be a surprise for everybody, because no one knows the day or the hour. But for Christians who know the times and the seasons, it *will not* be a complete surprise. No one knows the *exact* hour a thief will come, but some live in a general preparation against thieves. Paul tells us that those in Christ are *not* in darkness. We are to live as Sons of Light and Sons of the Day (1 Thessalonians 1:5). Paul explicitly states that the coming of the Lord would *only* be a surprise to those living in darkness.

If you are living in darkness (*caught up in some sin*), you are *not* ready. If this is you—you need to not wait another day but make yourself ready for Jesus' return. *"...I tell you, now is the time of God's favor, now is the day of salvation"* (2 Corinthians 6:2). Tomorrow might be too late, but it is not too late right now…put your complete trust in Him, depend on Him and *call on Him*! If you pay attention, you *will* see the Day of the Lord Coming. If you are reading and studying God's Word, and looking around the world at the current events in light of Bible prophecy, you *will* know the generation and the times and seasons.

Many people are blindly carrying on as normal because they don't see the signs that Jesus has given us in His Word. The coming of Jesus as described in Matthew 24:15-35 happens at a time of great global catastrophe, when no one could possibly say "peace and safety!" For when they say, "Peace and safety!" then sudden destruction comes upon them: The unexpected nature of that day *will* be a tragedy for the unbeliever. They will be lulled to sleep by political and economic conditions, but they will be rudely awakened. They will hear the frightening verdict "they shall not escape." As a people, we desperately *need* to get *right* with God, because we are in judgment time and Jesus is going to return soon to give His reward to those who have truly served Him or destroy those who did not obey the gospel.

The deceptions that Satan is going to manifest during the very last days are going to be so strong, that if you don't have a love for the truth and are not grounded in the truth of God's Word, then you will leave yourself wide open to be deceived. Don't think that your mere "belief" in Jesus will save you, because if you do *truly* believe, then you will be *living* every day for Him and *searching* the scriptures to find out the truth.

> *"Therefore, dear friends, since you have been forewarned, be on your guard so that you may not be carried away by the error of the lawless and fall from your secure position. But grow in the grace and knowledge of our Lord and Savior Jesus Christ..." - 2 Peter 3:17-18*

> *"All scripture is given by inspiration of God, and is profitable for doctrine, for reproof, for correction, for instruction in righteousness."-2 Timothy 3:16*

As Christians, we *can* be secure of our future. *"For God did not appoint us to wrath, but to obtain salvation through our Lord Jesus Christ* (1 Thessalonians 5:9). *"Seek the Lord while He may be found; call on Him while He is near"* (Isaiah 55:6). Jesus wants us to dig deep into His Word and know the truth. *"Then you will know the truth, and the truth will set you free"* (John 8:32).

Don't let the thief catch you by surprise...
God doesn't want you to be ignorant or fearful...
HE WANTS YOU TO BE READY!

Start Walking in the Favor Of God!

"Every good and perfect gift is from above, and cometh down from the Father of Lights, with whom is no variableness, neither shadow of turning."
-James 1:17

As members of God's kingdom and citizens of heaven, Christians have access to God's resources. This is particularly important to know during these times in which we are living. The systems of this world are failing, and we must know how to get undeniable results by doing things God's way. God is Our Heavenly Father, and He *always* provides. Our *faith* is the key that unlocks the blessings of God and releases His provision in our lives. We can be confident in the promises of God and *His* ability to take care of us.

If you want the *favor* of God and want to *walk in divine blessings*, you must have a personal relationship with Jesus Christ and be born-again. You must know what God's Word says about all the good gifts that Father God wants to give you. You need to start declaring with your mouth and calling out the things that you need—the spoken Word *will* activate God's promises and you will begin to see miraculous things happen.

The Word of God will transform itself and become whatever you need and whenever you need it. The Word of God will always restore your soul, no matter what condition you are in.

"But let all those rejoice who put their trust in You; let them ever shout for joy, because You

defend them. Let those also who love Your name be joyful in You. For You, O Lord, will bless the righteous; with favor You will surround Him as with a shield." -Psalm 5:11-12

The WORD OF GOD is whatever you need and whenever you need it:

Whenever you have lack..........He will be your abundance
When you are weak................He will be your strength
When you are hungry.............He will be your nourishment
When you are confused...........He will be your compass
When you are discouraged.......He will be your joy
When you lack knowledge........He will give you wisdom
When you are lonely...................He will be your companion
When you need protection........He will shelter you from the storm.

"But my God shall supply all your need according to His riches in glory by Christ Jesus." -Philippians 4:19

Your expectations have a lot to do with what happens to you in life. If you expect the worst, that is generally what you will receive. Proverb 23:7 says, *"as we think in our hearts, so are we."* It follows that the level of favor you experience in life will rise to your level of expectation. There is no way around it; if you are to grow in favor with God and men, you are going to have to raise your expectations. You must start believing God's Word is true and pray in faith and know in your heart that God wants you to be blessed with His favor.

"For whoever finds me finds life, and obtains favor from the Lord." -Proverb 8:35

It is God's will for you to experience His favor. Every promise He makes is for you, and as Jesus said, *"According to your faith will it be done to you"* (Matthew 9:29).

You must declare God's Word in faith and begin to live in the inheritance our Heavenly Father has so freely given. God's Word tells us that He has never seen the righteous forsaken or their seed begging for bread (Psalm 37:25). The Word says that God gives us the power to prosper (Deuteronomy 8:18). Yet we continue to live outside of our inheritance. It is time to claim our birthright! We are sons and daughters of the King. We must believe that we are entitled to His provision and favor. We must begin to think and live our lives like the royalty we are.

Command the floodgates of Heaven to be opened and watch an ABUNDANT OUTPOURING of God's provision be released in your life!

God WANTS to bless you, personally, with His favor.
As you enlarge your mindset to EXPECT and BELIEVE for His favor, and as you open your mouth to CONFESS God's promises,
You CAN find favor with God and man!

When You Speak God's Word... It Enables His Angels To Work On Your Behalf!

> *"For He will command His angels concerning you to guard you in all your ways; they will lift you up in their hands, so that you will not strike your foot against a stone."*
> *-Psalm 91:10-12*

Angels are the mighty ones who fulfill the Word of God. They obey His voice according to His word and they are servants that were created only to do God's Will. What wonderful promises we have for protection from God's angels. God commands them and they obey on our behalf. Angels are real spiritual beings. They are messengers sent from God to minister to God's children by protecting us from danger, strengthening us in times of weakness, and refreshing us in times of discouragement. Angels are sent forth from God's throne to be servants for all those who will inherit salvation. These angels are not for those who are lost, but are sent only for those whose names are written in the Lamb's Book of Life.

> *"The angel of the LORD encamps around those who fear Him, and He delivers them." -Psalm 34:7*

These Angels are before the face of God waiting for His orders to serve us. But one of the biggest challenges we face as believers in releasing our angels is by what we see, what we hear and what we feel. Things we experience in the *physical* often times conflict with what the Word of God says. The Word of God says that by what Jesus did on the cross we are *already* healed! As we speak or confess these promises of how Jesus has already healed you, saved you, and delivered you—*power and life* are given to your words. *"Death and life are in the power of the tongue"* (Proverb 18:21). God *"delivered us out of the power of darkness, and translated us into the kingdom of the Son"* (Colossians 1:13).

Darkness and the power of Satan should have *no* power over us. Because Christ lives in us we are now spiritually seated with Christ in the Kingdom of God. Jesus raised us up with Him and seated us with Him in the heavenly places in Christ Jesus. When Christians don't believe this, they are tossed to and fro by worry and despair. They choose to believe what they see instead of *accepting the truth in the Word of God*. Lack of faith and lack of boldly speaking the promises of God will restrict or bind His angels from leaving the throne room of God to work on your behalf.

We must learn from our Father in Heaven who *"calls those things which do not exist as though they did"* (Romans 4:17). We must learn to speak into existence what we have faith for and what God promised us through Scripture while at the same time casting down the things we see and feel in the natural that are contrary to God's promises. Bring every thought into captivity and filter it through the Word of God and you will start the process of renewing your mind. *"Do not be conformed to this world, but be transformed by the renewal of your mind, that by testing you may discern what is the will of God, what is good and acceptable and perfect"* (Romans 12:2). By transforming your mind from the natural things you see and feel to the mind of Chris, and how He sees it, you *will* start to boldly speak faith in what the Bible promises you.

Many Christians struggle through problems only to realize that they have not even asked for God's help and salvation for this problem. *"You do not have because you do not ask."* We get so caught up in our works and our efforts that we squeeze God out. Jesus wants to be our Savior in all areas of our lives. Angels are just waiting for us to *trust* in God so that they can minister to our needs. The choice is ours and when we speak life or confess the Word, we release our angels who stand before the Father. They are just waiting for us to believe and confess God's Word to others.

> *"Bless the LORD, O you his angels, you mighty ones who do his word, obeying the voice of His word! Bless the LORD, all his hosts, His ministers, who do His will!" -Psalms 103:20, 21*

When we call on Jesus as our Savior every day, we employ Our angels into action and get our prayers answered.

> *TRUST IN GOD IN ALL THINGS and*
> *He will always take care of you.*
> *Our angels are waiting on us*
> *to make the first move of FAITH!*

Renew your Mind with "The Word" and Reap All of His Benefits!

> *"And be not conformed to this world: but be ye transformed by the renewing of your mind, that ye may prove what is that good, and acceptable, and perfect will of God."*
> *-Romans 12:2*

God did not create you to remain the same. He created you to grow and to be transformed. He created you to make a difference in your environment, wherever you are, to be purposefully adding in a creative way… to regain what has been stolen from this world by the enemy—the LOVE of Christ Jesus! When you are transformed, it causes you to rise above and beyond anything that you thought you could accomplish. You are not capable of doing anything in and of yourself, but with God all things are possible. It is time for Christians to realize that we are children of God, and seek to live in the fullness of Who He is and walk in power and in His plans and purposes.

Do not struggle in a place where you feel bound. Do not settle for what you think is your limit. Do not listen to man who has spoken limitations and boundaries into your life. As you begin every day, set your heart on the Kingdom of God, and HIS Righteousness, and *He will add what you lack and what you need* to carry out His purposes in this earth. If you allow Him, God will mold you into *who* and *what* He had always intended you to be. God is a God of victory and so be prepared to receive success and to be transformed. Keep in mind that the success that the world perceives as success is not always what God considers success. The world is full of envy and pride. The world will despise you, discourage you, and dismiss you. But they do not know your God! *"……With God all things are possible"* (Matthew 19:26).

If you keep your eyes on God, He will lead you. Nothing you have ever imagined will compare to what He has planned…because our ways are not His ways. God's desire is for you to see the big picture and not to be disappointed by small setbacks. They are just delays that God will use to keep you in His timing. God alone sees the beginning from the end. Those who *will wait on God and keep His ways* will surely be blessed.

> ***"Wait on the LORD, and keep his ways, and he shall exalt thee to inherit the land; when the wicked are cut off, thou shalt see it." -Psalm 37:34***

God is "Love" and sometimes this may be a difficult truth for our human minds to grasp. But love is the Lord's very essence, and He is the source from which all true love flows. There are no restrictions, no limitations, *and no exceptions*. God's care for us is absolute and genuine, and through creation, He has unmistakably declared that love. Jesus brings light into the darkness in our world. God's truth is light for us. One of the most important gifts that God has given us for renewing our mind is the Bible- HIS WRITTEN WORD-a wealth of truth that clearly shows His way of thinking, and how He wants *us* to think. King David said, *"Your word is a lamp to my feet and a light for my path"* (Ps. 119:105). God has given us an incredible tool for renewing our minds-His written word. Now what are we going to do with this treasure?

When it comes to renewing your minds—*God has already done His part.* If we do our part, we will reap all of His benefits. God is a God of life and light. He is a creative God and the Word tells us that we are created in His image. BELIEVE IN HIM, believe in yourself!

Today is the day…Now is the time to receive a newness of life and a renewing of your spirit. You may be a Christian, and have accepted Jesus Christ as your personal Savior, but have you received Him as Lord and the "Master" of your life? Have you completely surrendered your life to Him? If not, maybe it's time for a change. You may be "bogged down" or "in a rut". Ask Jesus to breathe new life into the things that are dead or dying. Ask Him to set you on a new path, to give you a new perspective that helps you to see things the way He does.

RIGHT thinking guides us in responding with RIGHT actions.

> *"Therefore, holy brothers and sisters, who share in the heavenly calling, fix your thoughts on Jesus, whom we acknowledge as our Apostle and High Priest." -Hebrews 3:1*

What Holds You Captive? What Keeps You from Living the Life You Long to Live?

> *"For our struggle is not against flesh and blood, but against the rulers, against the authorities, against the powers of this dark world and against the spiritual forces of evil in the heavenly realms."*
>
> *-Ephesians 6:12*

The Israelites understood the feeling of harsh oppression by the nation of Assyria. This wasn't just physical discomfort – it was robbery, destruction, and murder. There was some serious pain and they needed a deliverer who would rescue them from their pain. Through the prophet Nahum, God spoke the most life giving words many of them had ever heard: *"I will now break off his yoke from you and tear off your shackles"* (Naham 1:13). We don't have an Assyrian enemy in our everyday lives today—but we *do* have an enemy.

Is there an issue in your life that causes you to feel stuck? Is it something that you just can't seem to resolve? No matter what you do, it's still there? Maybe there is sin in your life that you have not confessed and have not asked God to forgive you. Maybe you have unforgiveness against someone in your heart. If so—you are shackled. Shackles are any problem or situation that weighs you down and causes you to continue to revisit the same old issues over and over again. Whatever issues you have been carrying around for years— you must lay them at the feet of Jesus—for *only* HE can unlock your shackles and *set you free*.

Before we came to know Christ, we were held captive by the enemy. Sin ruled our hearts and kept us in bondage. Then Jesus came into our lives. Christ, in rising from the dead, became the liberator who frees us from our slavery to sin. Death's power over us—*both spiritual and physical*—is broken when we put our trust in Jesus, because of His sacrificial death on the cross and triumphant resurrection three days later. Sin no longer has any true claim on us, because our old nature has died with Christ, and just as He was raised to life, we are now able to experience a new life with Him.

> *"Therefore if any man be in Christ, he is a new creature: old things are passed away; behold, all things are become new." -2 Corinthians 5:17*

So then, why do you sometimes feel like you still are in shackles? Why does fear rule over you? Why do you still living in harsh oppression? It's because even though you are free in Christ—the enemy still wants to destroy you. He has lost your soul to Christ and he won't stop trying to take it back. So you must press in to the fullness of life God has for you. Jesus said, *"The Spirit of the Lord is on me, because he has anointed me to proclaim good news to the poor. He has sent me to proclaim freedom for the prisoners and recovery of sight for the blind, to set the oppressed free"* (Luke 4:18). We need to grab hold of the freedom that Jesus has purchased for us and allow ourselves to experience it. Nearly all of us hold onto things that, in turn, hold onto us. These things hold us captive.

Don't continue to allow yourself to be burdened down any longer with the weight of sin—accept His forgiveness of your sins, forgive others of their sins and unlock the shackles which bind you. Allow yourself to be forgiven; not by forgiving yourself first, but by allowing the redeeming blood of Christ Jesus to wash you clean. Then release the anger, hate, and fear that binds you by forgiving those who have hurt you.

God promises to help us overcome every chain, if we *seek him with all of our heart*. God gave Jesus the key to free you from the heavy chains that keep you captive—by His death on the cross.

When He did, He broke off the enemy's yoke from you and tore off your shackles. He neutralized sin's power over you and gave you the ability to live for Him! YOU ARE FREE! You are *no* longer in chains! Hallelujah!

Jesus Has The Key To Free You From The Shackles of Sin!!

> **To live in COMPLETE FREEDOM, You must be willing to TRUST JESUS—COMPLETELY.**
> **Trust that He will take care of you,**
> **do what is just on your behalf,**
> **and love you no matter what!**

God Will Speak to Those Who Will Take Time to Listen!

Nothing can satisfy our longing for God, except communion and fellowship with Him. Isaiah expressed well our own hunger for God when he wrote: *"My soul yearns for you in the night; in the morning my spirit longs for you...."* (Isaiah 26:9)

One of the greatest benefits of our salvation has to be that of hearing God speak to us personally. There can be no intimate relationship with Our Heavenly Father without hearing Him speak to us. Learning to clearly distinguish God's voice is invaluable. Instead of going through life blindly, we can have the wisdom of God guide and protect us. The Lord constantly speaks to us and gives us His direction. It's never the Lord who is not speaking, but it's us who are not hearing.

Are we taking the time to listen to what God has to say to us or are we allowing distractions with the things of the world to drown out God's voice? The world makes it easy for us to fill our ears with all kinds of things that drown out God's voice and push Him far, far into the background of our lives. Are you so busy that you don't have time to spare to sit quietly with the Lord and hear what He has to say to you? Is the busyness of your life getting in the way of developing your relationship with God? Are we *just too busy* for God? Are we so focused on other things that "obsess and exhaust us" that we don't hear from God, leaving us to our own devices?

What does Jesus say about busyness?

"As Jesus and his disciples were on their way, he came to a village where a woman named Martha opened her home to him. She had a sister called Mary, who sat at the Lord's feet listening to what he said. But Martha was distracted by all the preparations that had to be made. She came to him and asked, 'Lord, don't you care that my sister has left me to do the work by myself? Tell her to help me!' 'Martha, Martha,' the Lord answered, 'you are worried and upset about many things, BUT FEW THINGS ARE NEEDED—OR INDEED ONLY ONE. MARY HAS CHOSEN WHAT IS BETTER, and it will not be taken away from her.'" -Luke 10:38-42

Most of the time, we resemble Martha more than Mary. We rush around doing "what needs to be done," while missing the glimpses of Jesus all around us. As difficult as it is, and as contrary to our culture as it is, we must intentionally make the effort to slow down and model Mary because, as Jesus himself said, *"Mary has chosen what is better, and it will not be taken away from her."* The Bible places high value on rest and peaceful living. During Jesus' earthly ministry, He Himself escaped the busyness of the crowds occasionally to renew His strength. *"Then, because so many people were coming and going that they did not even have a chance to eat, he said to [His disciples], 'Come with me by yourselves to a quiet place and get some rest.'"* Mark 6:31 It is difficult, if not impossible, for us to hear God's *still, quiet voice* over all the unrest all the distractions around us. So, like Jesus, we must make time to rest and hear from our Lord.

We must be intentional about making time to rest in Jesus. Let the phone ring, the chores can wait, and social media could use a break. Those things are not eternal. Jesus is eternal. Let us make the effort to sit at His feet and enjoy Him rather than miss Him like Martha did because she was fussing over the dishes. *"Do not be anxious about anything, but in every situation, by prayer and petition, with thanksgiving, present your requests to God. And the peace of God, which transcends all understanding, will guard your hearts and your minds in Christ Jesus"* (Philippians 4:6–7).

We need to withdraw from things that obsess and exhaust us and spend time in solitude and silence. Our motivation should be to spend quality time at God's feet and to do with excellence and joy that mere handful of things God truly called us to do. Even Jesus took time to pray for guidance in places of quiet solitude.

> *"But Jesus often withdrew to lonely places and prayed." -Luke 5:16*

ARE YOU TOO BUSY TO SIT AT THE FEET OF JESUS?

God wants to talk to YOU and He has a plan for YOUR life that will lead to a path of peace and contentment!
**GOD WILL SPEAK TO THOSE
WHO ARE READY AND PREPARED TO LISTEN!**

Are You Sitting on the Fence? Now Is the Time to Choose Which Way You Will Go!

> *"...choose for yourselves this day whom you will serve, whether the gods which your fathers served that were on the other side of the River, or the gods of the Amorites, in whose land you dwell. But as for me and my house, we will serve the LORD."*
>
> *-Joshua 24:15*

Noah preached for one hundred-twenty years and he and his sons spent much of that time building an ark big enough to protect anyone who wanted to be saved. However, since it had never rained before this time, people scoffed at them as if they were so spiritually minded they were no earthly good. Many wanted to get aboard the ark after it started raining, but it was *too late*. God had already closed the door (Genesis 7:16).

When it comes to deciding if you are going to choose to accept Christ as your Savior and serve God, you don't want to be dragging your feet. The Apostle Paul says in 2 Corinthians 6:2 that *"now is the accepted time; behold, now is the day of salvation."* Sometimes we put off decisions for so long that when we finally make a move, it's too late. God created man and then made the most unselfish move – He gave us free will. That means we are free to choose serve Him or not. The opportunity to choose to spend eternity in Heaven with a loving God is one that you don't want to take for granted. We are all going to spend an eternity somewhere. If you don't choose Heaven, you'll get Hell by default.

The Bible declares that if anyone claims to be a Christian, yet lives a worldly life, they are liars. (Romans 8:9; 1 John 2:4) Many who claim the name of Christ in their life are oblivious to the destruction they inflict upon the Kingdom of God by their words and actions. (Matthew 7:16-23) A shallow consent to accept Christ will bring no real change to your life and requires no surrender for the glory of God. Christians are not content with just participating in ritualistic, religious motions. They no longer desire to live in the fleshly, carnal, worldly realm of life—they want to be filled with the Holy Spirit.

"Blessed are they which do hunger and thirst after righteousness for they will shall be filled."
-Matthew 5:6

Salvation is not an end in itself. It is the beginning of a whole new life (2 Corinthians 5:17). We need to exhibit the fruit of God's Spirit, (Galatians 5:22-23) which is the result of the refining fire of His sanctifying process in our life. Christ in us expresses the fruit of the Spirit in and through us. We are a vessel containing the Living Lord of the Universe with all the dynamic power of the triune God dwelling within us (Ephesians 3:20).

Many Christians today are "on the fence" for Christ. I mean they've got one foot in the world and one foot in the Kingdom. Don't allow the circumstances of this world to make you drift farther and farther from Christ. Get off the fence! Commit your life wholly and completely to the Lordship of Jesus Christ! Make a difference in His Kingdom by following the leading of His Spirit moment by moment throughout the day. Fall in love with Jesus. Living in the center of God's will is the happiest place on earth.

When you begin to fill your life with the things of God and get His Word into your heart, you will develop an intimate relationship with Him... then you will be able to walk on faith, not feelings. If you truly seek God--change *will* come. It will start deep on the inside and transform you.

But first, you must choose for yourself this day—whom you will serve. *It is now time for the children of God to arise*, and get ourselves up from the place of complacency in our Spirit and in our flesh, and 'get off the fence!' We must take our rightful place and become what God has intended us to be! God has a plan for us to become HIS FAITHFUL CHURCH!

It 'IS' like the days of Noah.. So don't make the same mistake!

> *"I know your deeds, that you are neither cold nor hot. I wish you were either one or the other!" -Revelation 3:15*

Do You Have Enough Faith For the Journey Ahead?

"Without faith it is impossible to please God: for he that cometh to God must believe that He is, and that He is a rewarder of them that diligently seek Him."
-Hebrews 11:6

The faith that we are going to need, can only come from God himself. Faith comes when we can wholeheartedly put our trust in Jesus Christ. Faith is trusting God in ALL CIRCUMSTANCES.... especially when things seem hopeless and troubling.

As Christians we need to truly understand that we *are* and we *have* nothing without our "Savior" Jesus Christ. We must become totally dependent upon God and trust him in everything. We can't do anything without the Lord.

Righteousness and faith comes as a result of knowing Jesus. Knowing Jesus comes as a result of spending time in communion and fellowship and relationship with Him. COME TO HIM! If you seek Jesus with all your heart, He will give you the genuine faith that you need.

"Now faith is the substance of things hoped for, the evidence of things not seen." -Hebrews 11:1

The knowledge of this world tells us that we should only believe when we see! Frequently you will hear people say, "I'll believe it when

I see it." God's way is different because God says that WE WILL ONLY SEE, WHEN WE FIRST BELIEVE! We must believe that God WILL do what He has already promised to do. Only then, will we see the promise fulfilled.

We are living in perilous times and now more than ever we must trust in Jesus as our "Lord" and our "Savior". Be prepared when times of trouble, persecution or testing come. Remain steadfast by trusting in God.

Our "eternal life" depends on "knowing" God and Jesus Christ. Once we have accepted Christ we have all that God promises us in His word. It is time to get serious about your relationship with Jesus Christ. In other words, make Him the number one priority in your life… communicate with Him daily and read the words Jesus has given us for instruction and edification. TRUST IN THE LORD by starting to walk in the Spirit and not by sight. God will make it clear to you what He wants you to do… but you must step out in faith and actually start doing it. God will guide your paths; and in any situation give wisdom to His children that ask.

Believe these comforting words given to us by God our Father:

> *"I lift my eyes to the hills from whence does my help come. My help comes from the Lord who made heaven and earth. He will not let your foot be removed, he who keeps you will not slumber, behold he who keeps Israel will neither slumber nor sleep. The Lord is your keeper. The Lord is your shade on your right hand; the sun will not smite you by day nor the moon by night. The Lord will keep you from all the evil. He will keep your life. The Lord will keep your going out and your coming in forever more."*
> *-Psalm 121*

> *"Therefore, since we have a great high priest who has ascended into heaven, Jesus the Son of God let us hold firmly to the faith we pro-*

> *fess... Let us then approach God's throne of grace with confidence, so that we may receive mercy and find grace to help us in our time of need." -Hebrews 4:14,16*

YOU CAN CHOOSE YOUR ETERNAL DESTINATION by choosing "Jesus." Following Jesus is the only way that will lead you to the eternal dwelling-place that He himself is preparing for you. Jesus is all that we will ever need. He is now -- and will be then -- our Alpha and Omega; our First and our Last; our Beginning and our End.

> *"Ask and it will be given to you; seek and you will find; knock and the door will be opened to you. For everyone who asks receives; the one who seeks finds; and to the one who knocks, the door will be opened." -Matthew 7:7*

Travel with the only ONE you can TRUST... JESUS!

> *"I am the vine, you are the branches; he who abides in Me, and I in him, he bears much fruit; for apart from Me you can do nothing." -John 15:5*

Are You Living Under God's Grace....
And Each Dawn Receiving Your Free
Gift And Every Day a Miracle?

> *"But grow in grace, and in the knowledge of our Lord and Saviour Jesus Christ. To him be glory both now and forever. Amen."*
> *-2 Peter 3:18*

God's Grace is an undeserved free gift, undeserved favor, and undeserved love. As Christians, we can have peace and comfort knowing that God's grace furnishes what is lacking in our lives due to personal weakness. Knowing that Christ fills our inadequacy is a great source of encouragement. We know that Christ is with us in any task we may have to face. Knowing that God is not asking us to do anything that he is not willing to accomplish through us is our greatest source of encouragement.

> *"My grace is sufficient for you, for my power is made perfect in weakness." Therefore I will boast all the more gladly about my weaknesses, so that Christ's power may rest on me. That is why, for Christ's sake, I delight in weaknesses, in insults, in hardships, in persecutions, in difficulties. For when I am weak, then I am strong." -1 Corinthians 12:9-10*

Our only hope rests in God who is working on are behalf. Trusting on God's grace at work in and through us is our greatest source of comfort.

> ***"Praise be to the God and Father of our Lord Jesus Christ, the Father of compassion and the God of all comfort, who comforts us in all our troubles…"-2 Corinthians 1:3-4***

Our strength comes from not relying on our adequacy but on God's sufficiency. Sometimes God has to humble us in order that He can reveal His greatest glory. We must always understand that our failures and weaknesses are no match for God's grace and love that He has for us. God will use our brokenness and some of the trials in our life to draw us back to Him to prepare us for his plan for our life. Through this he will help us see ourselves more clearly and help us to see others more compassionately. WE MUST NEVER FORGET WHO IS REALLY IN CONTROL, WHO IS REALLY INVINCIBLE AND OMNIPOTENT.

Trust in Jesus and try looking at your trials in a better light. Receive the blessing of an opportunity to grow in Christ and use your situation as a way to minister to another. God wants to reveal his power to make us dependent upon the One who is the master of all our circumstances. If we could do it all on our own, we wouldn't need God. He is the One who sustains us when we are too weak to stand on our own. God's grace is sufficient for all of our needs. GOD'S GRACE WILL SUSTAIN US—*WHEN WE SEEK TO DO HIS WILL.*

Faith in God allows us to go as far as we can while trusting in God's grace to overcome the insurmountable difficulties we face. Only God's grace can hold us together when we are under an attack from Satan. Satan can only control our circumstances, if we let him. Be obedient to Christ and let God be in control of your life. God is not asking us to endure our hardships alone. He is asking us to persevere, keep at it, carry on, stick and with it… as we trust in Him. In doing so, God will pour out His mercy and grace and lift us above our circumstances as he develops our character.

*BE OBEDIENT AND SEEK GOD'S
PERFECT WILL FOR YOUR LIFE.*

Only through Jesus Christ we are offered grace, a free gift. Jesus says, yes I gave you life and I gave you power to choose, it is your choice. So if we choose love and give our life to Jesus… we can find rest in Him. All that we are is a result of God's grace at work in us. *God has a purpose for your life so let Him direct your steps and LET HIS GRACE FALL UPON YOU.*

GRACE is the PLACE from which all BLESSINGS FLOW!

WHEN WE ACCEPT JESUS INTO OUR HEART
He sends the Holy Spirit into us to begin our spiritual life in Christ. Only then are we given the
FREE GIFT OF GRACE!

The Body of Christ... There Are Many Parts BUT One Body!

"So in Christ we, though many, form one body, and each member belongs to all the others."
-Romans 12:5

Christ' body is the church. The church is not a building nor is it any particular denomination. The church is made of people all over the world who have discovered the love of God as demonstrated by Jesus Christ.

Faith in the shed blood of Jesus brings a person into the household of God. We have access to God through Jesus. Repenting and forsaking of sin can only take place when we accept that Jesus died to pay the price for our peace with God. We are all joined to Christ in salvation and He is the Head of us all. Each person is important in the body of Christ. We all need to play our roles no matter how insignificant they may appear. Those singing, those praying, those ushering and so on, all are playing vital roles.

> *"Just as a body, though one, has many parts, but all its many parts form one body, so it is with Christ. For we were all baptized by one Spirit so as to form one body—whether Jews or Gentiles, slave or free—and we were all given the one Spirit to drink..." -1 Corinthians 12:12-14*

God has commanded us to love one another regardless of our back- ground, race, or ministry.

> *"There should be no division in the body, but… its parts should have equal concern for each other" -1 Corinthians 12:25*

Spending time with other believers gives you a greater awareness and understanding of the all-powerful God we serve. Our Spiritual growth will affect our hearts and attitude. It will give us a greater understanding of the teachings of Jesus. This is essential if we are to witness unity in the church. It will also help us in presenting the Gospel to the world. We have been all given the gift of His righteousness and all of us will be partakers of His inheritance. When a person trusts Jesus Christ for salvation, he or she is made a member of the body of Christ. For a church body to function properly, all of its "body parts" need to be present. Likewise, a believer will never reach full spiritual maturity without the assistance and encouragement of other believers.

> *"… If one part suffers, every part suffers with it; if one part is honored, every part rejoices with it. Now you are the body of Christ, and each one of you is a part of it." -1 Corinthians 12:26-27*

In order to gain spiritual growth, we need to attend church so we can worship God together with other believers. Church is the place where believers can love, encourage and edify one another. We need to lift each other up in prayer. True Sons and Daughters of God have a desire to attend Church, to worship God, receive His Word, and fellowship with other believers.

Especially now with the times we are living in…we need each other to stand strong in the "Body of Christ". We must be in unity with Jesus and be of one heart and one mind. It is necessary for us to mature in our Christian unity so we can help each other hold fast to the promises of God and escape the deceitfulness of sin. Exhort one another to stand firm in our faith!

If you are in Christ and in a Church, you have many brothers and sisters who love you
YOU ARE NOT ALONE!

> **We are… the FAMILY OF GOD
> and all ONE IN CHRIST.
> WE ARE SONS AND DAUGHTERS
> OF THE KING!**

Do You Really Want A Deeper Relationship with GOD?

> *"Search me, O God, and know my heart... and lead me in the way everlasting.*
> *-Psalm 139:23-24*

In the depths of God's heart....He is calling out to the depths of our hearts. Are you hearing His call? If we truly want to experience more of God in our lives, we will have to remove the daily distractions that seem to consume us. Deny yourself the things that you want and God will then deposit the things He desires into your heart—His purpose, the things He cares about, the deeper things of God. We need to open our hearts and minds to the power of the Holy Spirit and allow Him to do a deeper work in us—and when we do just that—we will experience a deep life transformation.

> *"You shall consecrate yourselves therefore and be holy, for I am the Lord your God."*
> *--Leviticus 20:7*

This is a time we must set ourselves apart—apart from distraction and apart from things of this world—in order to go before the Lord, fully prepared to be used by Him. It is about looking at your life and deciding to declare your life sacred and devoting yourself, irrevocably to worship God. Ask the Holy Spirit to inspect the condition of your heart!

When you wake up in the morning, let the first thing that hits the floor be your knees. Pick up the Bible early in the morning. If you don't do it first thing, if you don't prioritize it and develop a new habit, the day is going to get away from you as it always does. If we will endure and complete the work God has given each one of us, we will see blessings, miracles, signs and wonders. It is vitally important to make time for silence, solitude, and reflection. We must take time to become still and spend time alone with God in order to hear and receive the Word that God has for us. We must remain committed, consistent, and consecrated.

When you go into a deeper relationship with God, the devil will try to defeat you by putting thoughts of doubt and fear into your minds. But if we speak, believe, and live God's Word, the enemy will have to leave.

> *"Fear not, for I am with you; be not dismayed, for I am your God. I will strengthen you, Yes, I will help you, I will uphold you with My righteous right hand." -Isaiah 41:10*

WE WERE MADE TO WORSHIP—just as it is essential to breath, drink and eat. We must be in daily communication with Him. It is in our daily worship and reflection of His holiness, grace, mercy, and goodness that we gain an understanding of what it means to be like Him. It is in those intimate moments that we begin to tap in to God's heartbeat. As we continue to seek after His heart, the Holy Spirit will reveal the sin in our lives and will draw us into repentance. When we repent, then Our Heavenly Father will forgive us.

As we daily give Him praise, we begin to capture His heart and develop an understanding of who He is. Then He will begin to impart all that He is into our hearts—His goodness, His mercy, His grace, His patience, His purity, His compassion, His love, and His holiness. The more we worship Him, the more we will truly see His holiness and the more we will be made holy, setting us apart. The more we know Him, the more we will desire to know Him, and the more we will truly love Him. We will learn to love Him equally in times of great joy and in times of distress.

When we come to live in the comforting presence of God on a daily basis, it builds our confidence and faith in Who He has made us to be. Let's ask Him for the grace to do this, so that He alone might rule in our hearts. Let us be His entirely.

Jesus wants to meet YOU… at a deeper level!

When you wake up each morning… SAY YES TO GOD

to the *things* of GOD, to the *heart* of GOD, to the *discipline* of GOD, to the *pain and fellowship of suffering with* GOD JUST SAY YES!

It Is Your Choice on How You Want to Live In This Life... the Choice You Make... Will Determine Your Eternal Resting Place! Pay Close Attention to the Choices You Make Today!

> *"Why, you do not even know what will happen tomorrow. What is your life? You are a mist that appears for a little while and then vanishes."*
> *-James 4:14*

Living in the world you hear statements like this all the time: I make my own rules. I answer to no one. The universe revolves around me. It's all about me. This kind of attitude is leading you down a road to destruction.

One day—LIKE IT OR NOT—OUR BODY WILL DIE. When that time comes if you haven't made a choice to follow Christ, the decision will be made for you and you will spend eternity in damnation. Some people think they have a lot of time to decide what they want to do but none of us knows, when we will take our last breath—ONLY GOD KNOWS!

We are now living in perilous times. Jesus said that the End Times would be as in the days of Noah when everyone only cared about themselves. Look around and you can see how we as a nation are self-destructing. For men will be lovers of themselves, lovers of money, boasters, blasphemers, unholy, disobedient, ungrateful, unloving, unforgiving, slanderers, without self-control, despisers of good, haughty, proud, lovers of pleasure, having a form of godliness but denying its power. Does this sound like our present age?

Of the total earth's population at the time of the flood, only eight people survived. No one cared enough to listen to Noah and get on the ark. *All they had to do was get into the Ark.* That's a picture of the simplicity of salvation. The Lord Jesus Christ paid for our sins in full. The ark represents the Lord Jesus Christ. All we need to do is accept Jesus as our Savior and we'll be saved. But people today won't get on the ark. People today are receiving false bibles, false gospels, false doctrines, and false Christs. Jesus told us to *"SEARCH THE SCRIPTURES"* (John 5:39), because the Bible says *"YOUR WORD IS TRUTH"* (John 17:17). This lost world needs to know that there is a God. We need to tell them about the redeeming SAVIOR, JESUS!

We don't have to choose between pleasure and God. Serving God is the ultimate pleasure… *"At Your right hand are pleasures forevermore"* (Psalm 16:11). But we do have to choose between the *love* of pleasure and the *love* of God. If you are Living for God you will have many pleasures, but they only come as you love God first.

When we read God's Word and let Him speak to us, it changes us by making us complete and it transforms us. One way the Bible transforms us is through our understanding.

> ***"Do not be conformed to this world, but be transformed by the renewing of your mind, that you may prove what is that good and acceptable and perfect will of God. -Romans 12:2.***

When we let the Bible guide our thinking, our minds are renewed and transformed, so we begin to actually think… like God thinks. The Bible will begin to transform us spiritually as God works in us. The Bible gives us eternal life (1 Peter 1:23), it spiritually cleanses us (Ephesians 5:26); gives us power against demonic spirits (Ephesians 6:17); power to heal our bodies (Matthew 8:16); gives us all our spiritual strength (Psalm 119:28); and it builds our faith (Romans 10:17). The Bible will do its spiritual work in us, if we will let it. *We are to stand strong and stand on the WORD OF GOD.* Where is YOUR WALK *taking you?*

We have no choice to live in the world, BUT YOU CAN CHOOSE TO LIVE HERE WITH JESUS. This world is only temporary. Do you really want to have your choice made for you? If not....don't delay!

CHOOSE TO WALK IN THE LIGHT OF THE LORD!

**Don't buy SATAN's BIGGEST LIE OF ALL:
YOU HAVE PLENTY OF TIME!
Physical Death is just the beginning of Life**
Will you spend your eternity with JESUS?

Only One Master Garnishes His Servants with Robes of Righteousness, Crowns Covered with Fine Jewels, and Everlasting Peace!

> *If you belong to Christ, then you are Abraham's seed, and heirs according to the promise."*
> *- Galatians 3:29*

The Joy of Being a Slave to Christ—as slaves of Christ, God lavishes us with all of His possessions. He does it for *our joy*, and He does it for *His Glory*. We are adopted into His family. We are made Sons of God. We are called joint-heirs with Christ. In heaven we will sit with Him and rule with Him. There is *no* greater joy than to be a slave of Christ and *no* greater reward. When you accepted Jesus Christ as your Savior you became an heir to a fortune. You were born into the richest family ever known—a *Royal Family* that owns and operates the universe. Your inheritance is so vast it will take all of eternity to fully comprehend it.

Abraham believed God when there was no hope. He believed even when the world said, "It's impossible."

> *"And being not weak in faith... He staggered not at the promise of God through unbelief; but was strong in faith, giving glory to God; and being fully persuaded that, what he had promised, he was able also to perform"* -Rom. 4:19-21.

THE BLESSING of Abraham will enable you to prosper no matter what's happening around you. It will cause you to increase in the midst of any recessions, depressions or any other kind of calamity the devil can dream up. The devil will always try to steal your inheritance—if you let Him. If you are *Born Again*, you are the SEED OF ABRAHAM, you shouldn't even worry about such things. As Christians we can depend on our covenant with Almighty God—and that never changes! He never alters the Word that comes out of His mouth, and He has said you are BLESSED!

THE BLESSING of Abraham comes to us when we do what he did. It comes to us when we *believe* God's Word. As Romans 5:2 says, *"We have access by faith into this grace."* Faith gives us access to the favor and grace of God and it gives God access to our lives. It opens the door to our inheritance because faith comes by hearing, and hearing by the Word of God. The fact that God has sworn to give you the blessing of Abraham should be an anchor to your soul! You should hold fast to it. When Satan comes against you and tries to steal your inheritance, you can stop him dead in his tracks. "Fear not!" For just as Abraham took God at His Word, we can be confident we are not alone and that God keeps *all* His promises.

> *"Fear not, Abram: I am thy shield, and thy exceeding great reward" -Genesis 15:1*

We also have a covenant with God and God has promised to be an enemy to our enemies. We need to take this promise God made with Abraham and put our name on it. Since we are heirs with Abraham, those words are just as true for us. God keeps His promises.

> *"I will make thee exceeding fruitful, and I will make nations of thee, and kings shall come out of thee. And I will establish my covenant between me and thee and thy seed after thee in their generations for an everlasting covenant,*

to be a God unto thee, and to thy seed after thee." -Genesis 17:6-7

God's Word gives you complete instructions on how to *receive* your inheritance and how to *keep* it. Start enjoying the riches that God has promised *You*! Discover for yourself that you are truly an heir to the limitless resources of the family of God! There is *no* limit to what THE BLESSING OF GOD can do for those who *dare to believe*. It makes the IMPOSSIBLE—POSSIBLE! As a Christian, you are the seed of Abraham! Everything God promised to Abraham belongs to you. It has been passed down to you through Jesus. Abraham's blessing is your inheritance! It has been willed to you by the Word of God.

Either we will be bound to Satan or bonded to Christ; Who would be "your" best slave master?

> **Our inheritance is only made possible through Jesus Christ! Ask Him to be Your Master! JESUS is the WAY, TRUTH, AND LIFE!**
> *Make the impossible POSSIBLE!*

Trust in The Lord at All Times, Even in Times of Trouble!

> *"Trust in him at all times; ye people, pour out your heart before him; God is a refuge for us. Selah."*
>
> *-Psalm 62:8*

Life can be bittersweet sometimes. There are some days when it seems like every wish or dream is coming true. And then there are some days when the clouds begin to fill in and block the light. It's on these darker days when your faith is needed most.

In 1st and 2nd Samuel you will read about the life of King David. He had to deal with tremendous hardships and overcome serious obstacles just to stay alive. He was constantly on the run, constantly in danger, constantly in fear of his life. He knew fear and he knew anxiety. But David also knew where to take his fear and anxiety – to *the Lord in prayer*.

The Psalms of David provide us a wonderful example of pouring out our hearts to the Lord in times of trouble, asking Him for help and trusting in Him for deliverance. David calls out to the Lord for help in times of distress, but then even before his prayer is finished, he already expresses his complete confidence that the Lord will answer his prayer, and deliver him in his time of need. Even though David didn't completely understand why everything happened to him the way it did, in humble faith he trusted that the Lord had a wise plan for his life, that He would fulfill His good purpose for him.

David's hardships and trials kept him humble and taught him to rely on the Lord at all times so that he would succeed in life.

God was teaching David some important lessons about humility, trust and patient endurance. David learned that the only way he was going to make it safely and successfully through life was to stay close to the Lord, trusting His promises and relying on His goodness. Those faith lessons taught David to be a great king—a man after God's own heart!

The Apostle Paul tells us that "We must go through many hardships to enter the kingdom of God." Living in this sinful world, we can expect to deal with all kinds of hardships in our lives. Yes, even as God's chosen people, we can expect to face heartache, pain, and loss. But like David, we can rest securely in God's unfailing love. We can walk through trouble and not be defeated if we keep our focus on the Lord and His purpose.

The Apostle Paul assures us, *"Therefore, there is now no condemnation for those who are in Christ Jesus"* (Romans 8:1). *"If God is for us, who can be against us? He who did not spare his own Son, but gave him up for us all, how will he not also, along with him graciously give us all things?"*(Romans 8:31-32).

Being a child of God doesn't mean you won't have any earthly troubles--but in the midst of all those troubles, you can find peace and rest in the arms of your Savior and strength and encouragement in the promises of your God. Those promises uplifted David while he was on the run, and they will uphold you in your time of need today as well...*so in every situation, in every trial, let us put our trust in God, calling upon Him in every trouble, and counting on Him to deliver us according to His gracious will.*

Yes, *God is with us,* as He was with David.

God is working His good and awesome plan for our life—even when He allows us to suffer heartache, pain and earthly loss. Therefore let us not worry, give up hope, or lose heart. We can trust in the Lord to see us safely through all the trials and troubles that we face. Don't get discouraged. Don't be afraid. Put your trust in God at all times, *especially in times of trouble!*

"Because he has set his love upon Me, therefore I will deliver him. I will set him on high, because he has known My name. He shall call upon Me, and I will answer him; I will be with him in trouble; I will deliver him and honor him. With long life I will satisfy him, and show him My salvation" -Psalms 91:14-15

God is our refuge. He is our strength, so we should not fear. No matter what situation arises, God reminds us to be still and know that He *is* God; He *is* in control; He *will* provide and He *will* make a way.

"The Lord will accomplish what concerns me."
-Ps. 137:8

> **HE HAS PROMISED TO DO A GOOD WORK IN OUR LIVES,** *but sometimes the only way that He can complete it* **IS IN THE VALLEYS OF OUR HARDSHIP!**

Remember How Happy You Were When You Were First Saved... Ask God to Restore You to the Joy of Your Salvation!

> *"In the beginning was the Word and the Word was with God and the Word was God... and the Word became flesh and dwelt among us"*
> *- John 1:1,14*

God the Son took on human form as God's final, decisive Word to the world! All that God has to say is rooted in Jesus, and points toward Jesus, and is proven by conformity to Jesus. All the fullness of God is in Jesus (Colossians 2:9). All the treasures of wisdom and knowledge are in Jesus (Colossians 2:3). Beyond what the Old Testament told us, whatever we need to know about God and how he relates to our lives we learn from what we hear and see in God›s final, decisive Word—Jesus Christ!

Jesus Christ, the Son of God is the heir of all things; he is the radiance of God's glory and the exact representation of God's nature. He upholds all things by the Word of His power, He made purification for sins, He sat down at the right hand of God's majesty, and He is greater than any angel—angels bow down and worship Him. He *is* the mighty God!

We must heed God's Word and we must be diligent in reading the Bible daily. We cannot treat this casually. We cannot act as if we already know all we need to know, or that we have nothing to gain from listening to Jesus. "*We must pay the most careful attention, there-*

fore, to what we have heard, so that we do not drift away" (Hebrews 2:1).

It is *exceedingly necessary* that we give heed to what God commands us to do. It is not just an option that you can do if you are feeling especially spiritual or have a crisis in front of you. We need to seriously listen to Jesus—The Word of God, and consider Jesus, and fix our eyes on Jesus. We are commanded to Listen! Consider! Look! We must be joyfully vigilant in reading the Bible and learning all about Jesus in order to maintain an intimate relationship with Him. His yoke is easy and his burden is light. But if we neglect this great salvation, and drift into the love of other things, then we will not escape. We will perish.

If you are not reading God's Word daily, you are progressively drifting from the Word of God—from Jesus! If your thoughts are not on Jesus *daily*, you will continue to drift day by day. There is no standing still. The life of this world is a river. And it is flowing downward to destruction. If you do not listen earnestly to Jesus and consider Him daily and fix your eyes on Him, then you will drift further and further away from the *only* One who can save you!

God has spoken by His Son, so listen—*listen very carefully*. We fill our heart with so many vain and empty things, but Jesus wants to open the door of your heart—because it is in your heart where you can encounter God and be restored. He has power to change and transform your life from the inside out. Jesus brings love and He restores you to wholeness when you invite Him into your innermost being. Jesus comes with love and forgiveness. He comes with peace and restoration. He fills your heart with His love which will restore your hunger for His presence. Jesus passionately desires to reign as King in your heart. If you let Him, you will live a life filled with overflowing and abundant love. Even in the midst of challenges and difficulties that you may face, Christ will be ruling in your heart, giving you inner strength and peace.

I encourage you to set your heart and make a commitment to restore your relationship with God. The only way you can achieve the fullness of all that God has for you is through… spending time in His Word—Jesus Christ! A restored relationship with God must come through Christ, who is the *only* Savior. He alone has been given the keys to the heart that leads to peace. In Christ all the fullness of the deity dwells, in bodily form (Colossians 2:9). There is a void in the human heart, designed by God Almighty, which *only* Christ can fill. When you open the door of your heart to him…*He will come in*!

He is standing at the door…
He is waiting for *you* to call on HIM!

> **You will find "Joy" in THE WORD because… JESUS IS "THE WORD"**
>
> *"Do not grieve for the Joy of the Lord is your strength." -Nehemiah 8:10*

To Be a Light, You Must Know the Light and Follow the Light!

"'Let there be light,' and there was light. And God saw that the light was good. And God separated the light from the darkness... the first day."
-Genesis 1:3-5

The first thing that God did as He created the world was to separate the light from the darkness. But the Book of Revelation tells us that the last thing that God does is to separate the light from the darkness. There's a darkness outside of heaven, the Bible calls it *"outer darkness"* (Matthew 25:30) — in which there is no glimmer of light. That's the awfulness of this other destination of the human soul — a place where light never penetrates. This is what makes the gospel so utterly solemn, so absolute and so important. We shall all, one day, spend eternity either in the light or in the darkness.

Walking in the light requires the right response—YOU *must follow*. *"I am the light of the world. Whoever follows me..."* (John 8:12). As we follow the Lord as His disciples, He illuminates the pathway of life so we can find our way through the difficulties, problems and decisions that constantly confront us. Jesus lights our way and shows us the direction that we need to go. He lights our path to heaven. He lights our pathway to His will on this earth in this life. If we're willing to trust in Him for His direction, He will faithfully lead us.

Compared to Him and His perfection, we're dark and like filthy rags. *"None is righteous, no, not one...no one seeks for God"* (Romans

3: 10). It is not what we're like in comparison with others, no matter how religious we are—it's what we're like standing beside Jesus. What does the light in Him say about the darkness in us? The very presence of the light exposes the darkness. The life God wants is the life Christ lived. We're filled with darkness and the Bible tells us that if there is just an ounce of darkness still in our heart, God cannot accept it, and will not accept it. This is a dark, dark world. Perversion, addictions, racism, suicide, abortion, hatred, dishonesty, and crime permeate our society. We are seeing Isaiah 5:20 fulfilled before our very eyes.

> ***"Woe to those who call evil good and good evil, who put darkness for light and light for darkness..." -Isaiah 5:20***

Unlike any other man who's walked on this earth, Jesus Christ is unique. Outside of Him—there's not even a spark of true light. He continually sheds His light upon us and this darkened world through the Gospel, and by the power of His Spirit. Jesus alone has *"come down from heaven,"* speaking with God's authority to mankind. He alone can testify of heavenly things. He is *"The Light of the World."* The glory of the gospel is that the light that belongs to God has come into this world of darkness. The light of the gospel points us to the one who came, to the one who stepped into our darkness in order to save us. He saved us by enduring the darkness Himself that we caused by our sins. When Jesus died on the Cross He came right into our darkness, deliberately stepping into it, experiencing it in all its horror and terror. *He did this in LOVE in order that there might be LIGHT for us!*

And one day we will shine with Him for all eternity. Jesus said, *"The righteous will shine forth as the sun in the Kingdom of their Father"* (Matthew 13:43). Christians await a glory that involves a shining that will be so glorious beyond our imagination: *"We know that, when He appears, we shall be like Him, because we shall see Him just as He is"* (1 John 3:2). Not only will the light be in us, not only do we become light, we have the light to illumine our steps as we walk through life. Light comes into us so that it can go out to others, making us to be light and life to them.

If you are a Christian and have walked away from the light, stepping into any shadows of darkness—come to Jesus and tell Him in your own heart that you are coming back into His light. He will come into your dark and dying world with His forgiveness and grace and bring you back into His light. And if you've never come to Jesus—The Light of the World—run to the Cross and ask Him to be your Lord and Savior TODAY!

GOD has provided A WAY OUT
of the darkness… JESUS!

> *WE ARE ALL BLINDED BY OUR OWN SIN.*
> **If God did not "enlighten" us, if He did not seek us out and open our blind eyes, we'd never see…**
> **THANK HIM AND PRAISE HIM!**

Know That God Never Leaves Us Nor Forsakes Us... So Why Do I Sometimes Feel So Alone?

> *"Be Strong and courageous. Do not be afraid or terrified because of them, for the Lord your God goes with you; he will never leave you nor forsake you."*
> *-Deuteronomy 31:6*

Sometimes in life you feel forgotten. You keep bumping your head up against those same walls, chasing shadows down the same dead ends, and you wonder if anyone, anywhere, even cares. It can feel so dark and alone there. You look around and feel as if everyone else is getting the big breaks and moving ahead. Meanwhile, there you are—forgotten.

Loneliness is one of life's most painful experiences. Since God created us as relational beings, the absence of companionship can be very discouraging. At some point, all of us have probably dealt with feelings of isolation. But it's especially difficult when we're going through a trying situation and there is no one to help or encourage us. What we want at that moment is companionship, support, and comfort so that our emotional pain will go away. During these times don't give up hope because God will use your loneliness to achieve His purposes in your life. Sometimes He allows such situations because they are prime opportunities to develop godly character within us, train us to depend on Him, and bring us into a closer relationship with Him. When you are feeling all alone just remember He is the *One* who never leaves us.

A long time ago, Israel felt as if God had forgotten all about them. Everyone around them was getting blessed left and right, but not them. Everyone was getting ahead, while they were left behind. When they cried out, "The Lord has forgotten us!" Isaiah gave them these words from God: *"Never! Can a mother forget her nursing child? Can she feel no love for the child she has borne? But even if that were possible, I would not forget you! See, I have written your name on the palms of my hands; your walls are ever before me"* (Isaiah 49:15-16).

Even when you feel completely deserted, God has not forgotten you. We experience pain for several reasons—maybe we have pulled away from God and are out of His will, or perhaps that pain is building our character and pushing us to become a better person. God sees the pain and He feels the hurt. Scripture tells us that every single tear we shed is counted and collected. He cares so much; and He has not forgotten you. Your name is written on the palms of His hands. He's waiting on you to step out of that rut and *step forward* in faith. God has so much in store for you; and He wants to lead you to *a life that is overflowing with abundance and joy*. But, you've got to take that first step, and you do this by *lifting your heart in praise*—PRAISING GOD FOR *no other reason than* FOR BEING GOD.

It's easy to praise God when everything's going well, but not so easy when you feel down and deserted. But when you begin to praise God, something miraculous happens. Praise is an act of taking your eyes off of yourself and putting them on God. God responds to your praises and He will turn your life around. God hasn't abandoned you—He's right there. Lift your voice in praise to Him and watch Him push you ahead, far beyond anything you could do on your own. Sing a song to Him. Pray a prayer of thanksgiving. Quit speaking at what's wrong and start voicing all the things that are right about your life. Those hands of His are waiting to lift you up and push you forward—those same hands that carry your name.

In his lifetime of walking with Christ, the Apostle Paul had learned that times of weakness were God's invitation to depend on Him. When Paul was struggling with a "thorn in the flesh," the Lord said to him, *"My grace is sufficient for you, for my power is perfected in weakness"* (2 Corinthians 12:9). Don't allow yourself to feel hopeless in your loneliness. When you are emotionally, physically or spiritually weak, you are in a prime position to witness firsthand the power of God working within you. He'll give you the strength and courage to endure whatever you are going through.

We are never alone and WE CAN endure to the end because WE have JESUS CHRIST!

> **WE MAY LEAVE GOD… BUT HE WILL NEVER LEAVE US.**
> No matter how empty the feeling comes,
> God will never leave you!
> **HIS PROMISES AND HIS WORD ARE TRUE!**

"Who is whispering in Your Ear... Who Are You Listening To?"

> *"Be on the alert, your adversary the devil prowls about like a roaring lion seeking someone to devour. Resist him... be firm in your faith."*
>
> *-1 Peter 5:8*

We have an enemy of our souls. Don't allow Satan to have power over you. We can resist him by being firm and taking God at His Word. The word of God says, *"Greater is He who is in you, than he who is in the world"* (1 John 4:4). Satan is relentless! He tempts us to sin and tries to keep us from believing God. Jesus himself prayed for us that the Father would keep us from the evil one (John 17:15). God's Word says that Satan is the accuser, the slanderer, the father of lies, the murderer, the deceiver, and our adversary.

"Our struggle is not against flesh and blood but against the rulers, against the powers, against the world forces of this darkness, against the spiritual forces of wickedness in the heavenly places" (Ephesians 6:12). We do not have to fear for we know the victory that we have in Christ—the truth and security that is ours. Satan is in the business of trying to deceive us and trying to make something look like the truth but it's a lie; it's a deception. Satan's power is in the lie and if you don't believe in his lie... you will remove his power. You can confront Satan by looking at what God's word has to say. In dealing with Satan's lies, you have to know the truth.

You have to know God's Word before it will set you free. Faith is not a feeling. It is a choice that we must make to take God at His Word. To gain freedom in spiritual battle, we must take those thoughts, feelings and temptations, and ask what God's Word says about this: *"You shall know the truth and the truth will set you free"* (John 8:32). *"There is therefore now no condemnation for those who are in Christ Jesus"* (Romans 8:1).

Satan tries to cloud our thinking. But it is God who created us and loves us.

> ***"If we confess our sins, He is faithful and just to forgive us our sins and cleanse us from all unrighteousness." -1 John 1:9***

So when we find ourselves having negative thoughts about ourselves or about God or about others, what do we do? *"...taking up the shield of faith with which you will be able to extinguish all the flaming arrows of the evil one"* (Ephesians 6:16) and *"Resist the devil and he will flee from you"* (James 4:7). We have to actively take God at His Word. *"I pray that the eyes of your heart may be enlightened so that you may know…what is the surpassing greatness of His power toward us who believe"* (Ephesians 1:18-19). We can take our thoughts captive because God lives in us and empowers us. Satan cannot read our minds, but he can plant thoughts in our minds. *"…we are taking every thought captive according to the obedience of Christ"* (2 Corinthians 10:5). Take captive those thoughts that come to your mind that are contrary to what God says about you and what He says about Himself. Thoughts can become actions; actions can become habits. And it all starts with a thought so don't dwell on negative thoughts.

God wants us to trust His Word more than we trust our feelings… more than we trust how things appear. GODS' WORD IS TRUE. The Bible says that, *"The grass withers, the flower fades, but the Word of our God stands forever"* (Isaiah 40:8).

WE CAN STAND up to any situation, any thought or feeling and turn to our Jesus. Satan may try to tempt you, discourage you, and defeat you. But he is a liar, and we need to confront his lies with the truth of God's Word. When we actively take up our shield of faith in God's Word, we stand victorious in Christ. If you don't know God's voice, maybe you need to draw closer to Him so the deceiver can't tempt you into sinning. Draw closer to the Lord and live a life of LOVE, PEACE and JOY!

Choose a personal relationship with Jesus, Our Shepherd and you will recognize His voice.

"Thy Word... I hid in my heart...that I might not sin against thee." -Psalm 119:11"

YOU WILL HEAR SOMETHING...
If you aren't *Hearing the Voice of the Lord,*
you are probably *hearing the deceiver... father of lies.*

Are We Looking to Our Own Understanding or Are We Looking Through the Eyes of God's Word?

Jesus replied, "You do not realize now what I am doing, but later you will understand."
-John 13:7

We were not promised that our walk with God will be trouble free. There will be dark shadows falling on us and often we will be confused and disillusioned in not finding the face of God. Remembering the Bible passage where Jesus raised Lazarus from the dead. When Jesus arrived, Lazarus was already dead and had been buried in the tomb for four days. Martha said to Jesus *"You are late. If you were here, my brother would not have died"* (John 11:21). Martha could not understand this delay of God.

If God delays, it is always for our own good. Often we do not understand because we look through our own eyes and not the eyes of God. God looks at things from an eternal perspective. God is waiting so that we may trust in Him, that we may put our faith in Him, and that we may turn to Him.

Often we do not understand why God seems to delay. We pray for God's intervention but nothing really happens. We pray for guidance from God and there seems to be no response. We pray for a loved one who fell ill and he was not healed; not only was he not healed but he died. We pray for a financial problem and we waited for God to intervene but it was in vain - the problem became more acute. We wanted a job because we had to feed the family and yet God was silent. We wanted understanding, fellowship, friendship, companionship and we prayed for it all… but things turned worse. We do not understand the ways of God, the delays of God, and the silence of God. SO…WHY IS GOD SILENT AND IS HE LATE?

God does hear all of our cries and He is an on time God! When God delays…it is always for His Glory to be manifested in that particular situation. In John 11:4, Jesus tells us *"this illness is not unto death, it is for the glory of God, so that the Son of God may be glorified by means of it."* In John 11:14, Jesus says to Martha. *"Did I not tell you that if you believe you would see the glory of God?"* What does that mean? A delay in God's intervention is for the manifestation of God's glory. I believe that Jesus wanted Martha and Mary and the disciples to know that God was in control. God is in control of our sickness, of our life and of our death and that is why Jesus is challenging Martha, *"Believe and you shall see the glory of God."*

Often we want to control our situations in our own way even though we know that God's ways are better than our ways. GOD KNOWS EVERYTHING FROM THE BEGINNING TO THE END. At the right time, he will intervene. God will answer the cries of your heart, but in God's own time, in God's own way, and in God's own place. We must wait for God's glory to be manifested. God is in control and everything that He does is to manifest His own glory to us. Moments of trials WILL come. Even though we are confused and disillusioned with the silence of God, we can trust in God's Word and display our confidence in the love of God.

> **"I love the Lord for he hath heard my voice and my supplications." -Psalm 116:1**

God knows all about our sorrows and collects all of our tears. No sigh, no tear, no pain escapes God's attention. God knows everything and at the right time, He will turn everything to our good."

We don't really need to UNDERSTAND or even ask WHY….
Trust God and He will take your yoke upon himself!

"When I cry unto thee, then shall mine enemies turn back: this I know; for God is with me."
-Psalm 56:10

"If you believe ... then you shall see the glory of God" -John 11:40

"...We rejoice in our sufferings knowing that sufferings produce endurance and endurance produces character and character produces hope and hope does not disappoint us because God's love has been poured into our hearts, through the Holy Spirit who has been given to us." -Romans 5:3-5

Are You Living Abundantly? The Life that God Desires for You!

"Repent, then, and turn to God, so that your sins may be wiped out, that times of refreshing may come from the Lord..."
    -Acts 3:19

Spiritual refreshment is promised to those who repent and turn to God. In the presence of the Lord we will not only have love, joy and peace, we will also have our spirits, souls and bodies refreshed physically and spiritually. God has promised us these times of spiritual refreshing in order to revive our spirits and souls when we need it the most.

We are living in times when we are going to be in great need of spiritual refreshing and rejuvenation because of the trials, tests, disappointments and persecutions that we may suffer for the sake of Christ. As believers, we all go through fiery trials that can drain our spiritual strength. Not spending enough time in the presence of the Lord will leave you feeling spiritually unfulfilled and missing out on the power of the Holy Spirit.

In order to have a move of the Spirit, we must invite the very Person or the One that brings us the spiritual refreshment. When we are in God's presence, we will receive all that we could ever need or want. God has plans and purposes that he wants to fulfill in our lives. The Word declares, *"Those that are led by the Spirit of God are sons of God"* (Romans 8:14). The only way to fulfill God's will and destiny for our lives is by following and yielding to the Holy Spirit.

If we would just lose our own agendas and receive His…then we will experience the presence and power of the Holy Spirit! We must humble ourselves before the Lord and acknowledge our sins and repent! The Lord can only work with those who walk in humility and who will submit themselves to Him. We must be willing to let go of wrong thinking, attitudes and our own agendas and start conforming to God's will if we want to see the demonstration of the Spirit's power. If we submit and yield ourselves to the Lord, he will lead and guide us in the path that he wants to us to take.

> ***"Humble yourselves before the Lord and he will lift you up." -James 4:1-10***

God wants to lift his people up and take us to new heights spiritually. When we honor and revere the Holy Spirit, we are also honoring the One who sent him—JESUS! Everything the Holy Spirit leads us to do will glorify Jesus and draw us closer to him. When we allow Him to orchestrate our lives, *we will see Him move in great power and glory.*

> ***Jesus Said, "I have come that they may have life, and that they may have it more abundantly."***
> ***-John 10:10***

As believers, we can experience a time of refreshing by quieting our hearts in a devotional time of prayer and reading the Bible. When we spend time alone with the Lord, we can experience His peace and joy which will renew us in our spirits; and we will receive spiritual refreshment. When we draw near to God, our minds are refreshed and our strength is renewed.

God desires to pour out his Spirit upon you. *Make yourself right with God. Humble yourselves before the Lord by confessing your sins and ask for His forgiveness.* Listen to the Holy Spirit and ask Him to speak to you through His Word that you might hear him. As you submit to the mighty hand of God, you will see a mighty moving of the Holy Spirit in your life.

REFRESHMENT WILL COME FROM GOD.. WHEN YOU SEEK HIM!

Seek the Lord and receive his refreshment today!

"Blessed are they which do hunger and thirst after righteousness; for they shall be filled"
-Matthew 5:6

> *"I will refresh the weary and satisfy the faint." -Jeremiah 31:25*

How Do You Respond When You Feel Offended?

> *"A man's wisdom gives him patience; it is to his glory to overlook an offense."*
> *-Proverbs 19:11*

Thankfully we can take all our difficult questions to God and He always has an answer for us. If we rely on our own wisdom at the time we are offended we get hurt and angry. Only God's wisdom can give us patience after someone has hurt us. Godly wisdom helps us to have tolerance for the person who has offended us and through this patience we can find God's plan to restore the situation.

> *"He was oppressed and treated harshly, yet he never said a word. He was led like a lamb to the slaughter. And as a sheep is silent before the shearers, he did not open his mouth." -Isaiah 53:7*

Jesus is an amazing example for us. He was treated harshly, beaten and ultimately crucified, and through it all, *"He never said a word, He did not open his mouth."* Words are very important and the Bible says that we will be held accountable for every word we say. Many words are spoken that can never be taken back and later regretted… making the situation worse. There is a time to speak and there is a time to be silent. The key to Godly wisdom will help you know the difference.

> *"Let us fix our eyes on Jesus, the author and perfecter of our faith, who for the joy set before*

him endured the cross... Consider Him who endured such opposition from sinful men, so that you will not grow weary and lose heart."
-Hebrews 12:2-3

Jesus is our source of faith and strength during opposition. If our thoughts are fixed on Jesus...then they won't be focused on the person who has offended us. The Word of God encourages us to get our eyes off the situation and on to the hope that has been given us through Jesus' death on the cross. Our focus must be on the joy that has been set before us knowing that God is able to work together all things for our good.

"And the fruit of righteousness is sown in peace of them that make peace -James 3:18

It is impossible to have peace and be angry at the same time. Those who are the peacemakers will reap a harvest of righteousness into their lives. When we are at peace in our own life, we can then plant seeds of peace in others. Having peace is a choice. We must put aside the anger and overlook the offenses before we can be a peacemaker. When we are willing to do this, blessings will come into our lives.

Remember our sin offends Almighty God, but in Christ He had mercy upon us. We are all recipients of the mercy of God—a full and free forgiveness, gained by Christ's punishment for our sins, in our place, on Calvary's cross. Surely, knowing that God, in Christ, has forgiven us all our sins, our attitude towards others should be that much more merciful. *"Be kind to one another, tender hearted, forgiving one another, as God in Christ forgave you"* (Ephesians 4:32).

If someone offends you...pray for patience, choose your words carefully, look beyond your situation and count it joy, and be a PEACEMAKER.

"YOU" were granted MERCY... SO HAVE MERCY!

> **WHAT IF JESUS.. WOULD HAVE BEEN OFFENDED?**
> *Our lives would have been forever changed!*
> **THE WORD OF GOD IS LIFE CHANGING...**
> *Make sure that the only thing...that consumes you... is God's Word.*

Delight Yourself In The Lord...
And He Will Delight In You!

"The Lord takes pleasure in His people."
-Psalm 149:4

God has demonstrated His love for us by letting His only Son Jesus Christ die on our behalf. When you seek Him with all your heart, He will demonstrate His love for you in immeasurable ways. He will draw you nearer to Him and reveal more of Himself to you. The Bible says, *"The eternal God is a dwelling place, and underneath are the everlasting arms"* (Deuteronomy 33:27). The more you let yourself delight in His love, the more you will find freedom to believe. The more you believe, the more you will let yourself be open to experience His presence as He holds you close.

God doesn't want our interactions with Him to end at salvation; that's where they need to *BEGIN*. If we communicate with Him only on a surface level, we cheat ourselves and hinder fulfillment of the Lord's ultimate goal for us—an intimate relationship with Him.

The first step in our quest for intimacy with the Lord is getting to know Him—who He is, what He does, how He thinks, and what He desires. WE WILL NEVER ACHIEVE CLOSENESS WITH THE LORD UNLESS WE INVEST TIME AND EFFORT IN GETTING TO KNOW HIM. A neglected relationship simply won't grow in richness or depth. If you are too busy to spend time each day with God, the immediate demands of your schedule are robbing you of an awesome eternal treasure—deep, satisfying communion with God.

Every other pursuit in life should seem like a dry desert when compared to the fulfillment of an intimate relationship with God. Our souls and spirits will *never* experience satisfaction—*until* we discover the joy of devotion to the *only One* who can fill our emptiness. Our relationship with God should be the most important thing in our lives and take precedence over everything else.

God becomes our shelter in life's storms when we hide under His wings of protection and cling to Him in total dependence. Those who know intimacy with Him feel the safety that comes with submission to His will. Since they know His heart and trust His goodness and wisdom, they have no cause for fear.

God delights in hearing our prayers, He also wants us to be still and listen to Him. He speaks to us primarily through His Word—that's where we will most likely hear His voice. Interact with the Lord by praying as you read Scripture. Meditate on His words and ask Him: "What are You saying to me? How does this apply to my life?" Then *be still and listen*, giving Him time to speak to your spirit. Just remember that whatever He says will never contradict His written Word. The more you listen, the more you'll hear His voice, and soon your time with Him will become your greatest pleasure!

As we begin to understand who He is, our love for Him grows and motivates us to innermost obedience. Our experiences with Him teach us that He is faithful and can be trusted. We will find that His presence satisfies our souls as nothing else can. The greatest investment we can make in this life is a wholehearted pursuit of a deep personal relationship with Him. The immediate earthly rewards are greater than any sacrifice, but the treasure awaiting us in heaven is beyond our imagination.

When you draw near to Him, His love comes to rest on you and the closeness of His Holy Spirit becomes your delight. Bask yourself in His Presence. When you draw near to Him this way He will draw near to you. He is a Fountain of Living Water.

> *"How priceless is your unfailing love, O God!*
> *People take refuge in the shadow of your wings.*
> *They feast on the abundance of your house; you*

give them drink from your river of delights. For with you is the fountain of life; in your light we see light." -Psalm 36:7-9

Let God become your ONE and ONLY pursuit!

OUR ETERNAL LIFE IS NOW!
Don't wait for Heaven.
GET TO KNOW YOUR AMAZING LORD TODAY!

"Be still and know that I am God!"
-Psalm 46:10

If You <u>Are</u> Worrying... You ARE NOT Trusting in the Lord!

> *"Therefore do not worry, saying, 'What shall we eat?' or 'What shall we drink?' or 'What shall we wear?'... For your heavenly Father knows that you need all these things. But seek first the kingdom of God and His righteousness, and all these things shall be added to you. Therefore do not worry about tomorrow, for tomorrow will worry about its own things sufficient for the day is its own trouble.*
> *-Matthew 6:31-34*

We all have to admit that worry is a common temptation in life—for many it is a favorite pastime. Worry *is* a sin—and for the Christian—it is absolutely contrary to *faith* in Christ. To worry is to violate the Lord's command.

If you are a worrier, what kind of faith are you manifesting? The answer is *"Little Faith"*... according to Jesus (Matthew 6:30). If you are a child of God, you must not act like an unbeliever in God's eyes. Many Christians believe God can redeem them, break the shackles of Satan, take them from hell to heaven, put them into His kingdom, and give them eternal life, but just don't think He can get them through the next couple of days! Why is it so easy for us to believe God for the greater gift and then stumble—and not believe Him for the lesser one? This reveals our lack of faith.

God has made his divine power (2 Peter 1:3-4) available to us as believers through Jesus Christ. God does not expect us to live the Christian life in our own strength. He has made provision for all the help we need by His Word (promises) and by the Holy Spirit. Satan however has set out to steal these provisions that God has made. He accomplishes this by blinding our eyes to God's promises. He sows doubt and unbelief in our hearts. All this is done in an attempt to take our focus off God's provision and put it on his lies.

Worry is one of his *most effective* weapons that Satan uses to steal from us. Worrying about tomorrow denies you from enjoying today. Worrying steals your joy and peace. To worry is to say God is not faithful. Worrying will take your eyes off of God's provision and will fix them on Satan's activities. Worrying opens the door to fear. Fear robs us from having a sound mind (2 Timothy 1:7). We need a sound mind (or peaceful mind) if we are to hear from God.

God desires to speak to us through His Word and by His Spirit. When we allow worry and fear to rule us, we lose our peace and no longer hear God and Satan succeeds in stealing what is ours. We must guard our heart and mind against worry and fear. Remember, they are weapons Satan uses to steal from you. Worry and fear take away your peace and joy. Fix your eyes on God's words, not on Satan's lies.

When you worry, you are choosing to be mastered by your circumstances instead of by the truth of God. When you catch yourself worrying, go back to Scripture and let God open your eyes again.

> *"I pray that the eyes of your heart may be enlightened, so that you may know what is the hope of His calling, what are the riches of the glory of His inheritance in the saints, and what is the surpassing greatness of His power toward us who believe." -Ephesians 1:18-19*

God gives us *the glorious Gift of Life Today*. Choose to live in the light and full joy of that day, using the resources God supplies. Don't push yourself into the future and forfeit the day's joy over an anticipated tomorrow that may never happen. Today is all you really have, for God permits none of us to live in tomorrow until it turns into today. Stay fresh in the Word *every day* so that God is in your mind. Otherwise Satan is apt to move into the vacuum and tempt you to worry about something. God gives you strength one day at a time.

We don't have to let the devil steal our joy!

> **Read and Study God's WORD… and BELIEVE!**
>
> *"The Lord shall guide thee continually and satisfy thy soul." -Isaiah 58:11*

God Wants to Give Us All That He Has Promised—But First We Must Humble Ourselves!

"No eye has seen, no ear has heard, no mind has conceived what God has prepared for those who love Him"
-1 Corinthians 2:9

"Humble yourselves, therefore, under the mighty hand of God so that at the proper time He may exalt you, casting all your anxieties on Him, because He cares for you."
-1 Peter 5:6-7

Being humble for most people brings to mind a form of weakness. But maybe we've got it all wrong—and the one who practices humility may actually be the strong one! In today's culture, we're told if you labor and are heavy laden then you are doing the right thing. You are sacrificing for your family and friends. You are pulling yourself up by your bootstraps and working hard to hopefully one day achieve paradise (retirement) where you get to do nothing as you live out the rest of your days. This is not God's desire for you. Don't let culture tell you that putting everything on your shoulders is wisdom. Trust Jesus when He tells you that His burden is light.

God cares for us. He is mighty. He calls us to humble ourselves under Him—not because He is a controlling God that wants you to bow down to Him because you are nothing, but rather because He wants to exalt us and care for us. In humbling ourselves, we are truly worshiping God—trusting Him with what's going on in our lives and believing He is the only one who can and will provide *all* of our needs.

Many Christians are walking around tired and weary—taking on responsibilities and placing things on their shoulders that don't belong there. Jesus said, *"Come to me, all who labor and are heavy laden, and I will give you rest. Take my yoke upon you, and learn from me, for I am gentle and lowly in heart, and you will find rest for your souls. For my yoke is easy, and my burden is light"* (Matthew 11:28-30). Jesus doesn't want us living a life that is full of anxiousness and weariness as we follow Him. He makes a point to state the exact opposite on how we can find rest in Him.

Most of the time when we don't humble ourselves, we are really saying we don't trust God. There are times as a follower of Christ when we forget *who* God is and we doubt Him. We're told in Scripture to think on the things of God. We are to meditate on anything worthy of praise to Him. Jesus is our ultimate example of humility. Out of obedience to His Father, He humbled Himself all the way to the point of death on the cross. The Bible says because of this that God exalted Him, just like how it says... He *will* exalt us! (1 Peter 5:6-7).

We are not capable of doing anything on our own and never will be. As soon as we begin to live in a way where we are no longer dependent on God to do everything for us, we are forgetting our first love and proclaiming what Christ did for us was not enough. As a follower of Christ, no matter what circumstances you find yourself in, you can *always* give it to Him. This is because God's Word is true. What Jesus did *was enough*. You have the Holy Spirit and can trust Him to lead and guide you.

Humble yourself and pray to God—truly casting your anxieties on Him and trust that He does indeed care for you. God *chooses* to fill clean empty vessels, but He cannot fill people with the Spirit if they are already full of themselves. When we humble ourselves, God promises to hear and respond — and he never breaks that promise. You will never find a time in the Bible when men humbled themselves before God and that He did not hear and respond. When you humble yourself God will exalt you in due time. When we learn to humble ourselves, people will see more of Jesus and less of us... TRUST IN HIM!

GIVE UP CONTROL TO GOD
and watch the Blessings flow!

> **Humility says...**"*I must have a Savior.*"
> **and...** "*Without the Cross, I am Lost.*"

The Only Place You Will Ever Find True Peace... Is in God's Word!

> *"Now, O Lord God, You are God, and Your words are truth, and You have promised this good thing to your servant.*
>
> *-2 Samuel 7:28*

There is nothing like the Word of God to keep our minds and hearts in peace. During troubled times—when worry and depression try to overtake us—we can *always* run to God's Word. His Word is our safety in the midst of harm!

Gods' Word is our PEACE!

It is more important today than ever before that we build a strong foundation in God's Word and make His Word a daily part of our lives. Sometimes our schedules are so busy that we think we don't have time to read and mediate on the Word of God. But we always seem to have time to do the things we want to do! We find time to read the newspaper or watch our favorite television programs. We can always find time to do the things that are important to us.

But *are we making time* to do the things that will cause us to walk in God's peace? *Are we learning to be grounded in the Word* and not moved by what we see with our natural eyes? *Are we learning to trust in the Lord* and cast our cares on Him? If we're not careful, we will find ourselves living a powerless life, a life without peace, simply because we've neglected the very thing that will give us God's power and His peace—the Word of God.

So many verses in the Bible talk about the importance of God's Word (Deuteronomy 11:22-24). These verses say that if we're "careful to obey" God's commands (His Word)—He will drive the enemies out of our lives—enemies of sickness, financial lack, discouragement, depression, and fear, etc.

Sometimes we wonder why we're not receiving the promises of God. We wonder why we're being battered by one crisis after another, with so little victory and no peace. We wonder why our world seems to be crumbling around us. Yes, we're claiming God's promises and we're confessing His Word—but our confession is powerless. Why? Because we're not doing what these verses tell us to do. We are not obeying the rest of God's Word. The Lord said if we would hide His Word in our hearts and continually do what that Word tells us to do, then every place we set our foot would be ours. But instead of grabbing hold of what is ours to possess, we've become disappointed and disillusioned. We've decided. "This faith stuff doesn't work." It does work! But it won't work for us personally if we're not meeting the conditions of God's Word!

In John 15:7 Jesus taught us how to meet the conditions of His Word, He said, *"If you abide in Me, and My words abide in you, you will ask what you desire, and it shall be done for you."* How do we abide in the Lord? We abide in Him by reading His Word, communing with Him in prayer, and keeping our hearts and minds focused on Him.

When Peter stepped out on the water to walk toward Jesus, he wouldn't have started sinking if he had kept his eyes on the Savior! (Matthew 14:28). The same is true in your life. When you keep your eyes focused on the Word of God, His Word will help you walk on top of your circumstances. But if you begin to focus on your problems and troubles, you're going to sink. Of course, the waters of your life won't always be smooth. The winds may be howling and the waves may be crashing all around you. But don't let the enemy distract you with those things.

Recognize that God is on your side. Don't let anything keep you from receiving what God has for you. If you're facing problems and heartaches right now and if you're struggling and cannot seem to find peace, set aside time to fill your mind and heart with God's Word. When pressure comes or discouragement is clouding your mind, YOU CAN TRUST GOD'S WORD—AND HIS WORD WILL GIVE YOU PEACE IN THE MIDDLE OF EVERY STORM!

If we *abide in Him and abide in His Word* we will have what we desire. We will receive everything that we *need*.

> *"Let us hold fast the profession of our faith without wavering: for He is faithful that promised." Hebrews 10:23*

> *"Thou wilt keep Him in perfect peace, whose mind is stayed on thee: because he trusteth in thee."* -Isaiah 26:3

Resting in Jesus in Perilous Times!!

> *"Thou wilt keep him in perfect peace, whose mind is stayed on thee: because he trusteth in thee"*
>
> *-Isaiah 26:3*

Even though we are living in perilous times, we need to keep our focus on Jesus. We must continue proclaiming the love of God the Father and the tender mercy that our Savior Jesus has for us. God is in control of ALL things.

Darkness is certainly coming and judgment is at our very door. But as God's people, we cannot allow any cloud of darkness to hide the great light of His promises of love and mercy toward His people. We must be well informed of God's Word and his prophets, but we are not to dwell on prophetic knowledge so much that it takes over our lives.

> *"Finally brethren, whatsoever things are true, whatsoever things are honest, whatsoever things are just, whatsoever things are pure, whatsoever, things are lovely, whatsoever things are of good report; if there be any virtue, and if there be any praise, think on these things."*
> *-Philippians 4:8.*

This promise of rest applies to "all whose minds are stayed on him." When storms rage in your life, are you going to the Lord in Prayer? If you are, then you're gaining strength, because your mind is becoming fixed on your sovereign heavenly Father's love, and he is continually revealing his power to you and encouraging you so that you make it through.

> *"Peace I leave with you, my peace I give unto you; Not as the word giveth, give I unto you. Let not your heart be trouble, neither let it be afraid." -John 14:27*

LOOK TOWARD A GREATER VISION… THAT THE LORD IS COMING…..

> *"It shall be said in that day, Lo, this is our God; we have waited for him, And he will save us: this is the Lord; we have waited for him, We will be glad and rejoice in his salvation…He will swallow up death in Victory; and the Lord God will wipe away tears from off all faces; And the rebuke of his people shall he take away from off all the earth: For the Lord hath spoken it." -Isaiah 25:9, 8*

YOU CAN KEEP IN PERFECT PEACE DESPITE ALL THE UPHEAVAL AROUND YOU.

> *"Behold, God is my salvation; I will trust, and not be afraid: for the Lord Jehovah is my strength and my song; he also is become my salvation." -Isaiah 12:2*

Resting in Jesus does not necessarily mean that you will be removed from circumstances, trials, activities, or responsibilities. It means that as you submit to the power and authority of Jesus and commit your situation to Him, you are connected to Him and He bears the weight of your burden. He shares in your suffering.

Resting in Him empowers you to remain steadfast no matter the circumstances."

God knows all about the dark days ahead. He knows there is no darkness that can obscure his face from us. Indeed our clear path through hard times will be found only in trusting the Lord. He is calling us today to have a simple, childlike trust in His faithfulness. Let us all keep our eyes on Jesus. Let us trust his great love and care for us.

Cast all your care upon him... for he cares for you."

> *"For I am the LORD your God who takes hold of your right hand and says to you, Do not fear; I will help you." -Isaiah 41:13*

How Firm Is Your Foundation? Is Your Life Built on "The Rock" Jesus Christ?

> *"Whoever comes to Me, and hears My sayings and does them... is like a man building a house, who dug deep and laid the foundation on a rock. And when the flood arose, the stream beat vehemently against that house, and could not shake it, for it was founded on a rock. But he who heard and did nothing is like a man who built a house on the earth without a foundation...and immediately it fell."*
> *-Luke 6:47-49*

Nothing compares to the importance of having the everlasting foundation ... *"Eternal life in Jesus Christ."* "Is your life founded upon, sand or solid rock? If we only hear the wonderful words of Jesus and yet still go our own way and don't do what He says, then we are like a foolish person, who builds his house on the sand! The foolish man may feel safe, but when the floods come he will have no hope and his house will fall. What about our lives? When Satan brings temptations and trials to us it may feel like we are being battered by a flood! The Bible refers to the enemy as coming in like a flood:

> *"...when the enemy shall come in like a flood"*
> *-Isaiah 59:19*

Have you found yourself standing on sand before? A flood of temptation or trial comes along and you fall like the foolish man. You need not be troubled, if you choose to be a wise man and listen to what Jesus tells us in the Bible and do what He says! Jesus is our Rock! He is the firm foundation that we can build our lives upon. And if we obey Jesus, and everything He tells us in His word, the Bible, we have the assurance that no matter what flood beats upon us, no matter how fierce the storms of this life may get we will never fall nor will we ever be moved.

> *"The LORD is my rock, and my fortress, and my deliverer; my God, my strength, in whom I will trust" -Psalm 18:2*

> *"For other foundation can no man lay than the one that is laid, which is Jesus Christ." -1 Corinthians 3:11*

God wants us to build securely upon the eternal Rock, the word of God. We have been "hearers only" long enough! Let us now put the important lessons of Jesus Christ into practice. He who is a hearer only and not a doer of the word is like the man who built his house upon the sand. When your house is built on sand, a storm of temptation can come and sweep away the foundation that you believed to be secure. How great is the loss to these souls! They might have had eternal life—a life that measures with the life of God if had they built upon the immovable "Rock of Jesus Christ."

One day when life is over we will each have to answer to our Creator for how we have lived in His world. According to God's Word, if we have lived for ourselves and failed to love God with all of our heart, mind, soul and strength and our neighbor as ourselves, we will be cast into outer darkness. This is the danger of which Jesus warns us in the parable: building our lives on foundations of sand. Such shoddy building ends in eternal destruction. *".... no one knows the day or hour when these things will happen,... Only the Father knows"* (Matthew 24:36).

"Be not wise in your own eyes: fear the LORD, and depart from evil." -Proverbs 3:7

> **PLEASE CHECK YOUR FOUNDATION TODAY.....**
> **If you keep delaying that decision to live for the Lord,...**
> **You may miss your chances for "Eternal Life with JESUS CHRIST!**

PRAISE YOUR WAY... to a Breakthrough!

"Evening and morning and at noon, I will pray, and cry aloud, And He shall hear my voice."
-Psalm 55:17

How you respond to hard and difficult storms in your life will determine the surety and swiftness of your deliverance. The power of your praise will determine the magnitude of your break-through. God wants you to show your faithfulness in the midst of your trials.

"*...Paul and Silas were praying and singing hymns to God, and the other prisoners were listening to them. Suddenly there was such a violent earthquake...at once all the prisoners' doors flew open, and everyone's chains came off*" (Acts 16:25,26). Even though their backs were bleeding and they were in chains. Despite the pain and suffering they were going through, they praised God anyway; and as a result, God shook the very foundations of the prison, setting them free. Paul and Silas didn't wait for a break-through but in the midst of it all they praised God and received their freedom. GOD CAN AND HE WILL *shake the foundation of your prison; your bondage, your problem...if you make a decision to praise and give Him thanks, no matter what trials you may be going through.*

We were created to praise God, and it becomes a natural expression of your love for the Father when you spend time in the Word and meditate on His goodness. When you truly have a heart for God and YOU KNOW HE LOVES YOU, your confidence in His ability to deliver you soars.

The storms of life are going to come; but don't let them disturb your peace and affect your thoughts and emotions. Always maintain an attitude of praise. Your first line of defense is always "The Sword of the Spirit" which is *GOD's WORD. GIVE IT LIFE* by speaking it over your circumstances. Receive that Word in your spirit and begin praising God for your healing.

FOR THE WORD OF GOD DECLARES:
"Rejoice in the Lord always. Do not be anxious about anything, but in everything, by prayer and petition, with thanksgiving, present your requests to God. And the peace of God, which transcends all understanding, will guard your hearts and your minds in Christ Jesus." -Philippians 4:4-7

When you feel hopelessness, open your mouth and praise the Lord—and don't stop. Instead of grumbling give God praise because you know He has a plan for you that includes deliverance, restoration and peace. Thank Him for His goodness because YOUR PRAISE WILL STOP THE ENEMY AND MOVE THE HAND OF GOD.

When your deliverance comes, continue to praise Him because He has more in store for you. Through your authority in Jesus Christ, claim your promised breakthrough and watch God show up in your life in ways you would have never imagined.

WHEN LIFE GETS TOO HARD TO STAND... GET ON YOUR KNEES
and PRAISE GOD from whom all blessings flow:
PRAISE HIM... PRAISE HIM... PRAISE HIM!

> *"Oh, come let us sing to the Lord!... Let us come before His presence with thanksgiving... Oh come, let us worship and bow down...; Let us kneel before the Lord our Maker. For HE IS OUR GOD." -Psalm 95:1,2,6*

Are You Creating Ripples of Love With Your Tongue....?

> *"Death and life are in the power of the tongue."*
> *-Proverbs 18:21*

A ripple effect is the expanding series of outcomes or consequences that are the result of a single event or action. You can cause changes through a single word or a simple act that can bring change for good or for evil. Our actions can create unintended consequences through these ripples.

> *"But I say unto you, that every idle word that men shall speak, they shall give account thereof in the Day of Judgment." Matt. 12:36*

What our tongue produces has eternal implications, for it reveals what is in our heart. Jesus said that, *"A good man out of the good treasure of the heart bringeth forth good things: and an evil man out of the evil treasure bringeth forth evil thing."* (Matthew 12:35).

PRAY BEFORE YOU SPEAK!

We are commanded to control the tongue: *"Keep your tongue from evil and your lips from telling lies"* (Psalm 34:13). A Christian's speech should consistently honor the Lord with the tongue *"We praise our Lord and Father, and with it we curse men, who have been made in God's likeness. Out of the same mouth come praise and cursing"*

(James 3:10). The world is full of words of death. You may not mean any real harm… but spoken words can cause death and destruction. They can cause death to marriages, families, friendships, churches, careers, hopes, understanding, and reputations.

> *"The words of the reckless pierce like swords, but the tongue of the wise brings healing."*
> *-Proverbs 12:18*

Pray and ask the Lord to *"Set a guard over my mouth, LORD; keep watch over the door of my lips"* (Psalm 141:3). The tongue can be "a tree of life". *"The soothing tongue is a tree of life, but a perverse tongue crushes the spirit"* (Proverbs 15:4). Tongues reconcile people and make peace. Jesus said, *"Blessed are the peacemakers"*. Tongues can keep marriages sweet, families strong, and churches healthy. Tongues can give hope to the despairing, advance understanding, and spread the gospel.

WHAT FILLS YOUR HEART? Jesus said, *"… out of the abundance of the heart the mouth speaks"* (Luke 6:45).

> A CRITICAL HEART produces a critical tongue.
> A SELF-RIGHTEOUS HEART produces a judgmental tongue.
> A BITTER HEART produces a malicious tongue.
> AN UNGRATEFUL HEART produces a grumbling tongue…

But…

> A LOVING HEART produces a gracious tongue.
> A FAITHFUL produces a truthful tongue.
> A PEACEFUL HEART produces a reconciling tongue.
> A TRUSTING HEART produces an encouraging tongue.

Today, make your mouth *"a fountain of life"* (Proverbs 10:11). Be *"slow to speak"* (James 1:19). *Encourage* more than you critique.

Seek opportunities to *speak kind, tenderhearted words* (Ephesians 4:32). Say something affectionate to a loved one at an unexpected time. Seek to only speak words that are "good for building up," that "give grace to those who hear."

> *"Let no corrupt communication proceed out of your mouth, but that which is good to the use of edifying, that it may minister grace unto the hearers." -Ephesians 4:29*

> *"Whoso keepeth his mouth and his tongue keepeth his soul from troubles." -Proverbs 21:23*

BE A PERSON WHOSE MOUTH IS FULL OF LOVE AND OF LIFE.

> *"And now I commend you to God and to the word of his grace, which is able to build you up..." -Acts 20:32*

**Fill your heart with grace by soaking in your bible.
Soak in the following Books of the Bible:
Matthew 5
Romans 12
1 Corinthians 13
Philippians 2**

Let ripples of Love flow from the Words of your mouth. BE AN IMITATOR OF JESUS CHRIST!

Have You Ever Wondered Why God Created Us?

KING DAVID ASKED ESSENTIALLY THIS QUESTION:

> *"When I consider your heavens, the work of your fingers ... what is man that you are mindful of him, the son of man that you care for him?"*
>
> *-Psalm 8:3-4*

God chose to create us out of his great love: *"I have loved you with an everlasting love"* (Jeremiah 31:3). God loved us *before he even created us*. It's impossible to get our heads around that idea, but it's true; that's what "everlasting" love means. God *IS* love (1 John 4:8), and because of that love and his wonderful creativity, he made us so we can enjoy all that he is and all that he's done. In His infinite wisdom, God chose to make us a part of his eternal plan. God endows us with the capacity to carry out His will and do His work in the world, as we work together under His care. It is His intention that we should touch lives, enrich spirits, and bring souls into His care and management.

We are also a part of the war between God and Satan and *God's ultimate plan to defeat Satan*. We all must be loosed from the tyranny of the wrong owner. We must be released from servitude to sin, to self, and to the slave master Satan. Though we may not realize it, our decisions, our behavior and our lifestyles are not totally of our own free will. Rather, they are conditioned, shaped, and directed by the hands that govern them—God or Satan. Everyone who commits sin is a slave to sin. It is only the hand of God that sets us free. It is His strong hands that can train us to move in new directions. It is His gentle, yet strong hands that can handle us with skill and love and strength. It is His hands, which can change our character, alter our conduct, and send us out to do great and noble service. Satan, while appearing to give us liberty by allowing us to do whatever we wish in response to our own inherent selfishness or sin, watches us enslave and destroy ourselves. Many of us have been under the wrong management —in the wrong hands.

> *"For God so loved the world that He gave His only begotten Son, that whosoever believeth in Him should not perish, but have everlasting life." -John 3:16*

Jesus looks upon us with love and sees beyond our sins. He extends His knowing hands to take us into His care. It takes some of us a lifetime to learn that Jesus Christ, Our Good Shepherd, knows exactly what He is doing with us. He understands us perfectly. He manages us with incredible wisdom and love—both for our benefit and His. By putting our faith in God, we can defeat Satan and his lies (see Ephesians 6:10-18). The most important part that we can play in God's eternal plan is to bring people into the Kingdom of God so they will receive the free gift of eternal life with God—through his Son *Jesus Christ*.

We ALL have a *choice*. God gives us freedom to make this choice. God does not need us... but *we certainly need Him*. I hope you've made the choice to put your trust completely in Him—and play an exciting part in His loving, eternal plan. God loves you completely in Christ! Drink deeply of this glorious truth. Bathe yourself in His unconditional love. Immerse yourself in it and rest in it. Experience His great love for you to the fullest, and remember God loves you for who you are in Christ—not for what you do or have done. He created us because of who He is. "HE IS LOVE."

> *"You did not choose me, but I chose you and appointed you so that you might go and bear fruit that will last--and so that whatever you*

ask in my name the Father will give you." -John 15:16

We have been created in the generous Sovereignty of God to achieve great things with Him. It doesn't matter where you have been or even where you are right now…YOU CAN CHOOSE A *NEW BEGINNING* TODAY!

> *"If you confess with your mouth "Jesus is Lord" and believe in your heart that God raised Him from the dead— you will be saved." -Romans 10:9*

We all have a choice in which Master we will serve— Whom do you choose… God or Satan?

"DEPART FROM ME...I NEVER KNEW YOU" Who is Jesus Talking To?

> *"Not everyone who says to me, 'Lord, Lord,' will enter the kingdom of heaven, but only he who does the will of my Father who is in heaven. Many will say to me on that day, 'Lord, Lord, did we not prophesy in your name and in your name drive out demons and perform many miracles?' Then I will tell them plainly, 'I never knew you. Away from me, you evildoers!'"*
> *-Matthew 7:21-23*

Can you imagine those words falling from our Savior's lips? *Depart from Me, I never knew you!* This could be the saddest and most fearful Scripture of all; and it is the very words of Jesus himself found in Matthew 7:21-23. Here, Jesus tells us that at the second coming, there will be people who will fully expect to ascend to heaven with Him in the clouds of Glory, but He will have to tell them— *"Depart from Me, I never knew you."* The people Jesus will say this to will be those who never felt the need to TRULY KNOW HIM.

A personal and intimate relationship with Jesus is vitally important for your salvation. God created us for His pleasure. He seeks those individuals whom He calls to glorify His name and to spend eternity with him.

Do You Know "OF" JESUS
or
"DO YOU REALLY KNOW HIM?"

Do you know Jesus' personal attributes? Do you know Him like you know your husband, wife, brother, sister, friends? How personal is your relationship with Him?

Having a personal relationship with God begins the moment we realize our need for Him, admit we are sinners, and in faith receive Jesus Christ as Savior. The only way to really have a personal relationship with Jesus is to spend time with Him as you would with all of those who you cherish here on earth. We must seek the Lord with all of our hearts.

> **"Draw near to God and He will draw near to you..." -James 4:8**

We should pray without ceasing, read the Bible and mediate on the Word of God, go to church regularly and fellowship with other Christians… all these things will help us to grow spiritually. *"Taste and See the Lord is Good."* Trusting in God to get us through each day and believing that He is our sustainer is the way to have a relationship with Him. We need to be spending quiet time with the Lord and asking the Holy Spirit to examine our hearts and change us so we can become more like Christ. We should pray for godly wisdom which is the most valuable asset we could ever have. We should take our requests to Him, asking in Jesus' name. Jesus is the one who loved us enough to give His life for us, and He is the one who bridged the gap between us and God.

Jesus loves you and wants to know you personally. Talk with Him daily. Be sure not to do all the talking—LISTEN TO WHAT GOD HAS TO SAY TO YOU!

WHEN YOU SEE JESUS FACE TO FACE, YOU WANT HIM TO SAY TO YOU:

"Well done my good and faithful servant."
-Matthew 25:23

Sit quietly with the Lord and truly get to know him!

> *"Be still and know that I am God."*
> *-Psalm 46:10*

Are You Seeking God with All Your Heart?

> *"I have set before you life and death, blessing and cursing; therefore choose life, that both you and your descendants may live; that you may love the LORD your God, that you may obey His voice, and that you may cling to Him, for He is your life ... "*
>
> *-Deut. 30:19 20*

As Abraham was "a friend of God" by his submission and obedience to God, you too can come to know God and experience His mercy, peace, and blessing. Knowing God by truly submitting to Him in trust is the most important experience of life. How wonderful that God reveals Himself to all who seek Him with their whole heart! **SEEK HIM! SEEK HIM! SEEK HIM! WHERE IS GOD WHEN LIFE HURTS?** The truth is that Christ is on the throne with complete authority over all that believers face in this perishing world. Yet, so many Christians still are unable to stand in faith in times of trouble and strife.

Without a doubt, we are living in perilous times. The increase of evil puts us all within the range of attack. We are trying to survive in a time when so many have turned their backs on God. The hearts of many have grown cold. We seem to be living in more heartache and pain as the forces of darkness have increased their effort to destroy lives. Yet, in spite of all this, we can know that CHRIST IS STILL OUR HOPE.

As a believer, we are not alone in our battles. We may be attacked from all sides but the outcome of assured victory has been given to us because Jesus paid the price for us on the cross. We have been made more than conquerors. God uses our pain and our struggles to transform us into the image of Christ. In the midst of darkness, God's power helps us overcome every single weapon of warfare. The enemy has been rendered powerless and ineffective to destroy those who put their trust in the cross.

Christ is right by your side in every single storm you face. His angels have been commanded to guard your life. *He loves you unconditionally just as you are*! It is not dependent on what you do or how well you do it. The everlasting mercy of Christ is enough for all your needs.

Our painful trials are only temporary. The enemy wants you to believe that things will never change, but that is a lie. We can trust in God's plan for our future. Our struggles should reveal to us more of the love and power of Christ. All our battles are being led by the army of God. We are conquerors because *"Greater is He who is in me, than he that is in the World"* (1 John 4:4).

In the center of each storm, the magnificent power of God works all things out for our good. He has a divine purpose charted out for everything that touches your life.

> ***"For the eyes of the LORD run to and fro throughout the whole earth, to give strong support to those whose hearts are fully committed to him." -2 Chronicles 16:9***

God's power is not limited by the impossibility of your situation. If you turn from going your own way and truly submit yourself to God, His Holy Spirit will live in you. Nothing will separate you from His love as you trust His promises and follow Him in obedience. He will be your God, and you will be His own treasured possession.

JULIA BROWN

SEEK THE LORD WITH ALL YOUR HEART AND YOU WILL FIND HIM!

> **Do you choose life or death?**
> **Do you choose blessings or curses?**
> **THE CHOICE IS YOURS!**

God Is the Wind under Your Wings... You CAN Trust HIM!

> *"For I know the plans I have for you," declares the* L*ORD*, *"plans to prosper you and not to harm you, plans to give you hope and a future. Then you will call on me and come and pray you seek me with all your heart. I will be found by you,"*
> *-Jeremiah 29:11–14*

> *"And this is His plan: At the right time He will bring everything together under the authority of Christ -- everything in heaven and on earth."*
> *-Ephesians 1:10*

Being able to stand in the Presence of God and manifest His character should be our daily goal. Christ revealed in us is *holiness* and *righteousness.* If we are to persevere to the end, we NEED to recognize the importance of *repentance, forgiveness, and the power of the Holy Spirit* to make real lasting changes in our lives.

As we cry out to Jesus asking to make us more like Him, we are asking Him to make us righteous and pure and holy. We are asking Him to transform us. Please remember in all your comings and goings that GOD IS A HOLY GOD; AND HE ALSO ALLOWS US TO COME CLOSER TO HIM SO HE CAN REVEAL HIS GLORY -- HIS SECRETS -- HIS HEART -- AND HIS LOVE.

Make Him your first priority in the morning by spending time in His Presence. He will transform you into His likeness and your life will never be the same again -- nor will the lives of those around you.

> *"Taste and see that the Lord is good; blessed is the one who takes refuge in him." -Psalm 34:8*

> REMEMBER...*it is not about us.* IT IS ALL ABOUT GOD and HIS GLORY.

Choose to spend time in the Presence of your Lord and Savior. Talk with Him—but more importantly—LISTEN to what it is that He wants to say to you. We are living in a time that we are going to need to be living more godly lives; and be totally dependent upon God.

> *"I am the good shepherd; I know my sheep and my sheep know me..."-John 10:14*

It is really important that we draw closer to the Lord; and recognize our need for repentance for it is the surest way to real freedom. Praise God in all our circumstances. Wait on the Lord and learn to pray with expectation believing in our hearts that God's Word is true; and he has plans for our lives greater than we could ever imagine. *"..those who hope in the Lord will renew their strength. They will soar on wings like eagles; they will run and not grow weary, they will walk and not be faint..."* (Isaiah 40:31). Meditate on this truth and your spirit will begin to soar recognizing the lack of fear that exists in an eagle as he faces storms of every type throughout most of his life, yet never falters. We need the same ability to soar in the face of storms. We need to be sensitive to those around us, and we need to be able to adjust to the circumstances we are facing. Obstacles are always going to be with us. We must embrace our struggles and endure knowing that God will use these trials to build our character and make us more like Him. Every day we can learn how to trust God more by surrendering our struggles and getting on with His agenda. Every day we have opportunities to touch someone's day by taking a moment to listen and to pray for them. It would help us to remember that.

"Trust in the Lord with all your heart and lean not on your own understanding." Proverbs 3:5

> *I can do ALL things through CHRIST who strengthens me." -Philippians 4:13*

Stop Doubting... Trust in the Lord!

"For the word of the LORD IS RIGHT AND TRUE; he is faithful in all he does."
—Psalm 33:4

Faith is a gift of God. During times of doubt we often feel that it is difficult to have faith. When things seem to be collapsing all around us and our situations look dim, it is really hard to pray for something and believe with 100% certainty that God will answer that prayer. It is hard for us to *believe in* and *trust in* something or someone when we see no physical evidence. In order to have *faith* you must understand the meaning of the word. The word Faith *is* to hold a conviction to, to have reliance on, to have assurance of, to feel confidence about, or to have trust in something or someone. Faith is based upon something that might not be visible to the naked eye but still having a realization that it is substantial and real.

"Now faith is the substance of things hoped for, the evidence of things not seen." -Hebrews 11:1

When a man brought his demon possessed boy to Jesus he believed that Jesus could heal him by saying "I do believe" (Mark 9:24). So why did the father say in this same verse, "Help my unbelief?" He believed Jesus could heal him yet he still had some doubt and asked Jesus to help in his lack of belief. When you ask the Lord to help your unbelief you are asking him to strengthen your faith.

> *"But when you ask, you must believe and not doubt, because the one who doubts is like a wave of the sea, blown and tossed by the wind."*
> *James 1:6*

Faith is a *gift* from God and He will give you or increase your faith as you read His Word. Faith can only be increased by reading and hearing the Word of God. This means that faith comes from hearing the message at church from your pastor or teachers, during Bible studies, and reading your Bible.

> *"Consequently, faith comes from hearing the message, and the message is heard through the word about Christ. -Romans 10:17*

Persistent doubt and fear only reflects our lack of trust in our Almighty Father in Heaven as we allow our thoughts and emotions to be tormented and held in bondage by our circumstances and fear. (Romans 8:15) Overcoming doubt isn't just about feeling better; it's about getting back into faith that only comes from the Word of God. God wants you to trust Him—even if your prayers don't turn out the way you want. He is trying to help us grow in our faith, and in order to do that He continues to raise the bar little bits at a time. As we grow spiritually, He asks us to believe more, and when things become difficult—*He wants us to believe EVEN MORE!*

God is real and is very aware of what is going on with you and He knows that *most* of the time you doubt Him—even so He does desire that you take that one leap of faith to trust Him with your life. And when you take that leap, He is finally able to wrap His arms around you. Jesus asks us to have faith as a little child. Maybe we will never understand each other's' circumstances and our sense of desperation, but, each one of us can boldly approach the throne of grace, asking of the Lord to fill us with His *"Spirit of power, of love and of a sound mind"* (2 Timothy 1:7).

Trusting in God is vital to our spiritual lives, yet our faith is so weak. If we only knew the amazing way that the Lord would open up to us if we would just open up to Him in belief. God asks the hardest thing from us to suspend our common sense, close our eyes to everything around us, put aside our knowledge of earthly reality and logic and TRUST HIM.

When we truly trust the Lord with our hearts, we finally give Him permission and freedom to minister to us without us getting in His way. God wants to give you a full and abundant life--all He asks is for us to *believe* in Him. The Lord can then make you the person He wants you to be, a person of true faith.

> *"But I trust in you, LORD; I say, 'You are my God.'" -Psalm 31:14*

We can CHOOSE TO FEED OUR FAITH WITH THE WORD OF GOD, rather than feeding doubt with the devil's lies!

No Need to Worry about Any of Our Provisions for Those in Christ. He Will Provide <u>All</u> of Our Needs!

> *"My God shall supply all your needs according to his riches in glory in Christ Jesus."*
> *-Philippians 4:19*

Paul gives us the liberating promise of a future grace in Philippians 4:19. If we live by faith in this promise of future grace, it will be very hard for anxiety to survive. God's "riches in glory" are inexhaustible. He really means for us not to worry about our future. We should follow the example of Jesus and Paul. We should battle the unbelief of anxiety with the promises of future grace.

> *"Be anxious for nothing, but in everything by prayer and supplication with thanksgiving let your requests be made known to God."*
> *-Philippians 4:6*

Many of us attempt to meet our own needs apart from God. But this never works. It only leads to frustration and deep disappointment. There will be times when we wonder if He hears our prayers. He always does! And He also is the only One who can answer correctly and satisfy the desires of our hearts. So why do we struggle? Usually, it is because we think we know better than God. We fail to realize we cannot meet our own needs or we expect Him to comply with our personal desires, schedule, or concept of how we think something should be done.

Even though sometimes it can be very difficult—we must trust and wait for God and allow Him to work fully in our lives. Many times, God stretches our faith by allowing us to have a need. He knows how we will respond, but He wants us to learn how to say *yes* to His design—even when we do not really understand.

> *"Trust in the LORD with all your heart; and do not lean on your own understanding. In all your ways acknowledge Him, And He will direct your paths." -Proverbs 3:5-6*

We need to trust God completely with the entirety of our lives. He knows what is best for us, and His purpose in allowing any delay is for *our* good. Waiting will prepare us for a greater blessing. It strengthens our faith and reliance on Him and consequently rids us of a desire to be self-sufficient.

In trusting God, we must be able distinguish between *what is a need* and *what is a desire*. Many times small children want something they do not need. It is the wisdom of the parent which supplies the needs of the child. The same is true of us, God's children – we often want things which would bring injury to our lives. God does *not* promise here that He will supply all our desires or wishes, but He *does promise* that He will supply, and fulfill *all* our needs. Sometimes we get all caught up in worldly things instead of seeking God in earnest for guidance in all our circumstances. If we seek God with all of our hearts and keep our minds stayed on Him, we can be encouraged and comforted that our God will supply *all* of our needs. God's supply is according to His mercy — not of our debt, but according to His grace; not of our emptiness, but according to His fullness; not out of our poverty, but according to His wealth. The truth is, God wants us to trust Him and not look only for the blessing. In other words, keep our focus on the right thing, which is a personal relationship with the Savior. The *only* way to be fully happy is to have a *heart that is set on Jesus Christ.*

We must always remember that God is faithful. No matter if we feel discouraged or disheartened we must embrace the truth of God's faithfulness. If we focus on our problems and troubles instead of God's faithfulness, we are heading down the dangerous highway that leads to discouragement and unbelief. We must trust Him and know that he is faithful to us, His children. He will take care of us!

> God promises us that His Word will not return empty, but it will accomplish what He desires to achieve through us. (Isaiah 55:11)

"... The LORD will give grace and glory: no good thing will he withhold from them That walk uprightly." -Psalm 84:11

How Do You Live Your Life—Following God's Ways or Your Own Ways?

"My thoughts are not your thoughts, nor are your ways My ways,' says the Lord. 'For as the heavens are higher than the earth, so are My ways higher than your ways, and My thoughts are higher than your thoughts."
-Isaiah 55:8-9

"Enter by the narrow gate; for wide is the gate and broad is the way that leads to destruction, and there are many who go in by it. Because narrow is the gate and difficult is the way which leads to life, and there are few who find it."
-Matthew 7:13-14

Bring your supplications to God in prayer; use the Bible as your guide; and then following God's leading. He will make your paths straight by both guiding and protecting you. Trust in the Lord, spend time with Him. Reach out to Him—He is waiting for you!

When we have a close personal relationship with the Lord, and pay close attention to what He teaches us, then He will direct our paths. We must make things right with God by having a right relationship with Him. Receiving what God wants to give us depends on us being rightly connected to Him. And God will bless us if we do things His way.

If you are seeking guidance about His way of doing things, you will find clear instructions in His Word. If you desire to know how to enter into personal relationship with Him, with others and how to be in God's will, you will find all the answers in the Word of God. You will find the solution to all the troublesome concerns of life, large and small, in His Word.

TRUST IN THE LORD WITH ALL YOUR HEART…
WITH GOD ALL THINGS ARE POSSIBLE…
IF YOU WANT TO PLEASE GOD…
YOU MUST HAVE FAITH!

The Bible shows us God's character and His ways. We can also get to know God better by spending time in prayer, worship, and fellowship with other Christians. The Bible says, *"Be anxious for nothing; but in everything by prayer and supplication with thanksgiving let your requests be made known unto God. And the peace of God, which passeth all understanding, shall keep your hearts and minds through Christ Jesus." -Philippians 4:6-7.*

Notice that the peace comes when we give things to God in prayer. It does not wait for how he answers our prayers. It does not depend on the outcome.

THE PEACE COMES WHEN WE PUT THE SITUATION
INTO GOD'S HANDS.

We can continue believing that we know what is best for us and keep doing things our way which will bring about more sorrow. By choosing to do things without God, we often miss out on blessings.

WE CAN CHOOSE TO CALL ON GOD
AND LET HIM DIRECT OUR STEPS AND WATCH
ALL THE BLESSINGS COME FORTH.

"Rejoice evermore. Pray without ceasing. In everything give thanks: for this is the will

of God in Christ Jesus concerning you." -1 Thessalonians 5:16-18

LEAN NOT ON YOUR OWN UNDERSTANDING…
CHOOSE TO FOLLOW GOD'S WORD and LIVE IN PEACE!

I choose to call on GOD… who do you choose?

> *Submit to God and be at peace with Him; In this way prosperity will come to you." -Job 22:21*

JESUS CALLS US TO OBEDIENCE!

"If you love me, you will keep my commandments"
- John 14:15

From Genesis to Revelation, the Bible has a lot to say about obedience. Biblical obedience simply means to hear, trust, submit and surrender to God and obey his Word.

> *"Keep this Book of the Law always on your lips; meditate on it day and night, so that you may be careful to do everything written in it. Then you will be prosperous and successful." - Joshua 1:8*

> *For everything that was written in the past was written to teach us, so that through the endurance taught in the Scriptures and the encouragement they provide we might have hope. - Romans 15:4*

HOW CAN YOU BE OBEDIENT TO THE LORD IF YOU ARE NOT READING HIS WORD?

TAKE TIME TO READ YOUR BIBLE!

As a born again Christian, it is VERY IMPORTANT in your Christian walk that you take the time to read the Bible. It is the only way we can really get to know Lord and have personal relationship with Him. We are called to be Holy as He is Holy and the only way that we can do this is to know all about Him. We are living in a time when we are all going to need to depend totally on God. And to do that we MUST know Him!

> *"My sheep hear my voice, and I know them, and they follow me."-John 10:27*

Studying the bible develops an appetite for God's word and allows for spiritual growth: If we do not take in a regular intake of bible doctrine, we become worthless as servants to God. To be strong spiritually and be good stewards we need a steady diet of His word. By feeding on God's word we will become mature Christians. *As believers we have a hunger that can only be satisfied by God's word, anything else will leave us feeling hungry.*

Studying the bible gives us the opportunity to know God and to reveal His character: God is not an inanimate object but a living God. We learn through His word that He is a loving God offering comfort, peace, and mercy. He is our hope and the Father of our Lord Jesus Christ who is our savior. We will develop a greater appreciation and a thankful attitude toward God as we see Him unfold in the scriptures. *If we do not know God, how can we love and appreciate what he has done for us?*

We must not trust the authority of man, but search the scriptures to see what God says. *We must study the bible with diligence and prayer.*

> *"All Scripture is God-breathed and is useful for teaching, rebuking, correcting and training in righteousness, so that the servant of God may be thoroughly equipped for every good work. -2 Timothy 3:16-17*

It is important to have prayer and communication with God so that the Holy Spirit can teach us. Studying the bible allows us to be better servants of God. It equips us with the armor of God so we can quench the fiery darts of the devil and be more than conquers in Christ. Remember our citizenship is not on earth but in heaven. While on earth we are to represent Christ in everything we do. So represent Christ to the world and preach His saving message.

The Word of God will set you free, so discover His truth in the word and enjoy the freedom and peace it brings. Read God's Word to enrich your life and strengthen your faith... live your life like Jesus....
WALK in LOVE and PEACE.

Read Your Bible!

"Then you will know the truth, and the truth will set you free." -John 8:32

Prepare Your Hearts... the Time Is Now Here... We Are Living in the End of the Age... "Trust in the Lord with All Your Heart!"

Here is a description of the coming birth pangs Jesus predicted would occur shortly before his return: "Then He continued by saying, Nation shall rise against nation, and kingdom against kingdom, and great earthquakes shall be in divers places, and famines, and pestilences; and fearful sights and great signs shall there be from heaven. And there shall be signs in the sun and in the moon, and in the stars; and upon the earth distress of nations, with perplexity; the sea and the waves roaring; men's hearts failing them for fear, and for looking after those things which are coming on the earth: for the powers of heaven shall be shaken."
-Luke 21.10-11, 25-26

"When you go through deep waters and great trouble, I will be with you. When you go through rivers of difficulty you will not drown! When you walk through the fire of oppression, you will not be burned up the flames will not

consume you. For I am the Lord your God, the Holy One of Israel, your Savior."
-Isaiah 41:10

Peace and protection can only come from Jesus ...He is the only answer. God's Word is promised to all those who believe in his Son, JESUS CHRIST.

"May your unfailing love come to me, Lord, your salvation, according to your promise; then I can answer anyone who taunts me, for I trust in your word. - Psalm 119:41-42

"Because he loves me," says the Lord, "I will rescue him; I will protect him, for he acknowledges my name. He will call on me, and I will answer him; I will be with him in trouble, I will deliver him and honor him. With long life I will satisfy him and show him my salvation."
- Psalm 91:14-16

We are living in a time when we really need to be placing ALL of our trust in God and become totally dependent upon Him. Without Jesus as our Savior, we have no strength to fight the battles we are about to encounter. Like the people in Noah's time who laughed and mocked as he built the ark, the end of this age will come when the overwhelming majority are unprepared. Don't be deceived. The Lord is our refuge in times of trouble. The only place that will be safe is in Jesus Christ.

GOD... CAN MOVE YOUR MOUNTAIN
When things seem so impossible and life's so hard to bear,
God can move your mountain before you reach despair.
He'll never leave you or forsake you. *Trust in Him always.*
Be anxious then, for nothing and never cease to pray.
So keep on climbing higher and be patient while you wait.

For *God is never early and also never late.* -Author Unknown

Those in Jesus Christ have nothing to fear. If you haven't accepted Him as your personal Savior....DO IT NOW!

> *"For the LORD your God is living among you. He is a Mighty Savior. He will take delight in you with gladness. With his love, he will calm all your fears. He will rejoice over you with joyful songs." - Zephaniah 3:17*

MY GOD IS MIGHTY TO SAVE!
Do You Have A Ticket To Heaven?
Is Your Name Written In

> *"The Lord not slow in keeping His promise, as some understand slowness. Instead he is patient with you, not wanting anyone to perish, but everyone to come to repentance." -2 Peter 3:9*

The "Lambs Book of Life?"

> *"….for there is no other name under heaven given among men, by which, we must be saved."*
> *-Acts 4:12*

> *"I am the way and the truth and the life. No one comes to the Father except through me."*
> *-John 14:6*

Salvation is not a reward for good deeds, but there are many who are still trying to win salvation by their own efforts.

> *"For it is by grace that you have been saved, through faith and it is not of yourselves, it is a gift from God—not by works, so no one can boast." -Ephesians 2:8-9*

Many have joined the Church knowing nothing of the "Miracle of Grace" which must take place in their hearts. Jesus said, *"You must be born-again!"* A new birth must take place and through this spiritual birth we become partakers of Christ's divine nature—dying in the flesh and living in Christ. This means that you must deal with the sin in your lives because SIN SEPARATES US FROM GOD. You must cry out to God in repentance and faith.

If you receive Jesus Christ as your personal Savior, God will acquit you of every sin, receiving you as His child. As long as sin separates us from God, we can expect no real everlasting peace. You must surrender your life as you know it and give up all of your old ways. TO LIVE IN CHRIST MEANS YOU MUST DIE IN THE FLESH. Ask God to transform your heart Today! Accept this free gift from God and have eternal salvation.

When a man finds that he delights in studying the Bible and he desires a person relationship with Jesus, and wants to please God more than anything else in life, he can rightly believe that God has done something to change him. Only when God becomes the most important thing in your life—will you know that you have been born- again.

"The Spirit himself testifies with our spirit that we are God's children." -Romans 8:16

If we want true salvation, WE MUST REPENT AND FOREVER TURN FROM OUR SIN. "Believing" alone, without a real turning from sin will not bring assurance of your salvation. *With God's help*, we can turn from all of our old sins. A Christian can expect a deep peace in his heart. Real peace comes the moment one is born- again and the burden of sin is rolled away—"a peace which transcends all understanding."

When you are born-again God will give you a new power to resist and overcome sin. Bondage of your old habits of sin will have to go; and in its place will be a new power and joy and righteousness. The new Christian will desire to do only those things that are pleasing to God. His will, once enslaved, has been set free. Chains are broken, new and holy desires flood the soul, and the redeemed person is a new creature indeed—a new creation in Christ Jesus.

To all who believe on Christ Jesus, making Him Lord of their lives, God gives authority or right to call themselves the sons and daughters of God.

GET RIGHT AND DON'T MISS THE FLIGHT!

HAVE YOUR TICKET READY...
JESUS IS COMING SOON!

> **Heaven is PROMISED to ALL Who know JESUS as their PERSONAL SAVIOR!**

We are about to Become the Bride of Christ... Are You Ready to Meet Your Groom?

> *"Let us rejoice and be glad and give the glory to Him, for the marriage of the Lamb has come and His bride has made herself ready." Then he said to me, "Write, 'Blessed are those who are invited to the marriage supper of the Lamb.'" And he said to me, "These are true words of God."*
>
> *-Revelation 19:7-9*

This life we are living on earth is a courtship. The body of Christ is in a courtship with our Lord Jesus. Unfortunately, there are many believers who go to church on Sunday (some don't go at all), and then don't spend any time with the Lord throughout the week. There are many other Christians who spend some time with the Lord throughout the week, but not much. Some Christians, they go days, weeks, and months without quality time with Lord. Some Christians have never experienced deep intimate moments with the Lord. Many Christians, apart from a salvation experience, don't know Him. Without intimacy—there is no courtship!

Being the bride of Christ isn't about standing at the altar in a white dress; it's about *waiting and preparing* for His presence in our lives on a daily basis, focusing on our relationship with Christ instead of spending all our time talking about what heaven will be like one day when we get there.

Waiting for anything in life is difficult, but we learn that waiting is essential to becoming passionate followers of God. To wait for God means that we put our heart and soul into being prepared for Him and His calling on our life.

In Matthew 25:1-12, the Parable of the Ten Virgins tells us that there were five foolish virgins who were *not* ready. Because of their lack of intimacy with Jesus, those who weren't ready missed the feast. Being the Bride of Christ means we stand firm in our faith, expectantly awaiting Christ's return. As we prepare ourselves for that day, we must be diligent to learn more about the groom. Through studying God's Word and sharing our faith with believers and nonbelievers alike, we begin to grow in our relationship with Christ. We see who He is. We see His desire for us. We see glimpses of God's magnificent plan for our lives.

Throughout God's Word, He makes it known that He is a God who wants a relationship with His people. He is the one pursuing that relationship—just as a young man desperately in love with the girl of his dreams will do anything he can to spend time with her. God pursues us, hoping He can spend time with us. The Bible says, *"The eternal God is a dwelling place, and underneath are the everlasting arms"* (Deuteronomy 33:27). The more you let yourself delight in His love, the more you will find freedom to believe. The more you believe, the more you will let yourself be open to experience His presence as He holds you close.

We are to keep ourselves inside the substance of His love. Jesus says, *"Abide in My love"* (John 15:9). That means we should live inside it. The love of God is a substance that we can stay inside because the love of God… is God Himself: *"The one who abides in love abides in God, and God abides in him"* (1 John 4:1). When you are "in love" with God, you draw near to Him because you *want* to be near Him. When you draw near to Him, His love comes to rest on you and the closeness of His Holy Spirit becomes your delight.

Don't be like the five foolish virgins. Be intimate with Jesus. Spend time with Him and get to *really know* Him. Embrace His love and cling to His presence. You can trust God to lavish enough of His Presence to quench your thirsty need for love. The Christian who is truly intimate with Jesus will never draw attention to himself--but will only show the evidence of a life where Jesus is completely in control. This is the outcome of allowing Jesus to satisfy every area of life to its depth.

"That I may know him, and the power of His resurrection..." Philippians 3:10

> *"...That Christ may dwell in your hearts by faith; ...being rooted and grounded in love..." -Ephesians 3:18*

THE RAPTURE
Behold I Am Coming Soon!

And then shall appear the sign of the Son of Man in heaven: and all the peoples of the earth shall mourn, and they shall see the Son of man coming in the clouds of heaven with power and great glory. But of that day and hour knoweth no man, no, not the angels of heaven, but my Father only.
-Matthew 24:30-36

"....When shall these things be? And what shall be the sign when all these things shall be fulfilled?"
-Mark 13:4

The unfolding of the "end times" prophetic scenario, before our eyes, should prompt Christians to take the Bible seriously and to actively watch the prophetic shadows that are appearing in today's headlines. The primary purpose of God's prophetic Word is to point people to Jesus Christ, "the author and finisher of our faith."

One day born-again Christians will escape the grip of death and be ushered into heaven, the "final frontier." Christ's return is drawing near. As believers, our main focus should be on the heavenly realm.

> *"Eye hath not seen, nor ear heard, neither have entered into the heart of man, the things which God hath prepared for them that love him.'" -1 Corinthians 2:9*
>
> *"In my Father's house are many mansions: if it were not so, I would have told you. I go to prepare a place for you." -John 14:2*
>
> *"Watch ye therefore, and pray always, that ye may be accounted worthy to escape all these things that shall come to pass, and to stand before the Son of man." -Luke 21:36*
>
> *"For God hath not appointed us to wrath, but to obtain salvation by our Lord Jesus Christ." -1 Thessalonians 5:9*

Jesus is preparing a Heavenly mansion for all of those… He calls his own!

> *"Henceforth there is laid up for me a crown of righteousness, which the Lord, the righteous judge, shall give me at that day…." -2 Timothy 4:8*

NOTHING IS MORE IMPORTANT THAN THE DECISION TO FOLLOW JESUS. The cares of this world do not compare with the importance of being prepared for the world to come. If you miss out on the eternal bliss of heaven and end up in hell, it will be too late! As the world falls apart all around us, we should be praying more and more, studying God's Word passionately, and sharing our resources with others. God's Word is the truth and it shall all come to pass.

The coming of our Lord will be without warning, and at a time we don't expect Him. When he comes, our fate is sealed. We must therefore be prepared now by acknowledging our sins, our helplessness, our need for salvation, and by trusting in the death, burial, and resurrection of Jesus in our place. Being ready means, among other things trusting in Jesus and having our sins forgiven.

The devil wants you to believe that Jesus is not coming in our day and you have plenty of time to repent. The Bible says doubters and end time scoffers will be one of the signs of the last days. *"Knowing this first, that there shall come in the last days scoffers, walking after their own lusts. And saying, where is the promise of his coming"* (2 Peter 3:3-4). During these troubled times many false prophets will be seeking to turn men's attention and affections away from Jesus, the true Messiah.

Don't risk your Eternal Salvation....GET RIGHT WITH GOD NOW!

Every individual will be held accountable for his or her own choices. In the parable of the ten virgins we are being warned to be ready. So don't be one of the foolish ones!

BE PREPARED!

"In such an hour AS YOU THINK NOT the son of man cometh" -Matthew 24:44.

Christians Wake Up!...

> *"We which are alive and remain shall be caught Up together with them in the clouds, to meet the Lord in the air; and so shall we ever be with the Lord."* -1 Thessalonians 4:17

Let Us All Get Excited About Jesus! We Need A Revival!

"If then you have been raised with Christ, set your hearts on things above, where Christ is seated at the right hand of God. Set your minds on things above, not on earthly things. For you have died, and your life is hidden with Christ in God. When Christ, who is your life appears, then you also will appear with Him in glory. Put to death therefore what is earthly in you"
-Colossians 3:1-5

The Kingdom of God is peace and joy. It is a kingdom of LOVE, according to Colossians 1:13. The children of God must demonstrate His love out on the street and in their daily lives with signs, wonders, and miracles. As born again believers, we are to share the Gospel as a witness that JESUS IS ALIVE, and loves all the people of the world. Jesus wants us to live on earth, as we will in heaven. He did everything for us so that we could have an abundant life. If the gospel was just for us to get saved and go to heaven, then we would most likely all die right after we were saved.

"All authority in heaven and earth has been given to me. Therefore go and make disciples of all nations, baptizing them in the name of the Father and of the Son and of the Holy Spirit, and teaching them to obey everything I have

commanded you. And surely I am with you always, to the very end of the age." -Matthew 28:18-20

Our mission is to take dominion over all the devil's works. The Kingdom of God's rule, authority, and dominion is in you. This power heals the sick, casts out demons, and raises the dead. The Kingdom is in us, causing Satan's defeat and God's will to be done on earth. It is not us who performs these miracles, but the Holy Spirit living in us.

GOD'S PEOPLE NEED TO AWAKEN TO
WHO WE ARE IN CHRIST…
KNOW WHO YOU ARE IN CHRIST

YOU are THE RIGHTEOUSNESS OF GOD IN CHRIST, and because of that you can walk in all boldness!

"The Spirit of the Lord is on me, because he has anointed me to preach good news to the poor. He has sent me to proclaim freedom for the prisoners, and recovery of sight for the blind, to release the oppressed, to proclaim the year of the Lord's favor." -Luke: 4-18-19

It is the promise of God that His Word will not return to Him empty. He will accomplish His purpose. Our desert times wear on us. They would strip us of our passion and our vision, and our desire to press onward. Yet, though we may not see the evidence of the coming harvest, we must not grow weary and lose heart, but trust that the HARVEST WILL COME! We are to take authority on earth and command things to line up with God's will. Remember, we are the sons and daughters of the "King of Kings—JESUS CHRIST!"

"O send out Your light and Your truth, let them lead me. Let them bring me to Your holy hill and to Your dwelling place." -Psalm 43:3-4

"He put a new song in my mouth, a song of praise to our God. Many will see and fear and will trust in the Lord." -Psalm 40:3

> Let the Revival start in YOU;
> and then go out and
> PREACH THE GOSPEL OF JESUS TO ALL.
> JESUS IS COMING BACK SOON…
> We must move quickly…
> Let the Revival begin…..TODAY!

When Jesus Comes... So Does Judgment!

> *"For the time is come that judgment must begin at the house of God; and if it first begin at us, what shall the end be of them that obey not the gospel of God: and if the righteous scarcely be saved, where shall the ungodly and the sinner appear?"*
> *-1 Peter 4:17-18*

You don't have to feel hopeless. God gives all men an opportunity for reconciliation, mercy, and grace, which is available to us through repentance of sin and acceptance of Jesus' sacrificial gift of "Eternal Life."

> *"Therefore, since we have a great high priest who has ascended into heaven, Jesus the Son of God, let us hold firmly to the faith we profess. Let us then approach God's throne of grace with confidence, so that we may receive mercy and find grace to help us in our time of need."*
> *-Hebrews 4:14-16*

Our High Priest is Jesus Christ, who was fully God and fully man. He not only understands everything we are going through—Jesus has been through it; and He paid the price on the cross.

Jesus says, "Behold I come quickly!" He is coming for His body of believers first—THE BRIDE OF CHRIST; then He must punish all the wicked of this world so that He can establish His righteous rule. From His throne, His blessings will flow to the earth. Jehovah is the only "God" that exists that can save mankind. No other God loves us, nor can! We were created for His pleasure. God's plan was always to love and bless His creation. Satan's evil plan has always been to separate us from God forever by continuous demonic attacks.

God's Word reveals ALL of His perfect plans, purposes and promises for our lives. The B.I.B.L.E. tells you all you need to know (*Basic Instructions Before Leaving Earth*). His words *will* truly change your life forever…HIS WORDS ARE TRUE. Ask God to give you the grace to hold firmly to the faith that we profess.

> *"But whoever looks intently into the perfect law that gives freedom, and continues in it—not forgetting what they have heard, but doing it—they will be blessed in what they do."*
> *-James 1:25*

We are living in a time when there is an urgency to …SEEK THE "WORD OF GOD". God's offer of the free gift of Eternal Life in this age of *Mercy and Grace* is about to be over soon. The Bible tells us of *Jesus soon return*. It tells us that *"it is given unto man once to die, and then the judgment."* It also reveals a Righteous God whose justice requires Him to purge the world of all sin. His mercy is so great, however, that He has offered man total reconciliation with Him through Jesus shed blood on the cross. **We must believe in Jesus' death and resurrection!**

The only other option that God can offer to those who oppose Him is to 'perish'. In His Word he warns us of what is to come.

> *"How awful that day will be! There will be no other like it!.."* *-Jeremiah 30:7*

> *"For the wrath of God is revealed from heaven against all ungodliness and unrighteousness of men, who by their unrighteousness suppress the truth."* *-Romans 1:18*

God is a 'God of Love' and He wants all of us to accept His offer of eternal life. Soon you will have to make a choice.

"Choose yourselves this day whom you will serve." -Joshua 24:15

He even offers to do everything necessary to change us. He provides to each of us a measure of faith—Jesus' cleansing blood, the gift of eternal life, and a new mind and heart to enjoy His *"abundant life"* right now here on earth! If you have received his FREE gift of salvation, YOUR NAME WILL BE WRITTEN IN THE LAMBS BOOK OF LIFE and you will not have to endure His upcoming wrath.

> **You are being forewarned…**
> **be prepared for what is coming…**
> **Ask JESUS INTO YOUR HEART!**

If Jesus Were to Come Today, Would You Be Ready!

> *"Then the kingdom of heaven shall be likened to ten virgins who took their lamps and went out to meet the bridegroom. Now five of them were wise, and five were foolish. Those who were foolish took their lamps and took no oil with them, but the wise took oil in their vessels with their lamps. But while the bridegroom was delayed, they all slumbered and slept."*
> *-Matthew 25:1-5*

They all thought the Lord would return one day and started out in a state of readiness, because they ALL had oil-filled lamps. But only the wise went further. They made sure the light of the Holy Spirit was not only in their hearts and souls (the wick) but in their "vessels" also – that is, they topped up their lamps to make sure there would be enough for a long wait.

The Church is the bride of Christ—Jesus *will* return in glory for a pure bride:

> *"Let us rejoice and be glad and give the glory to Him, for the marriage of the Lamb has come and His bride has made herself ready. It was given to her to clothe herself in fine linen, bright and clean; for the fine linen is the righteous acts of the saints."* -Revelation 19:7-8

Make no mistake about it: Jesus Christ *will* come back again, and God has given us specific instructions for what we are to do while we wait. We are to be watching for Him. We shouldn't get caught up in the things that dominate the minds and hearts of nonbelievers, such as what we will eat, drink, and wear. Instead, we should be consumed with our pursuit of the Kingdom of God. We should seek, above all, the rule and reign of Jesus Christ in our lives.

"Blessed are those servants whom the master, when he comes, will find watching." -Luke 12:37

We *must* be ready! When it comes to being ready and dedicating yourself to the Lord, you're the one who has to do it. No one can do it for you. It's *our* responsibility to be prepared. God has given us *everything* we need. He has put His own Spirit within us. He has given us His written Word. He has given us teachers, preachers, pastors, evangelists, apostles and prophets to help us learn how to live by faith, how to live separated from the world, how to walk in the Spirit, and how to operate in the power of God. But we must decide to make those things the priority in our lives.

Every day we should strive to become more like Jesus Christ. According to 2 Peter 3:11-14, *"…You ought to live holy and godly lives… So then, dear friends, since you are looking forward to this, make every effort to be found spotless, blameless, and at peace with Him."*

Live every day watching for His return. If you're watching and walking in tune with the Spirit, you won't be in the dark. You won't be caught unaware at the time of Jesus' coming. You'll know in your spirit He is at the door. Those who love the Lord will make certain that they are ready for His return, by reading their Bibles, praying, and watching (observing and understanding the events of this day as they unfold).

Living for God successfully means staying close to Him so one can hear His voice and thereby obey Him and do His will, whatever it may be *"My sheep listen to my voice; I know them, and they follow me"* (John 10:2). As a Christian you must have communion with the

One who made you. Listening comes from reading God's Word and by allowing Him to speak to you through a particular passage. Jesus tells us to stay alert, stay awake, and fight against all evil. He tells us to stay prayed up, fasted up, filled up, read up, and lit up. Not only must we stay in His written Word, we must always stay close to Him—*The Living Word*. These things help us to keep our lamps and oil flasks filled. We were made to be filled with the Spirit of God. We must always keep our oil supply fresh and our tanks topped off.

> No one knows the day or the hour…
> only the Father! (Matthew 24:36)

But you must be READY!

BEING PROPERLY PREPARED FOR THE LORD'S IMMINENT RETURN IS THE MOST IMPORTANT THING

YOU CAN DO IN THIS LIFE!

The Truth Is In His Word... Are You Teachable?

> *"Hear instruction, and be wise, and refuse it not. Blessed is the man that heareth me, watching daily at my gates, waiting at the posts of my doors. For whoso findeth me findeth life, and shall obtain favour of the LORD. But he that sinneth against me wrongeth his own soul: all they that hate me love death."*
> *-Proverbs 8:33-36*

God commands us to watch, wait, and search for Him. He instructs us to do this *daily*! He wants to teach us every day, and our job is to be watching daily for those teachable moments from God. "Watching daily at my gates" is not about keeping a lookout for Christ's return but about looking for opportunities to learn from God. He then promises, "…whoever finds me finds life."

What God says about our needing to acquire knowledge?

> *"My people are destroyed for lack of knowledge…" -Hosea 4:6*

If we are not studying the Word, praying, and meditating daily, then we must pray fervently for God to give us a greater desire to obey Him, learn from Him, and have the proper fear of Him. We cannot properly fear God, if we do not include Him in every aspect of our lives.

In acquiring knowledge—

A teachable person *STUDIES GOD'S WORD*.
2 Timothy 3:16-17- *"All scripture is God breathed and is useful for teaching, rebuking, correcting and training in righteousness, so that the man of God may be thoroughly equipped for every good work."*

A teachable person is *ATTENTIVE*.
Isaiah 51:1: *"Listen to me, you who follow after righteousness, you who seek the Lord.."*

Matthew 13:16-17: *"But blessed are your eyes for they see, and your ears for they hear. For assuredly, I say to you that many prophets and righteous men desired to see what you see, and did not see it, and to hear what you hear, but did not hear it."*

A teachable person *SEEKS GOD*.
Proverbs 2:3-6: *"Yes, if you cry out for discernment, and lift up your voice for understanding, if you seek her as silver, and search for her as for hidden treasures; then you will understand the fear of the Lord, and find the knowledge of God. For the Lord gives wisdom; from His mouth come knowledge and understanding…"*

A teachable person is *MEEK AND HUMBLE*.
James 1:21: *"Therefore lay aside all filthiness and overflow of wickedness, and receive with meekness the implanted word, which is able to save your souls."*

Psalm 25:9: *"… and the humble He teaches His way."*

God loves us and desires nothing less than our highest good and conformity to the character of His Son. The truth in His Word provides us with the spiritual nourishment we will need to grow into the maturity of Christlikeness.

> *"In the past God spoke to our ancestors through the prophets at many times and in various ways, but in these last days he has spoken to*

us by his Son, whom he appointed heir of all things, and through whom also he made the universe. The Son is the radiance of God's glory and the exact representation of his being, sustaining all things by His powerful word..."
-Hebrews 1:1-3

If you read and study God's Word, your KNOWLEDGE will increase!

> *"Your word is a lamp for my feet, a light on my path" -Psalm 119:105*

Jesus' Second Coming! Is Your Salvation Secured?

"Jesus saith unto him, I am the way, the truth, and the life, No man cometh unto the Father, but by me."

-John 14:6

"Jesus answered, 'Truly, truly, I say to you, unless one is born of water and the Spirit, he cannot see the Kingdom of God.' That which is born of the flesh is flesh, and that which is born of the Spirit is spirit.""

-John 3:5-6

JESUS AS .....THE LAMB OF GOD

THE FIRST TIME JESUS CAME—He came unnoticed into the world. After being born in a stable in Bethlehem, Jesus humbly walked the earth. He endured the mockery of men who despised him for his goodness. God gave us his one and only Son, Jesus, who was made the perfect and ultimate sacrifice as atonement for the sins of His people. Jesus was the sacrificial Lamb, who died and rose again to give us eternal life—HE CAME AS THE LAMB OF GOD.

JESUS AS... THE LION OF JUDAH

"Then will appear the sign of the Son of Man in heaven. And then all the peoples of the earth will mourn when they see the Son of Man coming on the clouds of heaven, with power and great glory." -Matthew 24:30

THE SECOND COMING OF CHRIST will be "WITH POWER AND GREAT GLORY." The second time "every eye will see him." When he returns, He will come back as King of Kings and Lord of Lords. Jesus will rule the nations with a rod of iron. THIS TIME HE WILL COME AS THE LION OF THE TRIBE OF JUDAH.

Our heavenly Father sent his Son to this earth the first time to offer all of us who were dead in our trespasses and sins—the hope of salvation

In this age of the Holy Spirit, which came into existence after our Lord's death, burial, resurrection, and ascension on the day of Pentecost, OUR RISEN LORD IS STILL OFFERING THE HOPE OF SALVATION TO ALL WHO BELIEVE IN HIM AS LORD. Once we accept him as our Lord, he places us into his household and gives us spiritual gifts and areas of responsibility to spread the good news of our redemption through our Lord Jesus.

We are called to remain faithful to our Lord by being dressed in readiness and keeping our lamps lit with the oil of the Holy Spirit, so that men and women all around us will be drawn out of a world of darkness into the kingdom of light. We are also called to keep alert in the midst of waiting, knowing that the invisible but always present Lord will return. This time when he returns he will bring blessing to those servants who are faithful; and judgment to those servants who are unfaithful. The Lord wants all to come to him and be saved. (John 3:16).

Jesus is coming again soon. The *first time* he came with the offer of salvation; the *second time* the world will see him rule and reign on this earth as the Righteous Judge. If we reject his wonderful offer of salvation now, we will have to meet him as our Judge at the time of our death or in his glorious second coming.

Now is our time for the day of salvation. Please don't wait another day to accept his offer of salvation. You may not have another day, hour, minute or even second on this earth to make the right decision....

> *"For God so loved the world, That He gave his only begotten Son, That whosoever believeth in him should not perish, but have everlasting life." -John 3:16*

Accept Jesus Christ as your personal Savior... before it is too late! JESUS LOVES YOU!

Special Occasion Messages

Without the Resurrection, There Would Be No Christian Faith! a Place Called Gethsemane!

> *"For God so loved the world that he gave his one and only Son, that whosoever believes in Him shall not perish but have eternal life."*
> *-John 3:16*

The story of Gethsemane in the Gospel of Mark brings us ever so close to the moment when the Lord Jesus would give His life on the cross for sin and sinners.

A Place Called Gethsemane--On that night, Gethsemane became more than a garden where Jesus and His men spent some time. On that night, Gethsemane became a place where eternal business was transacted *for the Glory of God*. It was a place where Jesus could go to find a private moment to commune with His Father. It was a sanctuary from the attacks of His enemies. It was a place of refreshment from the long days of ministry. It was a special place for the Lord and His men. The broken body of Jesus was lifted from the cross at the end of the day of His execution and placed in a borrowed tomb. The doorway was covered with a stone and our Lord was sealed within. But death could not hold Him! When they returned to complete the burial—He was not there—for *He had Risen!* Forty days later, after completing His work here on earth, He ascended to Heaven.

The Word of God tells us that Jesus was overwhelmed emotionally and spiritually by what He experienced as He entered the Garden of Gethsemane that night. Think about the pressure the Lord was under. He knows He is about to suffer intense physical pain. He knows that He is about to become sin on a cross. He knows that, for the first time in eternity, there will be a breech in the unbroken fellowship He has enjoyed with His Father. He knows that He will be separated from His nation, His followers and His Father. He knows that He is about to be tried, rejected and condemned to death by the very people He came to save.

We can thank God that He endured the spiritual and emotional trials and made it to Calvary so that we might be saved. While Jesus Christ is God in the flesh, the body He lived in was a frail human body just like ours. His body knew weariness, He felt pain, He got hungry, sleepy and tired. As Jesus prayed that night, the emotional and spiritual pressures that came upon Him were almost more than His body could handle. But—H*e did handle it*! He survived the agony of Gethsemane and He made it to Calvary where He died for our sins! He could have walked away from us that night. No one was forcing Him to die. No one was forcing Him to become sin for us. No one was forcing Him to do what He did. He did it willingly! He did it so that we might have a way to be saved.

By His resurrection, He was powerfully revealed as the Son of God. The Resurrection declared who he had been all along. All of Christ's sufferings at Calvary did not come on Him by chance or accident, but they were fore-ordained by The Father. It was the only way to atone for our sins so that we could receive salvation. Jesus had to bear our sins and with His stripes alone could we be healed. This was the one payment of our debts that God would accept; this was the *great sacrifice* on which our eternal life depended. Jesus paid the penalty for our sins so we could wear His Righteousness! It is the cross, and what Jesus accomplished there, that gives the Resurrection significance. **WITHOUT THE RESURRECTION there would be NO CHRISTIAN FAITH… NO SALVATION….OR NO HOPE!**

The Cross was heaven's triumph. When Jesus Christ arose, the power of sin and death was forever shattered. Because of the Resurrection, Christians need never fear Satan or death again. The bible tells us: *"by being raised from the dead (Christ) was proved to be the mighty Son of God, with the holy nature of God Himself"* (Romans 1:4); *"If Christ has not been raised, your faith is worthless; you are still in your sin."* (1 Corinthians 15:17); *"For he raised us from the dead along with Christ and seated us with him in the heavenly realms because we are united with Christ Jesus"* (Ephesians 2:6).

The Resurrection is more than just an event that happened once in history. It's the source of the power you can experience in your own life, every day. The same power that resurrected Jesus from death to life is available to you, and if you tap into it, you'll see amazing transformation in your own life, too.

> *"Praise be to the God and Father of our Lord Jesus Christ! In His great mercy He has given us new birth into a living hope through the resurrection of Jesus Christ from the dead." -1 Peter 1:3*

This hope for resurrection isn't just for the future when you physically die and go to heaven; it's also for now, while you're living on earth and struggling with sin. Place your *hope* in a relationship with Jesus. As you live for Him, relying on His resurrection power at work in your life, you'll experience the fulfillment of all of God's good purposes for you. Instead of focusing on what you can do for God, *focus* on *what God can do through you*. Ask God to help you see your life from His perspective. Look beyond the world's values to what has eternal value. DIE TO SELF!

Remember that death must always precede resurrection. Be willing to sacrifice whatever selfish desires and agendas you have that conflict with God's purposes for your life. Decide to crucify your selfish attitudes and behaviors, so God will raise you to new life by transform-ing your attitudes and behaviors into healthy ones that will help you grow to be more like Jesus.

You can experience *resurrection joy right now*! The freedom from sin and hope in Jesus that the resurrection produced brings great joy into your life. If you allow the Holy Spirit to lead you, you'll experience the joy to see beyond your circumstances to the God who has ultimate control over them, and always acts according to what's best for you. Giving your allegiance *wholeheartedly* to God, gives you the confidence that can't be shaken—helping you through your circumstances. Regularly confess your sins, repent of them, and embrace the forgiveness and grace God offers you to keep growing. Ask God to flood your soul with the peace of knowing that you're in a right relationship with Him. If you want to experience the peace Jesus offers, you *must* come to Him on His terms, willing to live the way He leads you to live – the way that's best for you. Only then can you truly enjoy His peace.

We have been given the *resurrection power* of Jesus. Your salvation means that you don't need to fear death. *Expect* God to fulfill all the promises that He makes in the Bible, and *trust* those promises in your own life. *Live* with heaven in mind – pursuing eternal values – and *rejoice* in the hope you can experience every day.

Jesus calls and strengthens us to follow Him so that we might fulfill the commandment to carry this gospel to the world. Death has no hold on those who have accepted Jesus as their Lord and Savior. The *redeemed saints,* who have loved God and kept His commandments here, will enter in through the gate of the city, and have right to the tree of life. (Revelation 22:14) As we stand on the threshold of the eternal city, we will receive a gracious welcome by Jesus with His warm smile and open arms. It will be more glorious than our brightest imagination could ever fathom.

> ***"Eye hath not seen, or ear heard, neither hath entered into the heart of man, the things which God hath prepared for them that love him." -1 Corinthians 2:9***

All who trust in Jesus Christ will experience eternity in His presence. In Heaven, there will be no sorrow, death, crying, or pain. Heaven will have a beauty beyond our imagination. The Kingdom of God will be lighted by the *Glory of God.* Heaven is a place of continual blessings; blessings that will pour out into every area of your life, flourishing your strength and well-being. For the first time since the Garden of Eden, God's children may eat out of this tree in His paradise (Genesis 3:22, Revelation 2:7). We will be given new names, new imperishable bodies, and will be clothed in the white robes of righteousness.

We will be glorious living stones; pillars in the eternal temple of God. *Most important we will be with the Lord forever.* From His throne flows the River of Life. Songs of victory, joy, gladness and thanksgiving fill all of heaven, as the redeemed stand around the throne of God. All will joyfully sing, *"Worthy is the Lamb that was slain and has redeemed us to God."*

What a joy it is to know that our Savior fought all the battles for us and that He prevailed every time. Jesus achieved victory because He was vigilant and diligent in prayer. He leaned on His Father and His Father gave Him the victory. When the disciples leaned on themselves instead of God, and their time of testing came, they failed. If we want to enjoy victory in our times of temptation and testing, we *must* learn to lean on the Lord and His power.

We *must not* stand in our own strength, but in His alone (Ephesians 6:10-12). As long as we lean on self, we are doomed to fail. But, when we surrender to His power and His control in our lives, we will be successful as we live for Him and walk in His will. We *must* have a personal relationship with Jesus.

If this passage demands anything from us at all, it demands our worship. When we think of all that Jesus endured for us that night, it should drive us to our knees in worship and it should fill our hearts with His praises. It should make us want to lift holy hands to praise Him. It should make us want to rejoice in songs and shouting. It should fill us with a desire to worship and exalt Him! *"Blessed is He who cometh in the name of the Lord! Hosanna in the Highest!"* (Matthew 21:9).

We *all* must go through a Garden of Gethsemane—we *must* die to the flesh. We must die to our will and let *His will be done.* When we fully surrender ourselves to God's will we can safely fall into the arms of Jesus, *fully satisfied and fully at rest.*

JULIA BROWN

We *must* crucify our wills…

so, we can be resurrected with the KING OF KINGS, JESUS CHRIST!

> *"You should be known for the beauty that comes from within, the unfading beauty of a gentle and quiet spirit, which is so precious to God." -1 Peter 3:4*

Woman of God... You Are the Pinnacle of God's Creation! Mother's Day Should Be Every Day!

"An excellent wife, who can find? For her worth is far above jewels."

-Proverbs 31:10

"Strength and dignity are her clothing, And she smiles at the future. She opens her mouth in wisdom, And the teaching of kindness is on her tongue. She looks well to the ways of her household, And does not eat the bread of idleness. Her children rise up and bless her; Her husband also, and he praises her, saying: "Many daughters have done nobly, But you excel them all." Charm is deceitful and beauty is vain, But a woman who fears the Lord, she shall be praised."

-Proverbs 31:25-30

In His great wisdom and grace, He created man and woman. God formed Adam's body from the ground and breathed the breath of life into him. God caused a deep sleep to fall on Adam, and from him God took a rib and made a woman (Genesis 2:2 1). In that instant, Adam was fully aware, fully mature and totally equipped for his destiny – with one exception. God's plan was not yet *complete*. God had announced that everything He had made and done was "good." But, "The Lord said, *"It is not good that the man should be alone; I will make him a help mate."* (Genesis 2:18). God made woman—she was a direct gift *from the hand of God,* made *from* man and *for* man.

Proverbs 31:10-31 tells in detail what kind of helpmate the woman is to be. The supportive role of the wife to the husband is very evident in this description of the ideal woman. She "will do him good and not evil." Because of her honesty, modesty and chastity, "her husband doth safely trust in her." By her efficiency and diligence, she will be a blessing to her household. The basis for her virtue is found in verse 30: "*… but a woman who fears the Lord is to be praised."* This is a reverential fear that gives meaning and purpose to her life. Only as the Lord lives in her heart can she be the woman she was meant to be.

Woman was made with a purpose in life that only she could fill. To woman has been given one of the greatest privileges in the world, that of molding and nurturing a living soul. Her influence, especially in the realm of motherhood, affects her children's eternal destination. A mother is the heartbeat of her home. She helps lay the foundation of moral standards there. The warmth of her spirit quietly establishes security in the lives of her family. God has a beautiful plan for *all* women…a plan that will bring order and fulfillment—if it is followed in obedience.

The woman who wholeheartedly accepts God's plan will be blessed. As she exercises her inborn attributes of love, gentleness, and compassion, she is a living example of that which becomes godliness. May each woman fill her role with the grace of God in her heart, live in submissive obedience to His will, and humbly give of herself in the daily practices of life.

Mothers are truly a gift from God, and need to be held up and appreciated daily, by our words and actions of encouragement. God created families and gave *Mothers* a unique place in that unit. A *Mother* is filled with love for her family and she gives all of herself to them. Every day *Mothers* work endlessly (24/7) to provide all the needs of their children and their husbands. They are the first one up in the morning and the last one down at night. They juggle a lot of things including raising children, working at jobs, and managing a home.

Every woman is special. God has a beautiful plan and purpose for her life. And as the handiwork of God, made in His image and likeness, a woman must always be treated properly and with due respect. Remember, she is a treasure, meant to be attentively cared for and cherished for a lifetime. So whether you are married or single, take the time to let the women in your life – your mother, sister, wife, daughter – know how much you value and appreciate them. *"Dear children, let's not merely say that we love each other; let us show the truth by our actions"* (1 John 3:18).

The family is an essential part of God's redemptive plan for humanity. This is evident by the numerous biblical teachings about family relationships. God has commanded husbands to love their wives, wives to submit to their husbands, parents to train their children properly, and children to honor their parents.

Don't let a day go by that you are not grateful!
Honor your MOTHER and Honor your WIFE!

May your heart always know the Lord
May your feet always follow His path
May your life always be blessed by Him!

> *"If any man will come after me, Let him deny himself, and take up his cross, and follow me." -Matthew 16:24*

Can You Say You Are a Man Of God? A Fathers' Day Message

> *"But you, man of God, flee from all this, and pursue righteousness, godliness, faith, love, endurance and gentleness."*
> *-1 Timothy 6:11*

Joshua was the priest of the home (*He was the spiritual leader*). One of the main purposes of a priest is to be a go between for God and those he is serving. Dads, you are to be the priest in your family, who goes boldly before the throne of God on behalf of your family. Joshua said, *"....As for me and my house we will serve the Lord" Joshua 24:15.* His plan that he had for his family was that he would do anything and everything he could to help them to, not only know the Lord, but to serve the Lord.

"Man of God" is the description given to a man that follows God in every way, who obeys His commands with joy, who does not live for the things of this life but for the things of eternity, who willingly serves his God in giving freely of all his resources—yet gladly suffers as a consequence of his faith. Perhaps In the book of Micah, Chapter 6—he sums up how the man of needs to live in one neat verse: *"He has showed you, O man, what is good. And what does the Lord require of you? To act justly and to love mercy and to walk humbly with your God" (Micah 6:8).*

The man of God keeps his mind and heart pure by guarding his eyes and ears from the ways of the world; he is the *spiritual leader* of his family. He does everything opposite to what the world does or approves of; he goes "against the grain" of society because he knows these things displease God; he considers those who are "disadvantaged" or those rejected by society, those that are lonely or despairing; he is a listener to other people's problems and does not judge. Most of all, the man of God must understand that when our Lord God commanded him to *"be perfect, therefore, as your heavenly Father is perfect"* (Matthew 5:48), he is only able to accomplish that because God enables him to be "holy and blameless in his sight" through His power and the indwelling of His Spirit. On our own, we are incapable of holiness and perfection, but through Christ who strengthens us, we can "do all things.

> ***"I can do all things through Christ which strengthened me."- Philippians 4:13***

The man of God knows that his new nature is that of the righteousness of Christ which was exchanged for our sinful nature at the cross. *"Therefore if any man be in Christ, he is a new creature: old things are passed away; behold, all things are become new"* (2 Corinthians 5:17). The man of God must walk humbly with his God, knowing that he must rely solely upon Him to be able to live to the full and persevere to the end.

God is looking for men *whose hearts* are His—*completely*. God is not looking for magnificent specimens of humanity. He's looking for deeply spiritual, genuinely humble, honest-to-the-core servants who have integrity. It's what you are when nobody's looking. We live in a world that says that "you must make a good impression, that's all that matters." You can't fake it with the Almighty God. He is not impressed with externals. He always focuses on the inward qualities, like the *character of the heart*—those things that take time and discipline to cultivate. While Man attributes can be weakness, confusion, blindness and failure, God's attributes are *always* majestic, full of greatness and power.

To be "a man of God" is the greatest title that could be bestowed upon any man. Everyone who has the Spirit of God indwelling him has the desire to claim that title for himself -- to be a *man of God*—

not a man of the world; and not a man of the flesh—but a *man of God*. If you truly are "a man of God" and He is guiding you in all you do…you can't be anything but *'the best husband and father'* for your family and will experience God's blessings and extraordinary success.

The calling to serve God is a calling to a position of special honor.

A Father prayed this prayer, *"Our Father in heaven, I'm a father on earth. You have given me this gift and responsibility. Grant me wisdom to carry it out. Let me be there for my children and my wife when they need me, and get out of their way when they don't."*
--unknown author

CHARLES FRANCIS ADAMS, a 19th century POLITICAN and DIPLOMAT, kept a diary. One day ADAMS wrote in his diary…

"Went fishing with my son today—a day wasted."

His son, BROOK ADAMS, also kept a diary. Ironically on that same day, he wrote in his diary…
"Went fishing with my dad today— the most wonderful day of my life."

Be thankful and appreciate your family every day….
Time is one of the "greatest" gifts
that you can give your family

Are You Celebrating Thanksgiving Every Day?

In our country a special day is set aside each year for Thanksgiving. But for the Christian.... every day should be a day of thanksgiving as we are to *"always giving thanks to God the Father for everything, in the name of our Lord Jesus Christ"* (Ephesians 5:20).

God knows all of the trials you may be facing today and He loves you and is with you by His Holy Spirit. We must cultivate a spirit of thankfulness—*even in the midst of trials and heartaches.*

We should be thanking God especially for our Salvation in Jesus Christ. God has given us the greatest Gift of all—His Son, who died on the cross and rose again so that we can know Him personally and spend eternity with Him in heaven: *"Thanks be to God for his indescribable gift!"* (2 Corinthians 9:15).

The Bible tells us that we are separated from God because we have sinned. But God loves us—He loves you, He loves me—and He wants us to be part of His family forever. All we need to do is reach out in faith and accept Christ as our Savior and Lord: *"For God so loved the world that he gave his one and only Son, that whoever believes in him shall not perish but have eternal life"* (John 3:16).

From one end of the Bible to the other, we are commanded to be thankful. Thankfulness is the natural outflowing of a heart that is attuned to God.

> **"For everything God has created is good, and nothing is to be thrown away or refused if it is received with thanksgiving." -1 Timothy 4: 4.**

"I will give to the Lord the thanks due to His rightness and justice, and I will sing praise to the name of the Lord Most High." -Psalm 7: 17.

A spirit of thanksgiving is always the mark of a joyous Christian. *Are you a joyous Christian?*

Apostle Paul being separated from friends, unjustly accused, brutally treated—if ever a person had a right to complain, it was this man, suffering and almost forgotten in a harsh Roman prison. But instead of complaints, his lips rang with words of praise and thanksgiving! He was a man who had learned the meaning of true thanksgiving, even in the midst of great adversity. Earlier, when he had been imprisoned in Rome, Paul wrote, *"Sing and make music in your heart to the Lord, always giving thanks to God the Father for everything, in the name of our Lord Jesus Christ"* (Ephesians 5:19-20).

Think of it: Always giving thanks for everything—no matter what the circumstances! Thanksgiving for the Apostle Paul was not a once-a-year celebration, but a daily reality that changed his life and made him a joyful person in every situation. Thanksgiving—THE GIVING OF THANKS—to God for all His blessings should be one of the most distinctive marks of the believer in Jesus Christ. We must not allow a spirit of ingratitude to harden our heart and chill our relationship with God and with others. Nothing turns us into bitter, selfish, dissatisfied people more quickly than an ungrateful heart. AND NOTHING WILL DO MORE TO RESTORE CONTENTMENT AND THE JOY OF OUR SALVATION THAN TO HAVE A TRUE SPIRIT OF THANKFULNESS.

Ingratitude is a sin, just as surely as is lying or stealing or immorality or any other sin condemned by the Bible. One of the Bible's indictments against rebellious humanity is that *"although they knew God, they neither glorified him as God nor gave thanks to him"* (Romans 1:21). An ungrateful heart is a heart that is cold toward God and indifferent to His mercy and love. It is a heart that has forgotten how dependent we are on God for everything.

Do you let others know that you appreciate them and are thankful for them? Thank God for all who touch your life.

"Give thanks in all circumstances; for this is God's will for you in Christ Jesus." -1 Thessalonians 5:18

Have you Thanked God… Today!

"Consider it pure joy, my brothers, whenever you face trials of many kinds, because you know that the testing of your faith develops perseverance" -James 1:2-3

The Only Gift That You Will Ever Need— is Jesus Christ!

> *"An angel of the Lord appeared to them, and the glory of the Lord shone around them, and they were terrified. But the angel said to them, "Do not be afraid. I bring you good news of great joy that will be for all the people. Today in the town of David a Savior has been born to you; He is Christ the Lord….. Suddenly a great company of the heavenly host appeared with the angel, praising God and saying, "Glory to God in the highest, and on earth peace to men on whom his favor rests."*
>
> *-Luke 2: 9-11, 13-14*

The wise men brought the rather unusual gifts of gold, frankincense, and myrrh to Jesus. But the first Christmas gifts were not gifts *to* the Child. The first Christmas gift *was the gift of the Child.* Christmas, at its best and purest state, is a promise of something else, something that no holiday or experience or earthly thing can satisfy.

> *"But when the time had fully come, God sent his Son, born of a woman, born under law, to redeem those under law, that we might receive the full rights of sons" -Galatians 4:4-5*

"For unto us a Child is born, unto us a Son is given; and the government will be upon His shoulder. And His name will be called Wonderful, Counselor, Mighty God, Everlasting Father, Prince of Peace."- Isaiah 9:6

The full meaning of these words from Isaiah should give us enough strength, hope, and joy to face any crisis, endure any sorrow, and meet any trials or temptations. Jesus is *the Prince of Peace*, and He is the only one who can help you through all your circumstances of life.

JESUS *IS* THE GLORY OF CHRISTMAS. He is our provision for all that we need now, and all that we will ever need. When you begin to really take to heart all that He has already done for you and all that He wants to do for you, it won't be long before joy will begin to rule your thoughts which will put you in the right frame of mind to receive your blessing. *Remember*, the joy of the Lord is your strength. "Christmas time" is more than a season of the year – it is the celebration of God's work of redeeming mankind.

Today we can declare to the world that the Good Shepherd cares for all people and wants to give them peace. Christ came on that first Christmas for one great purpose—to die on the cross for our sins. Now God offers forgiveness, inner peace, and eternal life to all who will repent and believe in His Son. This is the Christmas message! Only the ones who hear and believe that… Jesus Christ is our Savior who came to redeem us from the slavery of sin and everlasting condemnation, rightly interpret and experience the true meaning of Christmas. Without the Gospel there is no Christmas. Our Heavenly Father gave us the most precious gift and most important gift anyone would ever want to receive.

The names Isaiah gave us describes a different aspect of the work that God wants to do in our lives.

THESE ARE FIVE CHRISTMAS GIFTS WE CAN OPEN EVERY DAY!

First, His name is *Wonderful*. This word comes from the root word "wonder," which means "a sense of awe." Jesus wants to bring a sense of awe and wonder to our lives. No longer do we have to look to the cheap substitutes this world offers to bring fulfillment, because Jesus Christ makes life wonderful!

Second, His name is *Counselor*. Did you know that God Almighty, the Mighty God, the Everlasting Father wants to give you His personal counsel and direction? As Psalms 73:24 says, *"You will guide me with Your counsel, and afterward receive me into glory."* No longer do you have to be baffled by the problems you face, because with Christ as your Counselor, you can know that God will reveal His will to you. His wise counsel is the only sure guide to enter into the Kingdom of God.

Third, His name is *Mighty God*. This means that Jesus has unlimited power for you as you encounter the demands of life. Living a fruitful Christian life *can* sometimes be difficult. In fact, *it is impossible* apart from the help of the Holy Spirit. *"...with God all things are possible"* (Matthew 19:26).

Fourth, He is called the *Everlasting Father*. Because Christ rose again from the dead, *never to die again*—you have an Everlasting Father, One who will be with you forever. He will never forget about you. You will *always* be His child.

Fifth, His name is the *Prince of Peace*. Certainly we live in frightening times. We look at our world and see so many things that have gone wrong. How we need peace in our lives today! True peace does not merely dull our pain. A person who has genuine, godly peace can endure an avalanche of hardship and difficulty and still enjoy an inner peace that surpasses all human understanding. True lasting peace can only be found in the presence of God. His peace is complete, adequate, and sufficient for anything you face. Christ *is* our peace**! God loves you and wants you to know Him so He can fill you with His peace and give you a more abundant life –** *forever!* "*Because of our Lord Jesus Christ, we live at peace with God*" (Romans 5:1).

We are so used to celebrating Christmas with gifts in beautiful packages that sometimes we forget the true meaning of Christmas.

> *"If you knew the gift of God and who it is that asks you for a drink, you would have asked him and he would have given you living water."*
> *-John 4:10*

On Christmas morning as we hand out those gifts—remember God's greatest gift to the earth. His Son, Jesus Christ—the *only* gift that truly keeps on giving *the gift of eternal life*. "*For God so loved the world, that he gave his only begotten son, that whosoever believeth in him should not perish, but have everlasting life*" (John 3:16).

As you think about Christmas, gifts, presents, giving and receiving—why not check and be sure that you have received the most important of all gifts? Only if we have received Jesus, who came to save us from sin, do we really have anything in our possession that matters. Every other possession and gift can be stripped away from us by death, disease, or disaster. Only Jesus will never leave us or be lost; only He can save and keep us forever. ***JESUS IS THE ONLY WAY!***

Where can we find the perfect gifts at Christmas? We find them under the tree—*God's Christmas tree*. It isn't an evergreen. **It is an old rugged cross**. It isn't decorated with lights or tinsel. It is **covered with the precious blood of God's Son.**

Everyone who accepts Jesus as their Savior
WILL FIND God's greatest gift, the GIFT OF SALVATION!
And this free gift will have their name on it!

> **JESUS IS SAVIOR for all the people,
> and this is cause for great joy!
> Don't keep this special gift just for yourself.
> Share with everyone....
> THE GIFT OF JESUS!**
>
> Don't keep this special gift just for yourself
> *Share with everyone... the gift of JESUS*

Ask God to Help You Make Your New Year's Resolutions... ONLY WITH GOD'S HELP Will You Be Able to Keep Them!

In January, millions of people begin their year with New Year's resolutions. Losing weight, getting organized, exercising more, eating healthier and managing finances better and etc. ... but how often do we really keep these kinds of resolutions?

In the Bible, James spoke of some people who can teach us a valuable lesson about great intentions that aren't aligned with God's will.

> *Come now, you who say, "Today or tomorrow we will travel to such and such a city and spend a year there and do business and make a profit." You don't even know what tomorrow will bring—what your life will be! For you are like smoke that appears for a little while, and then vanishes. Instead, you should say, "If the Lord wills, we will live and do this or that." But as it is, you boast in your arrogance. All such boasting is evil. So it is a sin for the person who knows to do what is good and doesn't do it. -James 4:13-17*

Our plans may or may not be God's plans. If we want to be successful with any New Year's resolution, we must seek God's will. By his strength we might lose weight, eat better, or become better stewards of our finances. But what does God want for our lives? When he convicts us, he also equips us in following through with His plan for us. When you follow God's plan you will have more strength to carry it out and in God's strength He will work well beyond anything you could even imagine.

> *"Therefore, brothers, be patient until the Lord's coming. See how the farmer waits for the precious fruit of the earth and is patient with it until it receives the early and the late rains. You also must be patient, strengthen your hearts, because the Lord's coming is near."*
> *-James 5:7-8*

When you wait patiently on the Lord… and do exactly what God wants you to do, *only then*, is God able to do the things that only He can do.

Try Seeking God's face, and pray David's prayer every morning for the next year.

> **"Create in me a pure heart, O God, and renew a steadfast spirit within me. Do not cast me from your presence or take your Holy Spirit from me."** *-Psalm 51:10-11*

Let's resolve to give our attitudes to the Lord. Commit to making a difference at home with your family and your neighbor, in the workplace, the marketplace, on the roads, and even at church. *"Above all, put on love—the perfect bond of unity. And let the peace of the Messiah, to which you were also called in one body, control your hearts. Be thankful"* (Colossians 3:14-15).

We live as though life is completely up to us. Yet if we are "In Christ" we are not alone. God is with us guiding each step.

Life is not always easy. Following through on simple commitments can even be difficult when bombarded by every day affairs. In addition, the attacks of the evil one will challenge us at every turn.

The start of a new year is a good time to stop and look at our lives -- and that's the first step in making any realistic resolutions. What needs to be improved in our lives? What needs to be eliminated -- or added? Most of all, what does God see when He looks at you, and what does He want you to do? What is His will for the coming year -- and for your life? The Bible says, *"Forget the former things; do not dwell on the past. See, I am doing a new thing"* (Isaiah 43:18-19).

Don't focus on self-centered goals; focus instead on what God wants to do in your life. Above all, make sure of your commitment to Christ. If you haven't yet accepted Jesus as your personal Savior -- why not begin the New Year by giving your life to Him?

Seek Him… Seek..His wonderful plan for your life!

> *"Set your affection on things above, not on things on the earth" -Colossians 3:2*
>
> *"Trust ye in the LORD forever: for in the LORD JEHOVAH is everlasting strength" -Isaiah 26:4*

"And do this, understanding the present time. The hour has come for you to wake up from your slumber, because our salvation is nearer now than when we first believed. The night is nearly over; the day is almost here. So let us put aside the deeds of darkness and put on the armor of light… Rather, clothe yourselves with the Lord Jesus Christ" -Romans 13:11-13

Now… is the time for us all to examine our hearts, repent and make ourselves right with God. Even though we know neither the day nor the hour of Jesus return, we do know the time is drawing nigh. When Jesus does return, I want to be ready… don't you?

JESUS DIED FOR YOU…
THE LEAST YOU CAN DO…
IS LIVE FOR HIM!

My grace is sufficient for this day! You have not known a day precisely like this in all your days upon the earth. It is a new day, full of promise and hope! Truly the Lord your God is guiding you through the rough places, and his hand is supporting you. When you walk through the valley, I am with you. When on the mountain-top, I am with you, in sunshine and in shadow. Take up your cross and follow me, for I am walking before you to make the crooked places straight. There is nothing that can harm you, for I am protecting you by the shadow of my wings. You have nothing to fear when I am with you, guiding your steps with my word. Be encouraged that I understand your struggles and know your heart. I am daily noting your progress! You cannot fail with your daily armor and my hand on your life! You are more than a conqueror! Amen and amen.

About the Author

Julia never had any intentions of writing a book or could never even imagine such a possibility. She is so very grateful to Gospel Lighthouse Church for giving her the opportunity and asking her to write these Bible teachings weekly for their church. She resisted at first because she didn't feel that she would even know how to begin writing. Her first thought was *she can't do this*, but then she remembered that *"She can do all things thru Christ who strengthens her"* (Philippians 4:13). The amazing divine intervention from God, through the Holy Spirit, had placed these messages on my heart. Each message that she wrote, she knew in her heart that the Holy Spirit was trying to teach her something. Also, she knew that was not only for her, for we all have many trials and tribulations that we are going through and need encouragement through the Word of God.

She wants to especially thank Pastors Jackie and Donna Chavers for encouraging her to write these Bible teachings which ended up being a blessing for her and for all those that read them. She really wanted to share these messages with as many people as she could because she found them helpful in her life and her walk with the Lord. Even when she reread them she felt hopeful and encouraged. She also wants to thank my very good friend Patty Prezzavento who really encouraged her to publish this book, and she will forever be grateful to her. But she cannot forget to thank her loving husband, Rhett Brown, who not only patiently sat down and read each Bible study, but contributed by helping her to modify and edit them when necessary. He encouraged her through it all.

There would not have even been a book without the Holy Spirit. She felt so blessed to be used by her Heavenly Father in helping to edify and encourage others. All the honor and glory for this book goes to God. Her prayer is that everyone who reads this book will not only find it helpful and encouraging, but she prays that they will be blessed! *"Give Thanks to the Lord for He is Good; His Love endures forever"* (Psalm 107:1).

CPSIA information can be obtained
at www.ICGtesting.com
Printed in the USA
LVHW042040010419
612606LV00002B/3/P